lobster

lobster

and other things
I'm learning
to love

hollie mcnish

FLEET
2024

FLEET

First published in Great Britain in 2024 by Fleet

3 5 7 9 10 8 6 4

Typeset in Garamond by M Rules
Printed and bound in Great Britain by Clays Ltd, Elcograf S.p.A.

Papers used by Fleet are from well-managed forests
and other responsible sources.

Fleet
An imprint of
Little, Brown Book Group
Carmelite House
50 Victoria Embankment
London EC4Y 0DZ

An Hachette UK Company
www.hachette.co.uk

www.littlebrown.co.uk

CONTENTS

to my loving and loved family,
please, never read
the oral sex section of this book

INTRODUCTION

This book is written out of both hate and love for the world.

The world, its people, creatures, cultures and concerns, fascinates, inspires and disgusts me every day. These poems were my attempt at learning to love those things which I do not think should disgust me or which I do not want to hate (any more), but which for some reason or another I have been made to feel that way towards. This sort of hate is a nonsense use of my time, time which is not infinite and, like everyone else's, far too precious to waste.

My body, for example, a body that has kept me very good company for many decades now; which has allowed me to sing, swim, skip, sweat, birth, orgasm, feed, dance and nap, among many other luscious activities. A body which, despite this, I have consistently and point-lessly bullied; largely because, somewhere, somehow, I have been told that it's worth my contempt, and I listened and I believed it.

Pleasure, a state which can be reached in many simple, safe, cheap, free and loving ways, yet is entrenched in centuries of stigma, shame, hurt and confusion – for those who are lucky enough to access it; what we should and should not find pleasure and happiness in dictated to us not by consent or kindness, thoughts and feelings, excitement even, but so often by those attempting to control or cap-italise from human insecurities and passion.

Certain words even, words that, despite being utterly harmless, we have been so duped into hating that we find them almost impossible to even whisper into the air; ask any friend if they find it easier to say the words moist or murder.

Such hatred and disgust, squeamishness and embarrassment are

1

so often constructed by outside forces. Unravelling these teachings from my mind and body has been – is – a long, ongoing process. To quote the greatest thinker of all time:

> Do not assume anything Obi-Wan. Clear your mind must be if you are to discover the real villains behind this plot.[*]

YODA

This book is about my attempt at reconfiguring my thoughts and my reactions, learning to stop listening to those who want power or money from me and starting to love the things I should damn well love. It is stuffed full with all the poems I've scribbled in parks and on trains and late at night in bed trying to convince myself to love more, trying to rejig my robot brain.

I hope there is much more love than hate in this book because I definitely have much more love than hate in me; more amazement than disgust; more fun than misery.

I hope you are also starting to love things other than those we've been told it's OK or cool or even necessary to love. I hope you've stopped hating things you don't need to hate. I hope you enjoy reading some of my thoughts on the matter.

I love writing, poems especially, and this book has taken years of my time. I am eternally grateful to have had snapshots of space in which to write it. Firstly, because writing brings me a lot of joy and relief, a bit like kissing but not quite as good. Secondly, because while writing this book, I have uncovered two new favourite words: arachibutyrophobia – a fear of peanut butter sticking to the roof of your mouth – and nebulophilia – an arousal by fog. Fucking brilliant. What wonderful weirdos we all are.

---

[*] Extract from *Star Wars: Episode II – Attack of the Clones*, 2002, directed and produced by George Lucas; screenplay by George Lucas and Jonathan Hales.

CHAPTER SUMMARY:
A Guide for People Who Just Want to Read the Poems

When editing this book, I kept thinking, *You could have said that in about three sentences not a hundred pages, Hollie.* If you also love a long-winded and winding chat, I've left lots of it in, dexterously edited with the help of Rhiannon, Amy, Helen, Howard, Michael and my mum.

However, if you just want to read the poems and not all of the prose too, then here are my summaries of each section. There is an index of the poems at the back.

The Body: Loving the Beast

Life is short. People profit hugely from our body insecurities. Try to remember that and tell them to fuck off. Scented candles aren't as calming as fair wages. Don't stress too much about self-love if it's doing your head in a bit. Call your friends. If you don't have friends, call mine. My mum used to call scabs 'nature's plasters'. Being juicy is not a sin, not for oranges, not for bodies. As far as we know, Jupiter has between seventy-nine and ninety-five moons, not all of which are named yet.

People: Hashtag, Not All

If one more person says *not all men* to me, I'll weep. It's easy to generalise about people and lump them all together in big balls of hate, but I don't think it helps anyone. At Cambridge University the fact I had a door number really excited some people. The queen was not your grandma. It's not any child's fault they're sent to Eton. Boys can also smell the sweetness of lilies. Falling stars are very common; the best way to see one is to stare at one point of the sky on a clear night for around twenty minutes.

Words: Moist Velvet Volvos

Being disgusted by the word vulva is normal. There is no French translation of 'tea-bagging'. Censorship and shame are very powerful things, even in language. Don't let anyone insult your volvo, it's a fine car. Writing image descriptions for Instagram posts made me question the entire world. Any product that tells you your vulva needs to be scented like lavender or orange blossom is a fuckwit piece of bollocks and you should run from it. One year on Venus is shorter than one day on Venus, by our measurements.

Motherland: Flags and Fiction

If your parents' background or country or culture differs to your own, you don't have to choose a 'side'. Heritages are not football teams. Also, you can support England and Scotland; yes, Hollie, you can. In general, flags scare me. My dad says you cannot get good vegetable pakora anywhere but Glasgow. My grandad was very friendly. Some people are so disappointed by Paris that they faint on arrival at seeing dog shit in the city. There are currently people arguing about who owns rights to the moon.

Oral Sex: Politeness and Pomegranates

A comic book workshop changed my sex life. Some ancient Greeks thought cunnilingus was the lowest and least masculine form of sexual activity. Pick rosehips after the first frost. Let them stay down there if they want to. If you don't enjoy something sexual, don't do it. Asking for a blow job by saying 'I bet you like sucking dick' isn't the only solution. I love the word fellatio and think it sounds like a French cake with lots of layers of buttered pastry. Sometimes female bonobos begin masturbating simply to distract the males from fighting. According to an article I read, Libras and Virgos are the most attentive oral sex gifters.

Happiness: Shit in Glitter

Adults are still allowed to skateboard. Pleasure is very personal. My grandad always said, 'If it's not hurting anyone, why are you bothering about it?' Sweety-flavoured vapes sold in sweet shops is a shitshow. I love sleepovers. One of my friends once asked me to be her best friend forever and I freaked the fuck out. If I could go back and relive my teenage years, I'd watch as much shit TV as my parents told me would ruin my eyesight. I'm happy there's a planet called Uranus.

Beginnings: Birthing Dragons

Peekaboo is a game of outstanding genius. Be kind to yourself. Babies don't give a shit what wallpaper you have. Ask someone to make you dinner. If I see any more new mums, bodies still healing, sat in the vestibule on the floor of a train I will bleed through my eyes. Pregnant people have a lot of nightmares. For months, I dreamt my daughter was born a goat. Unfortunately, I once imagined breast-feeding Boris Johnson and wrote a poem about it.

That's it. I hope you enjoy reading the poems as much as I loved writing them. Also, I hope you do read some of the rest, because it took me ages.

THE BODY

Loving the Beast

The Church says: The body is a sin.
Science says: The body is a machine.
Advertising says: The body is a business.
The Body says: I am a fiesta.

EDUARDO GALEANO, *Walking Words*

'i am a fiesta'

free, and bone-full of feast

shook champagne ready
bubbles uncorked to pour over faces
open-mouthed to the moon

let the wolf howl
stick out your tongue to the storms
lap the fizz till your lips
drunk with the sweetness
of no longer giving a shit about painful opinions
erupt into song

your body has done nothing wrong –
stop telling it off

put down your put downs
step away from the fuss

i know it is hard not to listen
to the constant cacophony
of not good enough
but you haven't much time
who knows why we're here
but we are, what ridiculous luck
to be stuck in these ballgowns of body
to party to love to dance until dusk
to footprint this chaos till the threads come undone
or the cotton turns dust

clocks stop for no one
birdsong your bones while you can

sunkiss your skull let your soles stamp
feel the glorious slap of the fat on your arse
as you jump and you land

you will land, every time, so laugh, it's absurd
how many moments you've had stolen already,
how many fucks you have given – too many

so laugh, loud enough to unbury the dead
laugh until even the most broken of corpses within you
remembers the fun of this flesh

YOU CANNOT LOVE OTHERS
UNTIL YOU LOVE YOURSELF

Despite never believing in the ability of horror films to make their way into real life through my television screen, I have still never said the word 'Candyman' in the mirror three times.

Candyman, Candyman. Say the word once more and, according to the 1992 film, the murderous Candyman will come to life, mouth full of bees, sweety wrapper weapons.

I have said it twice to myself in the mirror but not three times. I have said it once and then once again and then, three weeks later, once again, hoping that the break between recitals will keep me safe.

Candyman, Candyman. I'll stop there. I'm not sure writing it follows the same rules and I'm not risking my life for this book.

I watched this film for the first time at a sleepover at my house with friends, aged thirteen and far too young. For years afterwards the image of the Candyman infiltrated our nightmares, so much so that one of my friend's parents banned her from my house. This film and its impact on my psyche was a large part of my decision aged eighteen, the age I could legally watch any horror film I wanted, to never to watch another again. I've managed this, apart from the 2017 remake of *I.T.* and the film *Mother*, which I didn't realise was a horror film until a baby was ripped apart by an obsessive crowd.

I have stared at my face in the mirror many times wondering whether I would ever be 'brave' enough to complete the Candyman trio, telling myself over and over again that I'm being ridiculous, it isn't real, this is fiction, *just say it one more time and you'll see*.

At sleepovers, we dared each other to do it and watched as, one by one, we paused at two, giggled and refused to go any further. Even now, over twenty years later, there are some things I just don't want to test; this is one of them, bungee jump ropes are another.

The other time in my life I remember stammering over words as I stared at my mirrored reflection was after reading a 'top tips to body confidence' article in one of the many magazines I used to flick through for guidance as a teenage girl.

There were lots of different articles: how to bag yourself the sweetest guy; how to achieve a natural look in just three hours; how to look 'heroin chic' aka emaciated, insecure and addicted to anything but eating well; how to impress the boy you like; how to make face masks out of 'leftover' avocado; how to give a twister blow job; how to look sexy while reading a book.

In the article, a feature on loving your body crammed between a fashion page of clothes modelled by women with waists photoshopped to the circumference of the average penis, and a page covered in photos of female celebrities, red circles drawn around their 'shame' spots – armpit hair, gross! sagging knees, urgh! stretch marks, uh oh! – I stumbled on the recommendation of standing in front of a mirror, preferably naked, and telling yourself 'I love you.'

I tried it; stood in front of the mirror in my bedroom, naked and grimacing, and I stared. I cringed. I held in my stomach and cheekbones to see what I'd look like ill. In the end, I think I said something like 'You're all right,' but definitely not 'I love you.' In all honestly, at that moment, if I had to choose between the final Candyman and a full-body naked 'I love you,' it would possibly have been the former.

It wasn't that I had low self-esteem. My relationship with my body was OK. But telling myself that I loved it was going a bit too far. I have also never made a face mask out of 'leftover' avocado or met any friend or lover who gave a shit about the sort of tips I gleaned from

14

these magazines. It was only recently that I realised there were no magazines for heterosexual teenage boys dedicated to tips on how to please or impress girls, give twizzler fingering, make your skin shine, and so on. For boys, magazines seemed convinced of a holy trinity of football, music and photos of tits. And watches when you're older.

The most irritating thing looking back on that article was that I only imagined two choices: self-love or self-hate. There was no self-thinking-of-other-things or self-don't-give-a-fuck.

Self-love is a hot topic at the moment, but it's nothing new. People have been musing on self-love since masturbation was invented, which was a really long time ago, way before some puritans declared that wankers go blind.

Self-love. The Greek philosopher Aristotle (384–322 BCE) believed that self-love or philautia (φιλαυτία) was a prerequisite to loving others, but that there were both positive and negative aspects of self-love. He recorded these ideas in punchily titled books, *Nicomachean Ethics* and *Eudemian Ethics*. In the bluntest interpretation I can give, Aristotle argued that people who love themselves to achieve unwarranted personal gain are bad, but those who love themselves to achieve virtuous principles are the best sort of good.

I don't agree with everything Aristotle thought about self-love. He supposedly claimed women to be *unfinished men, monstrous, deformed*, a claim partly based on the then popular fallacy that women have fewer teeth than men. To then promote philautia seems a bit of a paradox.

The great Aristotle also theorised that women played a fairly minor role in reproduction because they 'simply' contributed the material while the father supplied the actual active force; a view that made both my womb and fist quickly cramp when I read it. Aristotle had two children. I don't know if he changed their nappies; it seems unlikely – he'd already contributed so much by cumming twice; he must have been exhausted after that.

In terms of female self-love, Aristotle seemed to be saying

something like: women, you are monstrous, but it would be really helpful to society if you learned to love yourselves. Also, you are stupid and should stay at home because you are incapable of abstract reasoning and therefore of entering into the public political sphere or becoming citizens. Also, our one ejaculation of sperm is more than your likely years of menstruation cramps, nine months of pregnancy, labour and producing the life source of milk in your own bodies like a fucking cellular magician. But, you know, #loveyourself while you're there, girls.

Jumping a millennium or so, it seems we've been grappling, and still are grappling, with these exact same issues:

- In 1848, a document entitled the 'Declaration of Sentiments', modelled on the 'Declaration of Independence', was signed by sixty-eight women and thirty-two men at what is recorded as the first women's rights conference organised by women in the US. It was written primarily by Elizabeth Cady Stanton as a guideline to demonstrate that women have been harshly treated throughout the centuries and that the ability to love oneself is possibly made much harder due to social inequalities and lack of rights. It states: 'all men and women are created equal; ... that among these [rights] are life, liberty, and the pursuit of happiness'; and that without these rights, the capacity to feel self-worth and self-love is scarce. As in, you know, if you have no rights, no respect, no economic independence, trying to love yourself is a bit fucking trickier.
- In 1956 psychologist and social philosopher Erich Fromm said, similarly to Aristotle, that loving oneself is different from being arrogant, conceited or egocentric. Fromm proposed a re-evaluation of self-love in a more positive sense, arguing that in order to be able truly to love another person, you first need to love yourself in the way of respecting oneself

and knowing yourself (e.g. being realistic and honest about your strengths and weaknesses).

- Just over a decade later, in the 1970s, the Black Power movement slogan 'Black is beautiful!' hailed a call for African Americans to escape and/or stand against the white or white European beauty standards, self-love here being a tool, or rather political campaign, in communities of colour in the United States.
- More recent online campaigns such as #blackgirlmagic have highlighted how our structurally racist standards are still far from being toppled, through both the necessity for such campaigns as well as the counterargument that, in order to have worth, black women somehow still cannot just be, but must be *magical*.

Alongside these issues, and many more, one of our predominant current self-love power struggles is the commercialisation of the body positivity movement.

Body positivity was, as Stephanie Yeboah says, 'spearheaded by larger fat, black and ethnic minority women [and] primarily focuses on the celebration and radical self-love of visibly fat bodies', but has more and more become 'a "free-for-all" movement monetised and politicised by brands and public figures in ways that often result in individuals above a certain size and of a certain ethnicity being excluded from the conversation . . . when they were the ones to effectively start it in the first place'.*

What started out as a grassroots movement has been hijacked by companies, as all good things are, and used to sell everything from underwear to sex toys to skincare to sofas. The idea of body positivity has been twisted back around so that our bodies are still being judged by some kind of standard of what's 'right'.

---

* 'Body Positivity: Why the Work Is Far from Finished', *Vogue*, 30 May 2020.

In 2021, model Karoline Bjørnelykke shared a video of how a modelling agency – one apparently embracing body positivity – insisted she wear padding so that she would appear plus-size in the way they wanted plus-size to appear. She claimed that she and others were hired for plus-size shoots and this padding, stuffed into 'fat suits', was used to make her arse and thighs and hips and breasts larger but her waist, neck and face still as slim. So, as long as she was an impossible plus-size hourglass that's all fine, but not plus-size in any other shape: not apple, or pear or whatever other fucking fruit our bodies should or should not supposedly resemble. The same is done for maternity wear, using belly padding on otherwise tiny frames.

It's a strange thing looking in the mirror these days.

In the mirror, I see my face and, largely, I still criticise it, almost subconsciously, instantaneously. I then tell myself off for criticising my face and tell myself about all the things my face does and why I should love it. I then feel guilty for having criticised it. And *then* I feel angry for having taken up two minutes of my very, very precious life having an argument with myself about whether or not I love my own face enough, as if I need to have a daily aesthetic opinion on my own fucking face. I sometimes wonder if the invention of the mirror or mobile phone had a bigger impact on human behaviour.

The rise in all these modern-day 'self-love' messages – printed increasingly, it seems, onto products from T-shirts, tea towels, post-cards and mugs to small bits of wood to hang in your bedroom, as well as all across a lot of the social media platforms I and millions of others enjoy using – however well-intentioned, has started to have the opposite effect on me.

Self-love self-love self-love. Every time I go to buy a greetings card or check my messages on Instagram or post a tour on TikTok or just want to scroll a while for a daily poem or a new skit from Kae Kurd or photos from a childhood friend, I get hit with self-love messages and quotes and people, mainly women, mainly white, mainly in their

18

underwear or yoga gear, mainly sitting on really nice beaches or in fancy and very tidy houses, telling me to love myself.

The extent to which society currently demands that I love myself before all other love has become almost more stressful than disliking myself, especially when these messages include the idea that I must love my 'flaws', which does nothing but remind me that some parts of my body are considered flaws.

Like, before I was reminded to love my 'mum body', I never knew I had a body that was now labelled a 'mum body'. I just knew I was a mum and that my body had been through a lot. Before I was reminded to love my lopsided labia I didn't think they were lopsided. I'm not a total cynical bitch – I know a lot of this also helps a lot of people, sometimes me included – but, fuck me, feeling guilty about not loving myself enough is too far.

In my teens, I'd criticise myself nearly every time I spotted my own reflection, which is of course a shit state of affairs. Twenty years on, I found myself instead taking the time to try to love my body, looking in the mirror and forcibly telling myself how gorgeous it is and then, after a day of seeing filtered film posters and faces that rid human life of all spots and lines and freckles (unless it is the filter that adds 'cute' freckles), I'd waver again. And then I'd feel guilty about wavering. Fuck sake, I have so much other shit to do.

'You cannot love others until you love yourself.' Thing is, I really think I can. If I hated myself, maybe not, but on days I'm just not that keen on myself, I think I'm still all right at loving others, pretty good actually; my kid, friends, boyfriend, family, strangers, a snail on the path outside my house, a friend's cat come up to sit on my lap, birds. I can love them. I can still scatter seeds for sparrows even on days I think my mind and conversation are dull as under-diluted diluting juice and my lobster-red face about as attractive as recurring thrush. And loving others often lifts my mood and makes me more likely to love myself too.

self ish

could try harder i suppose –
self-serenade *i love yous*
to each winking window pane

dash up and down the trellis
role-playing both parts
juliet above, romeo below
till i am utterly exhausted

but the baby needs changed
and the toddler face-palms,
screaming in the shop again

a friend's car is coughing smoke
and my neighbour craves a cup of tea
to save her from the solitude
that turns her weeks into a waiting room,

and in the oceans, people drown
politically abandoned
and mostly, we look the other way

waiting for the day, perhaps
we love ourselves enough
to love others just as much

At around the time the 'love yourself or you're a failure' messages
in shops and social media were starting to make me want to stick
toothpicks into my arse cheeks, I was asked to write a poem for a
meditation app. I've never meditated officially, though I feel that

20

many of my 'hobbies' – staring at clouds, lying with my eyes closed going over poems in my head, listening to music while stirring soup, masturbating into sleep, eating strawberries as if they are small red gods, hugs, walking through cities gazing at pigeons or people, and so on – are similar to meditation in some ways.

This app was specifically designed to encourage people to take time for themselves. It has a lot of great content about all the different ways we can do this, including a section for introducing your children to meditations of all kinds.

The app, if you opt in, sends notifications throughout the day to encourage you to take time out, even one minute, to find your own calm. I hadn't heard of this app previously, but I downloaded it to see if I liked it enough to write the poem. I signed up to the calming reminders.

Often, these reminders came at my busiest times of the day, like just before the school run. As I was desperately trying to finish an email before dashing to get my daughter, the app would pop up telling me to really feel my breathing for a minute.

I was asked to write the poem specifically from the point of view of a mother, because mothers, I was told by the team, get some of the fewest meditative opportunities. No shit, Sherlock.

I found myself more and more stressed out by both the app's soothing hints and the advertising team, who were not following the calming, self-loving message of their product but instead sending me emails all weekend about how tight a deadline it was and reminding me that the poem about how mothers need more time to themselves needed to be back in three days' time so if I could work on it over the weekend, super-duper.

When I posted it, on time, I put something in the comments about knowing the poem was a little 'cringy' but that I'd really enjoyed a lot about using the app, which is true. The advertising team were on me to remove this 'cringy' comment faster than the top-speed setting on a vibrator makes my muscles jolt in a half-orgasmic half-Frankensteinian electric shock. I have never enjoyed the higher settings of vibrators; they always feel like someone's moved the finish line of a race to the beginning for me to trip over almost unnoticed just as I leave the starting blocks – more clit hiccup than luxury cruise.

The fluster of collaborating on this calming meditation app was a running joke among my friends for a long time. I switched off the notifications after I was told, while working on a deadline before my daughter got home, to – ping – try to concentrate on the way my body felt in the chair. *Fuck off,* I yelled. I've heard that swearing also has a calming influence on the body.

I recently shouted at a similar meme online telling me kindly that I deserved to love myself. *Fuck off!* I screamed again, this time into a kind woman's Instagram square: *I don't want to fucking love myself, I just want to lick this peanut butter from the upside down spoon, hug my kid when she gets home, feed my neighbour's cat and work out when I'm going to get my taxes done.*

ascent

what joy it would be
not to think of this body
for even one day

not to mock or to praise
not to weigh up the size
nor the shape

the way clothing
creeps into its folds;
how it looks as i sit

how some body older
or younger or taller or curvier
might suit this skin better

what joy
for one single, good day
to wake as birds wake

feet perched
on the edge of the bed
before we ascend into sky

not one thought
how our wings look
in flight

skin, sometimes

it would be cool if you tanned a bit better,
holiday lobster, got you from my father,
at least i'm easy to spot on the nudist beach in france;

white breasts on burnt body like the most poisonous
of mushrooms, though i do enjoy my freckles now,
and using sunscreen made for children

in storms, you are incredible; waterproof but breathing,
seamlessly holding in my insides,
umbrella to the skeleton

how expensive you would be in mountain warehouse,
all-weather fabric; afforded only by those who go camping
despite having money for hotels

the hoover is full of you – and hair – when i empty it
seven layers magnificent, ever-shedding genius,
every seven years afresh;

do you remember that time in the forest
when i toppled from my bike when i was eight
and in a month our graze was gone?

sure, you have your limits,
but do you remember how much fun we had
last week with all those oils?

thrush has been a bitch and i don't love
the way you crack sometimes between my toes
and i can't work out if i'm in you or i am you

either way, i really love how well
you let sweat escape on sunny days,
or when i'm dancing, to stop me from collapsing

pass times

whilst worrying about my thighs
a nightingale flew past
        – i didn't see it

prodding at my skin
a book fell from the shelf
        – i didn't read it

sweating about my scent
a lover lapped me up
        – i didn't feel it

frowning in the mirror
friends told me lovely things
        – i didn't hear it

HOT ROCKET BODY

One day, after staring in the mirror wondering if I loved my smile lines or hated them and if I did hate them, why I shouldn't do that, and so on and so on until the water levels rose and all human life became extinct, I made a pact: I will not spend any more time criticising my body *or* feeling guilty about not loving it as much as I apparently need to. I will look at it and touch it and use it and enjoy it, but I will stop with the other shit.

When I slip back into the pointless stary criticism, I have a five-step strategy to snap myself out of it.

1. I think of billionaires laughing like horror-movie villains around a boardroom table.

Bahahahahahaha. Like that. They are laughing at me. Specifically, they are laughing at how much of my money and time they have stolen, now lining their Dalmatian-fur industry pockets. I think of them all as arrogant. I imagine they are. Billionaires are not a natural phenomenon. They're not oxbow lakes, they're manmade and, like bubblegum-flavoured vapes sold in sweet shops, really shouldn't exist.

I think of them, mouths open so loud in laughter I can see into their stomachs, which are filled with gold coins, giant belly safe locked by the combination: IMRICHANDYOUMAKEMERICHERBAHAHAHA.

No, no longer will they rob me, no matter how much money they spend to convince me my hips are too hippy or my belly is too

27

belly-y or my skin is too much like actual skin, or my breastmilk is too breastmilky or my body is too much like a body that eats or gives birth or has a shape they didn't cut out of a dollar bill. I just can't let them win this.

I realise this sounds like a simplification. It is. There are various levels to marketing and product design, and there are small businesses selling unnecessary stuff too, stuff like this book. And not all billionaires laugh like that. But many in the beauty and skincare industries do have board meetings sitting around tables working out what insecurities they can push on us and our children from a younger and younger age.

On a recent tour in France, for the first time I saw a huge number of adverts aimed specifically at young teens and pre-teens from various 'skincare' companies. These adverts were for pre-ageing products, skin 'training' products, targeting girls – I saw adverts only for girls' skin – to prepare themselves against their first wrinkles, as if ageing even into your early teen years was now a war we all need to armour ourselves against. So now, as well as women, little girls can walk city streets to school seeing these messages plastered like goading gods above their heads and panic about growing older from the age of eleven or twelve.

If you are part of these new product campaigns, fuck you. Seriously, fuck you all. And if you are selling this advertising space to these companies targeting little kids' minds, fuck you too.

So yes, I imagine them laughing, these billionaires. I imagine them swarming in the skies like seagulls on a beach trying to steal your chips as you lift them to your mouth, but instead of snatching your potato dreams they caw warnings about how the chips will make you fat and ugly or skinny and wrinkled so hand them over, caw caw bahahahaha.

Annoyingly, these seagulls don't only swoop in on self-hate, but also, now it can turn a profit too, on self-love, capitalising once again by convincing me I can only find the means to love myself through products they sell. Instead of more sleep and adequate childcare, what I really need are anti-puffy-eye vitamin pills and a scented pillow; or instead of just drinking more water, I need anti-wrinkle cream, Botox, or health-juice shots with ginseng or turmeric in plastic bottles big enough to hold about one ejaculation's worth of goodness; instead of closing my eyes for a moment, I need eye-mask packs and crystals to roll over my fat face; instead of believing I am beautiful, or just doing things I love more than thinking of my own reflection all the time, I must prove my self-love with an expensive naked photoshoot.

All these things are fine if you want them and can afford them and have fun with them but, despite what the adverts would have me believe, they're not essential for self-love. None of them. I will get the same results from sleep, water, friends, hugs, laughing, wanking, walking and smelling roses, all of which are very much cheaper and better at not fucking up the planet's own beautiful body.

2. If the evil laughing doesn't work and I am still standing looking at my body thinking *if only you had just slightly more bla bla fucking bla and slightly less bla bla fucking bla*, I turn away from the mirror, grab my phone and text a mate or family member instead. A bit like painting one nail red to remind you not to pick up your phone when driving (a technique my mum taught me), I text a friend a nice message to remind myself that maybe loving others is a more valid use of my time than picking myself apart.

3. Every time I waste more than thirty seconds staring at my flesh, mainly my face, being a bitch to it for no good outcome, or wondering if I love it as much as this morning's Instagram square says I must, I put a pound in a jar. Like a swear jar, if you had one of these. I did, growing up. At the end of the year, you take the money that you had to pay because you said shit seventy-three times to your brother and fuck twice (sometimes fuck was a two-pound swear), and you use

it for 'good': either giving it to an organisation doing better things than your cuss words, or buying crisps. I did this for a year, putting a pound in a jar every time I bullied myself too much. I can't remember how much I made, but it was a good reminder not to waste my own time. I also use this technique for avoiding bottled water. Every time I fill up my flask when out, I put the money I would have spent on a plastic bottle of water towards something less shit. Writing this has made me wonder what my parents did with our swear fines. Also, I don't actually have a jar any more, I transfer the money online into a savings account, but the jar sounded more poetic.

4. A bit more morbid perhaps, but this is maybe the one that I do the most; if I catch myself at it again, I think about how many years I statistically have left on this planet in this body if I am very lucky. Guilt and death are always good motivation for me. *What the fuck are you wasting time on this shit for, Hollie? Go and learn to do that twisty thing on roller skates you've always wanted to do. Death will come soon. Step away from the mirror and get on your fucking roller skates.* (That sentence would cost two pounds because it includes both a swear word and being a bitch to yourself, although I don't fine myself for swearing any more because I wouldn't be able to afford it.)

5. If none of the above works, I think of space exploration. I think of my body as a spaceship, a spaceship I have on loan for, if I am very, very, very lucky, ninety years. I think this would make the astronaut inside the spaceship my personality, or my soul, if I believe in that. I'm not sure.

Anyway, body = spaceship; a spaceship in which I get to explore our solar system until the spaceship is taken away and I can no longer breathe in that atmosphere.

I imagine the astronaut blasting through the beauty of space, able, if they look, to gaze upon the purple black between expanding stars. They are mesmerised.

Suddenly, the space police start chasing the astronaut, teasing them about the rocket, flaunting their top-of-the-range propellers and nose cones and laughing at the astronaut's smaller nozzles.

Astronaut: But my rocket's working really well, and I'm on my way to see Jupiter's moons – I've heard they're magnificent.
Space police: Not in that tatty rocket, I hope!
Astronaut: What's wrong with it?
Space police: Where do we start!
Astronaut: Really? But I think it will still get me to Jupiter, I can already see Cyllene.
(Space police, panicking, start pasting billboards onto comets declaring 'tatty rocket astronaut embarrasses the cosmos' all along the route to Jupiter until the astronaut decides to stop the rocket and cry and not visit Jupiter, at least not until they can afford all the new propellers and nozzles and airfoils, gyroscope and vernier engines, which will be never.)

I would love to visit Jupiter. Not only does it have a constant visible aurora – unlike Earth's, which you have to pay thousands of pounds to maybe see on a night-time bus tour in Iceland but won't if it's too cloudy – it also has at least seventy-nine moons (and maybe sixteen more, depending on who you ask), one of which, Europa, is ice-coated, apparently with more water than the Earth's oceans, and another of which, Io, is the most volcanically active body in the entire solar system with hundreds of volcanoes that erupt lava fountains up to twelve miles high.

As a parent, Jupiter makes sense to visit because its radiation belt can easily disable sensitive electrical appliances, which would mean that trying to limit mine and my kid's screen time would be much less problematic.

I do not want to die in a healthy body-rocket I never used because the space police told me it was too tatty. I want to have driven it across the universe, whizzing around Jupiter, floating contentedly until the rocket shoots its last flash of fuel to propel one final glittering orbit around the Sun.

Even with this astronaut death fantasy, it is still hard not to get pulled back in, because there is a lot of money being spent to make you think your rocket is shit. It isn't. Go and see Jupiter's moons. All of them.

love poetry on jupiter

with so many moons to marvel at
imagine how much romance could be written

how stressed would shakespeare be
as he frantically rewrote romeo and juliet
grappling to work out which moon is jealous
which is grieving, and if they all kill the sun –

would arguments erupt between the lovers
as, peering into one another's eyes
they attempt some moon-based flattery
not specifically enough,

oh romeo, swear not by that moon again!

christ almighty, which one then?
does it make a difference which one?

yes! of course it makes a difference!

and would juliet be bothered anyway
by which light was breaking
through which sodding yonder window
if, having recently started her periods
the tides of her shedding womb
were pulled in sixty-plus directions
by competing lunar cycles,
packing rags for exile,
how many days
are in a month when each year
is roughly twelve years long?

things i could think about instead of criticising my body

a medium-sized hedgehog you didn't expect to see there
rope swings dangling over rivers   different fancy hats
left-handed fountain pens   the surface of neptune
the belly of a pterodactyl   an empty railway station
small yellow flowers you do not know the name of
newborn baby toes   kaleidoscopes   poppy seeds
black velvet scrunchies   rose-scented hand cream
dark green nail varnish   cuba's healthcare system
pomegranate juice   paris   dry stone walls   turtles
a puddle you can't work out the depth of   porridge
an apartment in halifax   gorse that smells of coconut
dwarf daffodils   a jar full of pens, one of which works
the difference between satsumas and clementines
a glitterball in your bedroom   alphonso mangos
orange by wendy cope   scottish tablet with your coffee
gold melting into a mould and hardening into a gold ring
herons chatting   peanut butter   red cheddar   yorkshire pudding
salt and pepper   potential names for fairies
blackberries that look sweet but are still a little bitter
dolly parton not being richer because she's so generous
lipstick almost the same colour as your lips   cottages
cold water   a flame on a matchstick
the burnt edge of a pink marshmallow
a pineapple   sheep huddling in the corner of a field
a newborn dragon in a blue egg   the word emerald
hard honey   a peach tree with lots of peaches on
someone laughing in another room louder than traffic
cream of garlic soup   what to write on a postcard
ringlets drying higher   the horizon   time travel
any tracy chapman song   bradford literature festival
dandelions   kamila's cat, cookie   freckles   fern brady

when the king resigns in chess, and you win the game that way
cows sleeping but other cows not sleeping in the same field

inside, we are the brightest shade of red

my hair began greying in its twenties –
lazier than some,
could not be arsed to make colour any more

understandable; most days i feel the same;
better ways to spend your energy
when grey will do just fine
besides, the woods are full of bluebells
and soon again, to tuck in roots for winter's bedtime
forest greens will strip in slow motion auburn glitter

as the ever-ending sky yawns messy neon
each morning, and each night

and around my eggshell bones
this lucky blood still pumps; punctual and alive
its warm and heady maze of scarlet time

GETTING MY PRE-BABY BODY BACK

The saddest thing about having a child has been anticipating the inevitable moment that my body-loving baby, or rather just body-using baby, will be told by various people and platforms to think about her shape and skin and colour, often by those gaining from her demise.

I used to just love my body, in the uncomplicated way that most kids just love their bodies, because it enables you to do a variety of things such as sing, jump in puddles, fiddle, eat apple slices, hug your friends, pick up ladybirds and make daisy chains. I never thought I had a 'problem' with my body until I was told I did. By friends, by boys, by magazines and billboards and movies and my gran.

Watching a baby and then a toddler love its body so much, over-whelmed by every new thing it learnt to do, while I, as a new mother, was made to despise mine, was a tragedy.

There is a social obsession about getting your 'body back' after birth, to the level that I felt sickened by my own skin after it had done one of the most incredible things it ever achieved. I cannot get my body back to what it was before it grew and fed a baby because that old body doesn't know half the shit this new one does. It's like asking me to get my brain back to how it was before I read the ending of *The Lion, the Witch and the Wardrobe*. It's not fucking possible.

Of course, this 'get your body back' obsession isn't just related to mothers. Generally, this phrase seems to be used when people are older, romanticising about the body they had when they were younger. This idea of 'younger', however, does not seem to have a set age; my friends in their thirties talk about their teenage bodies, despite hating that body as a teenager; my sixty-year-old neighbour tells me she wants my thirty-year-old body; my gran, at eighty, wanted the body my mum had at sixty, and so on.

There are health reasons for some of these body-back longings. Birth complications creating actual physical trauma – prolapses, for example – are never going to be embraced with body-loving elation. At ninety, my grandma said to me that getting old was shit, but only once you're actually *old*-old and your bones feel it and grazes take ages to heal; or don't.

I did a school event near Glastonbury recently and took my daughter. We went into the town in the break between the workshops and the gig. Glastonbury high street is pretty amazing. It is full to brim with crystal shops and fairy glades and mermaids and pixies and people who are witches and druids. I was so glad, almost ten years after writing about how shit it was last time I took her there, that there were more and more fantastical figures depicted as something other than white people.

I'm not a big fan of stuff that you can't either eat or read or wear. But for the first time in years, I bought a small ornament. It was of Gaia, the figure depicted as birthing the Earth or personifying the Earth in Greek mythology. She has a moon on one breast, sun on the other; her pregnant belly is depicted as the Earth. I'd never seen an image of pregnancy so positive in my life.

Seeing this figure, Gaia, made me cry a little in the shop, embarrassingly for my daughter. I thought back to my pregnancy and how powerless and scared and just shit I often felt; not just physically but mentally; how many comments people made about me not being married or too young or not ready or looking fat or strange or so on.

I think pregnancy might have been just a little bit easier if I'd seen this figure of Gaia then. The only godly figure of motherhood I'd been brought up with was the Virgin Mary, an impossible-to-emulate figure of mothering. Gaia wasn't impossible, she was beautiful. If I'd imagined myself in that way, I might have appreciated the hugeness of what I was doing more, could have imagined my bulging belly as a world growing within me, the breasts I was so embarrassed to feed my kid with as something other than shameful or weird, they were the moon and sun and life.

I put the Gaia figure on my bookshelf and I look at it occasionally when I find myself lamenting the fact my body looks like a body that had a baby, as if that is a failed body. *Don't hate your body, Hollie. Hate the culture that tells you to hate your body. Move the hate.*

I wouldn't have my daughter or this mindboggling understanding of holding and delivering life into the world without this body.

I don't want my pre-baby body back. I also don't want my awkward-as-fuck twenties or teenage body back, the body that I also thought was shit at the time, and was taken advantage of on several occasions often because of this desperate desire to be told I was worthy or attractive or, better still, hot.

What I want, what I wish for most in the whole world of bodies, is my toddler body back; the one that has not yet heard the whispers of the world and does not give a fuck about itself as puddle-water spills over its bright red restless wellies.

the toddler

red wellies and a party dress, the toddler marches up
and down the path, singing songs about a giant greedy goose
as if the sun has told her secrets about all that empty air;
how song, in joyous freedom, may awaken lazy angels;

meanwhile, the adults chat, pass flasks of lukewarm coffee
laughing, as if someone made a joke

too warm now, the toddler flings off her gauntlet dress,
faints dramatic on the grass, faking her own death
self-resurrects, applauds herself –
a robin smiles then hops away. she chases it but cannot fly

her parents call her over, *a little quieter*, dress back on her,
offer her a sandwich; she shakes her head incredulous

sandwiches!? there are puddles to be stirred!;
she finds a better stick, inspects every muddy ripple
till, silent at the fifth, sees clouds far below her feet
she crouches for a closer look, then gasps,
as if reading rainfall's palm

deliverance/delivery

for years, i was searching for this body you tell me to get back, as if a simple case of missing bones, as if a cat not yet come home. i pinned a poster to every tree trunk on each street: *have you seen my missing body? have you seen my missing body?* a photograph of me, smiling, before pregnancy, no piles of dirty washing in the background, no milk sick on my shoulders, no pink tulips in the vase.

four days pass and nothing. one week until a sudden knock. i answer as my toddler sits suspicious behind me, clinging to my ankle bones. a stranger holds a cardboard box, they hope it is the right one, they found it in the bushes near the notice in the park.

in the lounge, we open it, bloody and elastic, my old pre-baby womb. i put it back inside me, feel the empty weight of it as a second rattle of the letterbox sounds and an envelope lands, soggy full. two pre-baby eyes drop, roll across the doormat, brighter, better-slept, tear ducts not yet raw with years of stinging stars, not yet sobbed sun-scorched storms as my baby smiles, then laughs.

next, my pre-baby arms are awkwardly pushed through with a shout of *sorry* from the other side, wrist-first, elbows cause some issues as i yank them and manoeuvre, shouting *thank you*, reattach them to my shoulders, slimmer, softer, unmothered, muscles not yet moulded by rocking sonnets into calm, not yet carried sleepy limbs across a million mislaid thresholds, no clammy hands held across every busy street.

next my lips, less kissed than ever; my cheeks, less kissed than ever; my throat, no tickle of birth's opera; my old,

41

unfountained breasts, chest undented by the sweat patch of a dreaming baby's heat; my pre-baby ears, no murmur of the thrill of those first mumbled calls of *mum*.

each pre-baby finger is delivered one by one, lightly thudding on the mat like ten plump raindrops, unwrapped by newborn grasps, unheld by shyly frightened fingers. i look at them, replait the broken ligaments to the stubs.

a final flurry now: my old pre-baby lungs, unlullabied by bed-time song; my pre-baby hips, unchaired by sideways holds; my pre-baby brain, no longer ridiculed as mushy or forgetful or mummy baby thick, both ecstasy and aches forgot; my pre-baby blood, unmingled forever from the hug of your existence.

i say a final thank you, close the door. my pre-baby body now finally restored, socially acceptable, unmothered to its core; i look down, the grip of my giggling toddler no longer clinging to my ankle bones, cot covers unruffled, house pre-baby silent, baby vanished back to thought.

shade

for clae eastgate, thank you

poem written after being told, once again, by perfect strangers,
that my daughter and I look nothing alike

once, i had my portrait painted
never realised my face was so colourful before

perhaps the painter was looking elsewhere, i thought
– three shades of green on their palette

in the street, my daughter and me
are never mistaken for mother and daughter

people ask who we are, as if strangers,
forever assume her blonde friends are my blood

unable to see the roundness in both of our faces
the cheekbones we share; the way we both laugh

with our hands to our mouths,
as if embarrassed by happiness

paint us both colourless, and maybe you'll see
the green we both hide in our cheeks

a estas alturas

*a estas alturas is a Spanish phrase meaning 'from these heights'.
I learnt it from a brilliant poet, Sandra Cisneros. It is used by
those who are older, looking back on life, as if getting older is like
climbing a mountain and having a clearer and wider view of the
world with each year that passes.*

at eleven, she discusses
what she sweetly calls her *childhood*
comments on how cute she was at three

when she is twenty, she laments
the self-consciousness of teenage years;
wishes she could go back, tell her young self to believe

at thirty-three she flicks through photos
from her twenties, how glorious she was
never thought it at the time

at fifty-three, she looks admiringly at forty;
did not realise
how well she suited early middle age

by seventy, she refers to her fifties
as her *younger days*; marvels at the strength
in her dancing legs back then

at eighty, she tells me her seventies were best
lunches at their cheapest;
friends free every weekday

by ninety-four, her eighties were a dream
she grips my hand, sighs, says she
wishes she still gripped it like she could at ninety-three

WHEN I FELL IN LOVE WITH JOE WICKS, BUT DIDN'T DO THE SIT-UPS

The thing I find really tiring about parenting is being in charge. I don't like being in charge, telling people what to do, confrontation. I never have, and having a baby didn't suddenly transform my personality.

Every morning waking up knowing you will piss off someone (aka your child) by waking them up when they want to stay in bed, making them wash and get dressed, making them eat food they don't like as much as other food, stopping them eating food they like more than other food, telling them no every five seconds to toys or checkout sweets then, later on, every new iPhone update or sportswear brand you're a loser if you don't have. It's exhausting, and often fairly upsetting. Every day as a parent I wake up knowing that, out of intense love for my child, she will dislike me, momentarily perhaps, perhaps for an hour or the whole year.

It's also just dull being the one in charge and responsible all the time. Getting a break from your child isn't something to feel guilty about. It's really a break from parenting I want. I love my child to heights that are frightening in their intensity, and I love hanging out with her. Even then, I don't want to be parenting all the time.

Because of this, I fell in love with Joe Wicks during lockdown. For those who don't know Joe Wicks, he is a very cheery personal trainer who did a series of live workouts aimed primarily at the kids who were off school during lockdown. I loved him for many reasons, but mainly because he provided half an hour each morning where someone other than me was telling my kid what to do.

Other people hated him, but we always seem to hate people that are trying to be helpful, especially when they smile or make money while they're doing it. I also love Jamie Oliver.

For that half hour each day, doing what Joe Wicks said, like some sort of pre-breakfast exercise dominatrix, it was bliss. In reality, my kid didn't do much of the class, mainly shouted at him through the TV whenever he mentioned 'Captain Serotonin' and joined in with occasional moves. Either way, I enjoyed it a lot.

Once lockdown was over, I thought, *I'll keep doing this. Yeah, fuck yeah, I'll keep doing this and I'll get so fucking toned and I'll do the abs workout too and I'll get a six pack and not this mum belly* (as I still annoyingly referred to it in my head).

I love feeling like my body is strong and healthy, and there are so many activities I really enjoy – dancing, roller skating, cycling slowly while staring at the sky – but this wasn't about that. It wasn't about staying fit. It was the stomach ripples I was thinking of, and that shit is both difficult to achieve and irrelevant to a healthy body. Nonetheless, for a moment I really wanted to have them.

When lockdown was over, the first morning in weeks I was properly alone, my daughter at her dad's and off to school, I woke up with no alarm, the sunlight tickling hot across my chest at the wink of open curtain, my naked, warmed, sleep-crinkled body splayed out like a cat in a patch of summer sun and I thought, *No, I can't be arsed.*

I've seen the effort it takes to get a fully rippled six-pack body. I lived for four years next door to a lovely policeman-body builder and his family. During lockdown, when the gyms were closed, he had to do all of his workouts in the garden, separated meagrely from our terrace patch by a small fence. For the whole summer, all my daughter and I heard were grunts and groans of what sounded at first to be some sort of loud, difficulty-in-orgasming outdoor sex struggle but what we soon realised were a series of fairly painful exercise routines coming from next door, as he lifted weights and skipped and ran back and forth across the communal drive and did sit-ups for hour upon hour, as his young child sat giggling on his back. It was arduous work.

So I didn't get up to do the Joe Wicks workout. Instead, I lay in bed and read a few chapters of *Gormenghast* and made a cup of tea and took it back to bed and thought about all the options in life that lay before me now the world was opening up again; a kind of giant golden set of scales balanced between 'things I definitely want and will work for' versus 'can-I-honestly-be-arsed-with-the-work-needed-to-get-this-and-if-I-can't-then-stop-fucking-bothering-about-it'.

In the throes of looking back on life, many of my loved ones have said things to me like, 'Oh, I would have loved to have travelled more/been a go-go dancer/met Idris Elba'.

I don't want to look back on life like that, especially about things I could easily do.

Similarly, though, I don't want to spend all of my time looking jealously at other people who have what I deem 'better' bellies or faces or houses or eye make-up, thinking *I wish I could do that/have that/be that*. I'm not talking about people who are billionaires and have lifestyles and ice trays I could never afford, or want. I mean people around me who have roughly the same options I have.

So I made a list of things I moan about not having and then I spent a while really, really thinking about, if they were affordable and achievable, whether I actually wanted them enough to spend the time and money they would take. Like really, do you really want that, Hollie?

Like, OK, you'd like toned legs like Angela Bassett when she played Tina Turner in the film of her life that you watched obsessively for about three years between the ages of ten and thirteen. Fine. So, do you actually want to spend more time doing leg lifts or whatever, and cutting down on dipping toasted bread in melted Camembert cheese? If so, do it. Shut up and do it. Work out more and cut down on the goo. If not, accept that this will never happen and shut the fuck up about your lovely juicy thighs.

Do you really want to spend more time cleaning your house so you have a spotless house that makes friends say, 'Oh, your house is always so tidy' but also secretly feel less at ease sitting down in? If so, clean your fucking house more often, it's not difficult, clean it and shut up. If not, stop giving a fuck about the sort of tidiness your friends don't give a fuck about anyway.

Do you really want to spend an extra forty minutes a day applying products and straightening your hair so that it shines more sleekly? If so, great, get up a bit earlier and do it and enjoy the process and enjoy the shine and the sleek and the more frequent compliments about your sleek hair. If not, accept the dull nature of your wavier locks, and go spend your time on something you do want to do. Like sleeping more. Or learning to do an eyeliner flick, or getting fluent in French.

If you want these things, really want them, do them. Do them. You have the time. But if you don't, just accept it and stop comparing yourself and your life to people who do decide to spend more time or money working out or cleaning their house or redecorating or learning to crochet or putting products and heat on their hair or whatever other differences stand between you and them.

That's their choice. This is yours.

honestly,

i would love a flatter stomach
but not as much as i love
not doing sit-ups

and i'd love the silhouette
of chain-smoking parisians
but not as much as i would love
to share your sticky toffee pudding

and i'd love the sort of skin
people look at and say *wow*
how do you stay so young?
but not as much as i would love
to spend the cash needed for botox
on romantic trips to peterborough
and a waterproof vibrator

and i'd love a fancy wedding
where someone promises to love me
until the day i die; but not as much as i love
not being anybody's wife

and i'd love to learn japanese
but not as much as sleeping

and i'd love to study art
so i could join in conversations
with friends who go to galleries
then invite them back to mine
for fresh pasta coloured pink

from purple beetroot
i grew from seed myself

but not as much as boiling supernoodles
and then reading a book

and in the evenings
once my emails have been sent
once my daughter is asleep
the plates are put away
and i've brushed my hair and teeth
once the washing is hung up
the lunchbox and the fruit snack packed
i would love to spend that time
learning about poetry
so i could edit all my poems
with meticulous precision
till i am proud that these poems
are the best poems i could write;

but not as much as i would love
to lay back on the sofa
watch reruns of jen brister
flick through photographs of space

poem written after hearing: *'she could have read the entire works of shakespeare in the time she spends doing her make-up each day'*

perhaps she doesn't want to read
the entire works of shakespeare; perhaps for her
the pleasure of one fleeting jolt on planet earth
is more gloriously served with paintbrush to her face
calm before the mirror, meditating the mathematics
of which inky curve to sweep upon each excited eyelid
reminiscent of that photograph she fell in love with
from a 1960s french film or the glittered trail of comets
or the trace of snails on pavements she saves along her walks;
her face a moon-blank canvas she can escape to
amidst shape and line and colour to start afresh anytime
erase with soap and water; perhaps she is an artist too,
and why is it always shakespeare that you quote?
perhaps you could have learnt the entire works of ryoki inoue
or maya angelou or nigella lawson in the time you've spent
slagging women off for spending too much time on make-up
or other things you deem inadequate or mindless
as you fill your entire life with purely purposeful tasks

perhaps, she doesn't want to read
the entire works of shakespeare

perhaps, she already has

shattered

and once my stomach has been sculpted
into undulating waves two thousand sunset sit-ups
three thousand sunrise crunches   once each eyebrow
neatly plucked to chosen phase of waning moon
daytime face painted to monochrome perfection
bedtime face primed in unceasing skincare routines
once each storyline injected back to newborn-botox-blank
hairs ripped from every limb in coagulating wax
once another bowl of pasta has been pushed out of my reach
pudding swapped for powder   passion swapped for pose
when at last, our bodies bulldozed into photo finish flesh
sculptures on a stripy lawn   shhh, hold in your breath
what happens next?   *what happens next?*
WHAT
          HAPPENS
                    NEXT?

what great pleasures can i expect
from this portrait-perfect skin,
that i cannot get exactly as it is?

'what's it like having so many soft bits on your body?'

in the riverbank nook
your tongue tickling riddles on my neck
you ask me what it's like
harbouring such softness in my flesh
self-conscious in your hands
fallen dress strap lets the sun spy chest
your own skin sailboat taut
moored slim against the water's edge, i
feel it as an insult

a heron turns then stalls
sun hides shy behind the bullrushes
your hands, to prove me wrong
gently map out all my softer bits
palms caress my belly
till muscles rest, stop holding breath in
you gorge on thigh and boob
let sunshine soothe our naked skin, till
trembling, i believe you

'IT'S WHAT'S ON THE INSIDE THAT COUNTS'

No it's fucking not, I thought, rolling my eyes and adding another layer of mascara to teenage lashes already too clogged for me to properly see through.

I knew what whichever well-meaning adult had declared this to me meant – you know, like, your personality and how caring and interesting you are and all that good stuff in life – but this phrase rarely made a difference when I was younger. In our society, especially for young people surrounded every day at school by other young people, their brains saturated by the must-be-cool messages of youth advertising culture and a fashion industry now unfortunately focused on people from babygro age onwards, the outside counts a lot.

When I was feeling shit about my appearance, it didn't help to be told it was the inside that counted because that didn't seem true. It wasn't what people whispered about or what I was getting teased for; it was my tiny tits, scabby feet, sweaty red face and the fact I couldn't be in the Kickers club or Levi's club because my parents wouldn't buy me Kickers or Levi's.

To this day, I have no idea how kids in schools with no uniform policy cope with the force of the fashion industry encroaching into every day of their young lives.

'It's what's on the inside that counts.' My mum never used this phrase with me when I was younger. Instead, as I purposelessly criticised my appearance, she sympathised, bored as she must have been, and spent a lot of her free time standing in teen clothes shops as I tried on wrap skirts and T-shirts that said 'babe' or 'hands off' in sparkly gold letters. The boy's T-shirts did not say these things or sparkle. They said things like 'Don't show any emotion other than anger' (slightly paraphrasing here) or 'NASA' or 'Eat. Sleep. Football. Repeat'.

My mum has worked as a nurse all her adult life, surrounded every day by people with a variety of ill-health conditions. Although I did on occasion cry and complain about my body, in general I mainly felt very lucky I had one that worked as well as it did. If I moaned too much, or too pointlessly, my mum would put me right.

As a medical practitioner, my mum is fascinated by the body, which made it very difficult for me not to be fascinated by it too. If it wasn't for her interest in human flora and fauna in all its marvellous modes, I can only assume that the power of adverts and the beauty industry and fashion and so on would have bitten into my self-confidence much more than it did.

The stories she told me growing up about what she saw and knew of the body made me absolutely certain that a) she was wonderful, b) my body was pretty cool and c) I never wanted to work as a nurse. It was impossible to avoid body talk with my mum. And I don't mean the sort of standard body talk I had with other people, like how your hair looks or how to put on or lose weight or whether nipple hair is normal for girls (yes). I mean anatomical, internal, biological body talk: boils, snot, blisters, verrucas, warts, abrasions, vaginal infections, foreskin rashes, prolapses, fungal foot treatments, and so on.

I loved my mum's job. I used to have to wait for her to finish work after school a lot. I'd walk from my school to the doctor's surgery and tell the receptionist I was there. Then I'd wait in the waiting room with all the other patients until my mum came out and hugged me and everyone knew that I was not in fact a normal patient but the actual daughter of their favourite nurse. I felt very special.

If there was a gap between patients, I could weigh myself or get my blood pressure checked. If not, then straight up to the staff room where I'd sit for a couple of hours doing my homework and helping myself to the staff biscuits.

In the waiting room, I'd look around and wonder which people's bodies and what parts of their bodies my mum had seen and treated and whether the people were there for the wart clinic or the genital check-ups or the flu jab. As the surgery was very close to my secondary school, rumours also flew around my friendship groups about which teachers' body parts my mum may have seen, mainly whether she had seen my PE teacher's bum. Obviously, she never revealed anything.

As well as giving me a lot of great ammunition for grossing out my friends, my mum's stories also gave me a real appreciation of the working body. Still today, when people use the phrase 'it's what's on the inside that counts', I most often don't think about personality, but the actual insides of the body: intestines, stomach, blood, bladder, my functioning digestive system.

If I had a cold as a child, and my nose was blocked and snotty and I felt like a gory bag of phlegm, my mum would say things like *isn't the body amazing, producing all that nasal mucus to fight the infection*, as she stared at my snot-covered tissue and explained the colour-coding possibilities of snot diagnosis. *Did you know we swallow mucus all day long without knowing it?*

If I got a rash, my mum would say *isn't the skin amazing – it's the body's biggest organ you know and isn't it great that it's waterproof! How fascinating it all is!*

If I was stinking with sweat, she'd say *go and have a shower, Hollie* but also, *Wow! What a super cooling mechanism we have. Do you know if we didn't sweat, we'd overheat and get very ill?* It seems Prince Andrew doesn't know that.

Of all of these stories, I remember my mum's fascination with scabs most vividly.

If I was staring disgusted at a manky scab forming on my bloody knee after I'd tried once again to cycle down the hill with my feet on top of the handlebars, my mum would look at that scab as if it were a newborn baby learning to talk.

Scabs, my mum said, *are nature's plasters.*

I remember being told not to scratch or pick at scabs not because it's gross, but because you are disrupting a most perfect bodily process during which the genius scab, after a cut, scratch or scrape, magically forms once your blood has clotted and the surface of the wound starts to dry out. It covers the wound as it heals, preventing infection by keeping out bacteria. It is a masterpiece of the body and should be praised not insulted and certainly not fucked with in any way by children's picking fingers.

Look how amazingly your body heals itself, my mum would say, every day commenting on the scab's progress, fascinated at the speed with which my younger skin healed.

And your nose, if your nostrils were at the top you'd drown in a drizzle.

And if your eyelashes didn't guard your eyes, and if your eyebrows didn't catch the sweat, and if your nose stopped making bogeys, imagine!

I'm sure my mum regaled me with a lot more information about my wonderful body than I took in, because I, as every child who could actually learn things from their parents does, often stopped listening and got distracted by other thoughts or told her not to continue talking about pus because I felt like I was gonna vomit.

I have also never worn thongs because of my mother's stories.

Thongs were very much in fashion when I was mid-teen, with many girls my age wearing them above the trouser waist so as to show the thong above the level of the trousers. This is, of course, the opposite of the original purpose of a thong, which was to pretend that we weren't wearing knickers below trousers because if people knew that girls or women wore pants by seeing the VPL then they would self-combust. I've never heard the phrase VPL used about boys' pants.

I was told on several occasions by my mother about the ease with which these up-the-arse strings move tiny particles of faeces from your arsehole to your vagina, thus increasing the chances of various bladder infections. I simplified this medical lesson to my friends as: *thongs can move shit to your vag.* When I see thongs, all I see is a UTI-potential shit string and have thus never found them in the slightest way sexy.

I do not know if this medical assessment is true or if my mum was trying to put me off this variety of underwear at thirteen in a world where thirteen year old girls are made to want thongs, but it worked. I wore one just once and kept pulling it out of my arse, forgetting it was meant to be there.

Knowing all of these stories about our bodies as a young girl made the concept of being 'ladylike' even more laughable than it would have been already as I approached my teens.

From the age of eleven, my body felt less like it was approaching some sort of ladylike potential and more like a volcano. As a woman, I feel like I've spent a lot of my physical life waiting for eruptions.

From eleven to fourteen, before our periods started, us girls were waiting, just waiting every day for blood to possibly cloud our pants or school skirts, swimsuit or pyjamas with the most embarrassing mark of bloodstain. We shared stories over midnight feasts about the most embarrassing places we'd heard of girls 'starting':

- on sheets at a sleepover of a family you don't know that well – *Oh my god!*
- on a school trip – *No! What if it was with Mr Hart!*
- on holiday in front of a guy you fancied – *I'd literally die!*
- at the swimming pool – *Oh my days, they had to clear the pool!*
- on a chair in the classroom just before bell rang and you couldn't stand up or leave the room and everybody asked why you weren't coming for break and you couldn't say but

you just knew you were sitting in a pool of blood – *I'd stay with you, I swear down, I would!*

Half my teenage days were spent nervously waiting in case today would be that day that I'd have to ask the question to a friend or to a teacher or to someone else's mum, *Do you have any um you know um um um* . . . Should I start to carry towels and a clean pair of pants everywhere I go just in case? Every day? Everywhere?

Once our periods did start, we still nervously waited just in case they weren't clockwork regular and started unexpectedly. And when we were on our period, we were fully aware of a sudden heavier flow which could possibly occur, perhaps during PE while wearing those fucking tiny girls-only gym shorts or white tennis skirts or during the horrendous classes in which students were not allowed to go to the toilet during lessons.

the ladylike volcano

vents coyly,
holds her breath
as lava rushes bloody from her core,

hopes no one gets too close;
stuffs clouds into her magma chamber
prays they cool the flow of earth-fire underwomb;

she does not fuss
about the threat of overheating
nor the simmering, shattered cramping
rocks fault-lining beneath her; *sits soundless,*

pretending
to be dormant,
pretending her extinction

praying
she might get away
as merely being mountain,
if she just stays very still and smiles

Early motherhood was a real pinnacle of waiting nervously for my body's stupendous volcanic ladylike eruptions.

First, I waited for pregnancy sickness (formerly known as morning sickness until too many pregnant woman laughed that title out of favour) and, when it came, I waited each hour to see what time the next bout would call.

Then, for my waters to burst – again inundated with stories of those 'ladies' whose waters burst in Tesco or in a work meeting or onto a friend's floor. I was constantly worried that this would happen in public and, in my case, it never happened at all: my waters never burst and I now feel slightly like I missed out on the water-bursting film moment.

Third, for labour to start in all its bloody glory – this waiting game was mostly terrifying, the excitement of having a baby definitely taking a back seat to the pain that would likely mark this moment, the humiliation of the piss-and-shit-yourself prospects and the very possible complications of it all. I still feel those frissons in my skin about this waiting game and have had many post-birth dreams, or rather nightmares, that I was still waiting for labour to start.

Finally, for my breastmilk to 'come in' as my breasts swelled and then suddenly released their love in leaking patches through every outfit I tried to gracefully cover my ladybody with. And they didn't wait until the baby actually needed feeding. They leaked when any baby needed feeding. Or cried. Or looked at me.

While editing this section of the book, I did a gig at Wilderness Festival and a lovely woman ran over to me as I was eating my lunch and told me that her milk had had a hard time coming in. She was told to look at her baby (as if she hadn't been doing that), at photos of her baby, at videos of babies feeding or crying, as you're told to do in this situation. Nothing worked. Then, she told me she watched one of my poetry videos related to motherhood and the milk began to flow. That is a compliment I never thought I would receive. Just in case it works for someone else. I don't know which video it was though.

With motherhood, as with life, it is not necessarily all these explosions that are the issue – though they're not all joyous – but the obsessive covering up and the worry; about any small puddle of blood or breastmilk or sweat or whatever will deem you the opposite of what a good lady must be. If I could have just gone out without panicking that my breast pads plus bra plus shirt or dress may at some point not prove enough of a barrier for occasional milk overflow, knowing no one would give a shit, I would not have been so uncomfortable at every restaurant/café/house/street/the world. Ditto with periods.

Oh, I forgot the placenta. That too. Yes, motherhood, so fucking ladylike.

Now it's the perimenopause I am waiting for, told that, once again, this volcano of a body will, without good warning, possibly begin erupting in new ladylike ways, overheating, flows of blood suddenly stronger and more erratic than ever from wombs winding down for the summer holidays.

Yes, I am calling post-menopause the summer holidays because I'm so sick of that time in life being referred to as autumn or winter and, although I haven't experienced it yet so I really don't know shit, I do chat to a lot of women who are post-menopausal now and I also work from cafés most Mondays and wherever I go when most of the working world is at school or employment or looking after pre-school aged children, I see retired, post-menopausal women sitting calm as fuck with a tea or wine or laughing with friends like they're having the time of their lives.

Of course, I see the ones who are out, but it's still a very different idea of being an older woman than I was ever made to believe through TV and films and stories.

retiring

for my grandma, who said her seventies were best

don't be such an old woman!
says the younger woman to her friend
and i wonder if she's seen them,
these older women, *an actual one*

the cafés are fucking full of them
laughing with their friends
who also free for half-price weekday lunches
clink wine glass or coffee cup

check any sea front,
between the seagulls and the scant sun,
dipping into oceans, all season,
gloves and socks and swim-hats on

sure, some days grandkids grab their ankles
but these ones they can give back
once the day is done, treat to chocolate ice cream
deny it to the parents

or else, finally alone, browsing newspapers
or books they've waited half a life to finish
now the serving and the sucking up
of womanhood has lessened;

i know i know, you wouldn't think it –
television rarely shows them, music charts disown them
statues are almost never resurrected in their praise
unless royalty, or from younger, naked days

but stray into the real world
and i assure you, there they are;
bleeding over, living longer,
giving fewer fucks than ever

I met a woman in Cardiff who said how great she found sex after the menopause, not only because the threat of pregnancy and contraceptive side effects or failures were no longer ticking constantly like the libido killer they are, but because sex felt more centred on her actual desire than menstrual cycle hormones. Also, because she was past the young vulnerable underconfident stage of pretending you like shit you don't. Thank fuck. I'm holding onto her story for dear life because the only menopause sex story I normally hear is all about dry vagina. Good to have some balance.

Some people have a very uncomplicated menopause. Others have a horrendous time. I have several friends whose working life is currently severely disrupted by sporadic and much heavier flows. Like teenage girls dropping like flies from sports teams when menstruation begins, so perimenopausal women have been dropping for years from long-term employment when menstruation winds down.

Who knows. Another fun game of 'I wonder which one I'll get.' I can't fucking wait. Or rather, I can and I am. Once again, I am just waiting and waiting for the unannounced eruptions of blood, sweat and tears.

It's almost laughable how women have historically been the ones encouraged via social and cultural shaming to be 'ladylike'. It would have been so much easier if the job of being a lady was given to guys.

Ladylike, I think, every month as I sit on the toilet with period diarrhoea. Yes, splendid Hyacinth.

oh period diarrhoea!

do you have to come as well?
is the bleeding not hilarious enough?
nor the cramps? the fear of leaking
into pants, stains puddling my jeans?
do you have to join in too?
make the wiping every month
just that little more disgusting?
toilet paper now a slippy sludge
of splattered red on brown
like a child's first try at painting
minus any proud applause

Yes, others must deal with things my body doesn't; like erections, which we can comfortably hide clit-sized inside our pants (one of my absolutely favourite things about my body), and ejaculation, which can come at unwanted times, in sleep, and must feel worrying, embarrassing, humiliating sometimes.

A side note: I remember the first time I saw sperm come out of a penis, literally expecting it to shoot water-pistol summer style across the room after years of seeing the over-exaggerated cumminginyour-face hand gestures from schooldays. It did not. My breastmilk, however, when I lifted up my arms in the shower, yes. Boom.

I often think how helpful it would be to know exactly when these spills and flows and floods will come and go; but that's not going to happen, so the second best option is to de-shame all of this stuff as quickly as we can so that when we do see the first signs of discharges or blood or water or milk or sperm on bedsheets or unexpected bleeding through trousers, we are not racked with the hellfires of some sort of lady-like failure or self-disgust.

My body, even when it oozes and juices and bleeds and screams, is not filthy. We seem a bit stupid about this stuff, especially about the difference between certain bodily fluids.

Urine and faeces, yes, they are full of bacteria. Faeces especially is full of harmful bacteria. That is why sewage systems were invented, which have decreased disease in most parts of the world to phenomenal levels. All praise to plumbing. And soap.

But just because things like sweat, breastmilk, menstrual blood are also excreted by your body does not make them the same. Sweating is not the same as shitting. Breastfeeding in a café is not the same as pissing on the street or ejaculating into a lover's mouth at a restaurant, both of which I've heard used as comparisons to why breastfeeding in public isn't OK. Tears are often forgotten in these debates on bodily fluids, though in many ways we do also shame tears a lot too, especially when they fall from men's eyes. Not sure there's anything that comes from our bodies that we don't shame. What pointless disgust we have created for so long about our bodies' natural and necessary functions.

placenta

no matter how i try, i cannot paint you beautiful;
jelly birth; blood clot copy;
second coming no one warned me of;
you plopped between my legs all bloody purple bruises;
you looked fucking disgusting

i know, i do,
without you she is cells still;
you were everything, you monster,
store room full to brim;
tinned tomato soups stacked to infinity inside me;

perhaps i'm just too vain to sing your praises;
cannot love ugly like i want to;
the memory of your departure
slumped there after birth,
remains of nine months' dinnertimes
still makes my insides spill

i'm so sorry,
i did not make you into pills
did not store you for my menopause
like more loving mothers do;
there will never be lasagne made of you

my body isn't dirty, it's just that i'm not dead yet

and sometimes it gets sweaty and sometimes it gets wet, but fuck me if those aren't some of the days my body loves the best; this flesh is not a show home, it's the home in which i play, i am done with your whispers, done with your shame – from the first fright of white in pants to the make-believe of menstrual filth; how many gods can we convince to write our bloods into a week of sin? do you see the way the tree sap drips? do you see the way the honey runs? when i fuck i sweat, when i love i cry, when i don't, i'll die and turn to dust; how many boys today are panicking, skin hardening between their legs; how many blushing cheeks are scrubbing dreams from off their sleepy sheets? how many scarlet stains have made a young girl weep? did you hear the one about the mother who nursed her kid in filthy toilets ashamed of her own milk? did you hear the one about the vulva scrubbed with so many fem fresh chemicals it turned into a lemon? i am sorry, i am really sorry children, how long we have been living in these bodies made of ocean still pretending we are nothing more than salt

UTI

is it funny, dear bladder, pretending you are full
when we've just been to the loo and i have
proven you a liar for the thirteenth time today?

do you fancy yourself somewhat of an illusionist
as i squeeze three single droplets liking giving birth
to needles until you chuckle *false alarm*

knowing in a moment you will coax me back again
to believe that you are bursting? a constant cheating lover
desperate for another chance, tugging at my zip –

i cross my legs. i cry again. i try my best to not give in

**awkward conversation with my previous poetry editor
about a poem i wrote called 'thrush'**

he said
he was
expecting
ornithology

if

if you can go online to airbrushed bodies
filtered skin and silken hair
and still believe your own are worthy
or better still, not care
if you can greet each morning's naked grin
with whatever clothes feel nice
as the world belters slut or bore
for skin, both in and out of sight

if you can pass, each day, shop shelves stuffed
with fem fresh wipes and vulva sprays
walk by them with shoulders shrugged
and middle finger proudly raised
if you can bleed – and not believe it sin
if you can scream and not deem it mad
if you can hear a joke that makes you wince
not feel the need to fake a laugh

if you can wank wonderfully alone
then face the wrath of haughty men
who tell you there is something wrong
because you do not orgasm with them
if you can grit your teeth each time they say
it made all of their exes cum
not punch them in the dick or face
still believe your body's horny songs

if you can sit through films where thirty
is too old to play the role of wife
for actors over fifty
and still believe desire a friend of time

71

if you can relish fleshly pleasures
as billions are spent each day
convincing you unworthy
convincing you decay

if you can save your cash not waste your time
take guidance just from those who love
believe, despite the constant grind
that what you feel is good enough
if you can see yourself as best friends see
make mirrored peace with pointless pain
then please, my love,
lend us your eyes, your brain

Footnote

I edited the section above in a café in Ely, Cambridgeshire. I finished it, closed my computer and got ready to go and collect my daughter from school. As I was packing my rucksack up, the woman next to me, newborn baby strapped to her chest staring up at her lovingly, uttered the words, as the baby gurgled a little: *Don't be too expressive my love, or you'll get all the wrinkles Mummy has*. Literally, those exact words.

It was quite a weird thing to say, I thought, and also perfect timing to make my heart implode, throw the computer out of the window and scream *fuuuuuuccccckkkkkkk*. Sometimes, it is like that. What is the point when the enemy is so very ingrained into our minds?

This is too hard.

Don't be too expressive my love, or you'll get all the wrinkles Mummy has. This cannot be the future we allow for the next generations to grow up in, or the present we allow ourselves to be brainwashed by any longer.

I opened my computer up again and I wrote another poem about babies being gross, mainly to ease my pain at hearing her say that and also because we need to stop idolising babies and youth over living and life.

I then wrote a poem about cats because writing about idolising babies made me think about all the people I know and love who do the same to their cats.

These poems have nothing to do with this topic but I am including them because they were written directly after all the hope I had was sucked out of me. If I do not make myself laugh in these situations, I will cry constantly until all the water in my body is sobbed through my tear ducts and I shrivel up into my own inevitable wrinkled dry death prune.

Don't be too expressive my love, or you'll get all the wrinkles Mummy has.

Fuck. This. Shit.

your baby is gross

for people who talk about how beautiful their baby is all the time

yes, she looks cute in those booties
but there is literally piss on her arse,
and your arms

wrap a bow round her head
if you like
– she's still bald

i beg you, stop buying white clothes,
she is gross, and will be gross for a while
i'm sorry, i love her despite this, and you

and yes, it is great
she's starting to try other foods
but please don't make me watch

as you spoon cold mashed carrot
into her mouth, i will vomit
as she spittles it back down her bib

plastic curved at the end
to collect all the dregs
the most horrific of drip trays

the high chair now covered
in dribble of orange
she swirls with her thick baby fingers,

then licks them, staring at you
as she smiles in her nappy
straining to push out a shit

your cat is a murderer

for people who talk about how beautiful their cat is all the time

a cute face and the softest of fur
cannot cover the fact that
your cat is a murderer

last week,
she left the full head of a mouse at your door
decapitated and twitching, not even a nibble

aw, look, so sweet, you purr, as she curls on your lap
her guillotine limbs all cocky and yawning
as your left-hand runs through the gold of her fur

your other hand holding the phone
flicking online through other photos
of other cats, equally cute, equally murderous

a million fresh mouse heads delivered
to back doors all over the world,
gift-wrapped and stinking

the sweet taste of their screams on her tongue
as she licks the palm of your hand,
then her arse

PEOPLE

Hashtag, Not All

I was born, just as you,
a love letter addressed to the world

GEET CHATURVEDI,
'Letters from a Kashmiri Boy'

praise

there are angels all around me –
clicking kettles; popping by

angels who will listen
admit they cry when i cry

with hugs for hands
and ears for wings
we chat through fears
like angels sing

you may not see your halos
but, please know
to me, you're everything

becoming the mother of a teenager

you go out alone these days. no, not alone
there are too many men alive for that
men who see your body as a bird, searching
for the smallest of the prey,
to whom a broken wing, or feathers
not yet accustomed to the gusts of outside winds
is exactly what they search for

my skin itches as you close the door
insides rise up through my throat
vomiting the contents of my womb onto the mat
knowing there are men like that,
not all men, but enough of them, plenty
that i must warn you of the perils
of a top that shows your belly, and of smiling

so no, you don't go out alone
but you do go out without me now
in packs of hopeful safety, and you wave
and you are happy, i hold my breath
till you come back; ready to hold
my breath forever

when you were littler
i bought you a costume of an astronaut
in the hope that you would see
you could be anything you wanted
now i pray you don't remember that
what was i thinking? forget the moon
even the bus to town is killing me

but you are gone,
and you will keep on going further
and that's the whole point of this love
so i must re-learn how to breathe
despite constant ruptured lungs

and i must learn what delights
to fill my own intermittent freedom with
now time sneaks back up on me
i have forgotten how to have a conversation
with people who aren't parents
how to talk about things
that weren't once inside my womb

often, i wish you back inside again
however sick it made me
just until i rid the world of wolves,
just until i make sure your wings
are fool-proofed for flying, bear with me,
it will only take a lifetime

then you're back, and we chat
as if time went on as normal
i ask to see the top you bought
it shows part of your belly;
i tell you it looks lovely, because it does,
because that has to be ok now

you ask me how my day was –
i pretend not to have spent it
sobbing into tissues
my molten bones melting at your feet,
pleading *don't ever leave again*

you do not need to tell me it's *not all men*. you do not need to thrust this phrase between my ribs, scream young men's horrendous suicide statistics every time there is discussion about violence against girls as if pain is competitive. boys hurt too. are harmed too. i know this. i care. i am not stupid. women can abuse. i know this. i know it's *not all men, not all men* is not the issue, *not all men* never was. *not all men* is not what makes me want to squeeze children and teenagers back into my womb so they may safely cross the globe, it's *not all men* that makes me shudder as my daughter walks alone and i try to work out how to sit at home without biting through my fingertips, it's *not all men* that made my father every time i left the house frighten me with facts, it's *not all men* that pastes posters in every airport in every bus station in every country on the back of every nightclub toilet door urging vulnerable people whose passports may be stolen, bodies in demand, that there are numbers they can call if they are trafficked here for rape, that there are numbers we can call when dates go wrong, when drinks taste odd, when we might need chaperoned home by someone we are not scared of, it's *not all men* that makes every walk home longer, that makes toddlers cover nipples in bikinis, that makes belly tops dangerous for daughters, that makes me question every priest and every teacher, every scout leader and stranger, that makes all carers tell young kids to ask a woman if they're lost it's *not all men* in every century in every country in every city in every household who demand human flesh enough to make the trafficking of people still a profitable business it's *not all men* that make the most atrocious headlines an unsurprising read as if we've just come to expect this oh another grooming gang, oh another politician, oh the prince of fucking england it's *not all men* that means we need actual written laws to stop men trying to marry children it's *not all men* that fuel the creepy, legal need for an age of sexual consent, and then wait for that to come, it's *not all men* that make jokes about the sleazy boss or unrequited uncle's touch relatable to all, of course it's *not all men,* it's *not all men* who rape, *not all men* who pay to rape, *not all men* preying on the ignorance of youth *not all men* who abuse *not all men* who make it dangerous to be a child or be a teenager or marry or divorce or turn down dates or turn down flowers or be pregnant or give birth or be sober or get drunk or go outside or walk home, we know it's *not all men* it's *not all men* it's *not all men* it's *not all men* that is the problem, it's *not all men* that ever was, it's just that there's enough.

MEN/HASHTAG, NOT ALL

I write a lot of poems. To my knowledge, I have never written or shared a poem about hating men. I have, after sharing poems about loving women (hashtag, not all women) or enjoying being a woman myself (hashtag, not always, especially during bouts of period diarrhoea), or criticising certain things some men or groups of men have done, been called a man-hater.

Recently, I received a DM on Instagram with poems a guy had written and sent me in which he described his sex life and orgasms. I hadn't seen the message and hadn't replied (and don't always see everything and don't always reply). On this occasion, within a week of me not giving him feedback on his poetry, he made an official 'statement' on his account that I was in fact a hypocritical bitch who cared nothing about the people who support my poetry, and that he was publicly 'unfollowing me'.

When I replied (don't reply, Hollie) to say that DMing a stranger sensual poems is quite different from sharing poems publicly in the hope it will normalise female pleasure for people who choose to follow your work and that, also, I do not see all the messages and cannot read all the poems sent to me because I have a full-time job and child to look after, I was, unsurprisingly, accused of being a man-hater, among other comments, and I gave it up as a pointless quest. In his view, I didn't reply, not because of these reasons I just explained but because I hate men. As soon as I am told I hate men, which is often, it's pointless, because they have made up their mind and everything I say will come back to that.

86

Another man DM'd to tell me, incredibly politely at first, that he was writing to me so that I could understand that my poems were shit and that people only read my poems (and here, the politeness waned) because I'm female and write about CUNT (his capital letters to accentuate).

A comment beneath one newspaper review of my book *Slug* stated that I was 'probably another fat, dyke man-hater', but they hadn't read the book. Cool, good research.

The most recent messages I got after commenting below someone's post about the Russell Brand allegations was a DM telling me that 'You clearly have a hatred for men, for whatever reason.' Whatever reason. Hmmm. I'm pretty sure even most men could think of a reason why 'men' as a category might not be at the top of the love list for many folk. But no, I do not, and have never 'hated men', except men who tell me I hate men. I do really dislike those ones a lot.

I say this, not to take the piss out of these men – I don't know their background or mental health status – but it is annoying that this is so often their go-to retaliation. Man-hater. It's so lazy.

Not just because I do not hate men. There are so many of them, it would take far too long to think about them all and I need to make the dinner. As is often said, some of my best and closest and most gorgeous friends are men. Some of the men I admire most are men.

My boyfriend Michael who introduced me to Rodriguez is a man. Rodriguez was a man. The man in the concert crowd who pushed away the other man when I was fifteen was a man. Roger Graef was a man. James Baldwin was a man. My grandfather was a man who like many men had friends who never got the chance to become men. My dad and brother are men. My daughter's dad is a man. Yomi Sode is a man. David Attenborough is a man (please God, don't let him fall). But sometimes, even David Attenborough is not enough.

The main reason I find being called a man-hater most annoying, is not because I don't think I deserve the label, I know I don't, but because I have worked very hard not to be one.

Fuck me, it would be so easy to actually hate men, to generalise, lump them all together with the guns they have fired and the wars they have started and the people they have beaten and raped, and the pregnancies they have been allowed to run from, and the money and lands they have stolen, and the girls they have forcibly married, and the boys they have abused and the opportunities they've been gifted, and the shit love poems they've been praised for, even for all the times they have not been asked 'Who's looking after your kid?' when they go to work. Even for that. Even then, it would be so easy to throw up my hands in the air and think, *fuck this, you got me. I hate them. I fucking hate them all.*

But I don't, because it is inaccurate and stupid. As stupid as news reports that state how many children and women are killed in atrocities as if male deaths are less sad. They are not.

Sometimes though, even knowing this, I have to walk the streets repeating inside my head *not all men not all men*, thinking of all the individual loving and brilliant men I know. Then I switch on the news and have to do it all over again. *Not all men. Not all men.*

When I walk the streets, repeating this, I am scared of men. If men walk the streets, they are mostly scared of other men. The most likely person to kill a man is another man he knows. The most likely person to kill a woman is a man she is intimate with. From school age, the ripples of this were felt every time you turned a boy down for a date and were told you were a slag anyway.

Hard for the boys, I imagine, always meant to be the ones to ask girls out. To put themselves out there, to open themselves to the possibility of rejection while we stood in the corners of the school hall waiting to be asked to dance. But please, can we teach sons how to deal with rejection in another way? I hate that friend-zoning has become an insult, as if it is an intentional diss. Fuck that phrase. No one owes anybody their body or their intimacy. No one should have to apologise for wanting to just be friends with someone. Or not.

Perhaps the most sickening of these *not all men* moments in my life was when studying. I did a master's degree in Development Economics. The research papers we had to read were full of stories about men: courageous men; men forced to migrate; risking their lives for their friends and families; men paid pittances with no respite by huge corporations; men corralled into diamond mines for bastard billionaires so our fingers could sparkle while walking down aisles; men leading human rights legal battles; men conscripted into warfare.

Men go through a lot. Men are treated like shit by many different unjust systems. Men are bullied and beaten and underpaid. Often, in these scenarios, the aggression and shame and hate are then taken out on others. Children. Often intimate partners. Often women. Women are often beaten because men are underpaying other men, overworking other men, bullying other men.

One of my exam modules was on forced migration, including child trafficking. In 2022, when the Home Office appeared to have 'lost' over fifty young people from asylum-seeking protective custody in Brighton, it reminded me of one lecturer's unforgettable message to the class.

When you search the internet as to why child sex trafficking happens, what is the cause of it, the answer often comes back as poverty. Poor parents sell their children to traffickers, or people flee and work for traffickers, or children are picked up on streets and from boats and from British government-sanctioned hotels in Brighton because they are in helpless situations. In the classroom, we all suggested the same. *Poverty is the cause. Vulnerability.*

No, the professor informed us. *This is not the cause.* Poverty does not cause child sex trafficking. It just makes it easier to carry out. The economics of child sex trafficking are based on supply and demand. There are some things we do not demand and so advertisers create false demand for things we didn't initially know we needed or wanted. Like Coca-Cola. Like sweets shaped like watermelons made out of pig collagen. If our economic system was based solely on supplying what people demanded, adverts would hardly be necessary.

But child sex trafficking exists because it *is* demanded, even without advertising, and more so with it.

The reason there are so many children still stolen and sold into slavery, including sexual slavery, is because there are enough men, mainly men, not only men but mainly men, and in fact huge, huge numbers of mainly men globally, who demand it; who pay to rape children in high enough numbers to make a global trade profitable enough to run as a business; *demand* is the cause of child trafficking. Not poverty, *demand*. This lesson has never left my bones.

I understand most men also aren't part of this, but enough of them are and have been for centuries that the demand for child and teenage trafficking remains high enough that 'Have you been trafficked?' posters still line every airport arrivals zone I go through, suitcase in my hand, *not all men* mantra repeated on a loop in my head.

Approaching the age of sixteen filled me with a strange sense of dread. For years, I had heard talk and jokes and read articles about men waiting for girls to be 'legal'. The countdown in the *Daily Mail* to Charlotte Church being 'legal'. At a festival, thinking it would put a man off by telling him my age when I was fifteen and seeing him move even closer. So many men have seemed continuously fucking gross since I was about ten years old and it is constantly a struggle to balance those memories with the lovely men I have also met or loved. I simply haven't had to do the same with women. I know there are people who have.

Once I reached sixteen, I felt like I was even more at risk. I worried there would now be no protection from this sort of intimidating older guy. We were now legal, fair game for older men to openly salivate over and stalk. I cannot imagine what it is like in countries where the age of consent is lower. The fact that these laws are necessary to protect children and teenagers from those adults around them is its own horror show. Turning sixteen didn't affect whether or not I wanted to have consensual sex with anyone my age. I knew loads of people who'd already had sex. My main idea of sixteen was this 'legal' old-man trope. I have never, ever told my daughter to respect anyone simply because they are an adult. Fuck that. Respect people if they deserve it, for god's sake don't just respect someone 'cos they're older than you'.

It's so shit being frightened. It is horrible. It's horrible being angry. It's horrible being scared that your anger might anger someone more. And it is so horrible being suspicious of every unknown guy you see, because people don't come with lights on top of their heads that warn us of an attack of rage or power hunger.

We don't come with labels, only names, all different names, because all men are different. Like snowflakes. Like penises. Like people. All men are different. All men are different. Not all men. Not all men. Not all men. I am so tired of spending time repeating this to myself, and the world, only to be told by men who know nothing about me that I hate men anyway.

streetlights

we chat about fear like we are passing round chocolates –
my grandma goes first; talks of the blackouts in war,
more scared of the streets than the bombs sometimes

was advised to dress 'dowdy' those air raid evenings
to not draw a gaze to her womanly shapes in the shadows
when sirens sounded – not only the planes to avoid overhead
when rushing alone to the shelters,

my aunty goes next, then my mother, then me
now my daughter asks questions, shows scrunchies on tiktok
that double as covers for drinks
as if date rape accessories are part of the nightlife experience

i don't want to begin this again
i don't want to be giving advice i was given
my mother was given, my brother my grandma

i'm so tired of being on guard; the beauty
of darkness and stars stolen over and over again
by men who just used to be boys

how to stay safe; every walk home
a constant cacophony of what to avoid
lest you be blamed for the actions
of men who just used to be boys

each noise a new risk; each footstep,
each breath closing in and then passing, please passing,
each rustle of leaves in the breeze, each splinter
of moonbeam in puddle; heart falters at every new shadow

and the advice keeps on coming as it has all our lives
do not talk to strangers, keep to the streetlights
yell *fire* not *help*, practise your screams when alone
leave your hair down, ponytails are more easily grabbed

ditto rucksacks ditto hands held at sides
ditto footsteps in shadows, *keep to the streetlights*

walk down the centre of roads if cars line the pavements
take out your earplugs, drown out your music in silence
call up a friend – do not talk on your phone
hold your phone in your hand, hold your keys between fingers

be ready with blunt metal edges to open your front door
before you have even arrived, look ahead /
check behind at all times, do not walk in shadows
keep to the streetlights

do not walk alone, get a taxi instead
if you cannot afford one, get the night bus instead
if the night bus looks rowdy, beg for a taxi /

do not get in cars with a stranger
sit directly behind any driver
you are harder to catch there
check that the doors stay unlocked

do not walk, if you must, *do not wear a short dress*
or a tight dress or a dress which shows skin
keep skirts above knees to more easily run in /
keep skirts below knees because knees are alluring

do not be alluring
do not wear a tracksuit do not wear pyjamas
do not wear a raincoat

it's such a repulsive dilemma, that game we've all played
trying to work out which unlabelled man
is more likely to rape us and which of our careless mistakes
will be blamed if one of them does:

the man in the taxi? the men on the night bus?
the man who is hid in the bushes again?
the men shouting 'sexy' who tell me to smile?

and why did you smile? why don't you ignore them?
who?
the men who are calling me bitch for ignoring them?
why did you speak to them? isn't that flirting?

as we grapple to learn that perfect positioning
between being too friendly and not being friendly enough
what do you expect if you don't take advice?
– there is so much advice that is given

in our sex education classes
we learnt how to put condoms on carrots
learnt that sex was preparing a penis to put in our bodies
how skin can be seen as a come on

how morals are measured in inches of hemline to knee
how some boys, from the first time you turn down a date
will label you slut, disappointment so quickly switching
to anger: *and why did you smile at that stranger?*

not once in my school were boys taught how to give pleasure
how to touch a girl's body
how girls are allowed to touch their own bodies
how girls are not slags if they own their own bodies

how nobody owes them their body or time
or a date or a kiss, no matter how much they might want it
how being a friend is not leading you on
how 'friend-zoning' someone is not to be punished

how often we sat in the headmaster's office
told off for short skirts and bra straps and make-up
bombarded with rules on how to grow up
scrubbing off lipstick and sin

stop flirting keep smiling do not smile too much
do not lead men on do not be too sexy
do not be offensive do not make men sad
do not make men angry

always have money for taxis always have time
for the longer way home

how much time i have wasted taking the longer way home;
how many falling stars have fallen without me
sweeping the sky with their firefly wishes
so i will not be blamed for walking in shadows

attacks are always taught in the passive –
how likely we are to be followed;
how many of us possibly raped
if we do or we don't pay attention
nothing is active – no lessons left boys in a panic

no parents sat sons down to chat
about how not to wake up with necks in their hands
how not to take naked legs as a come on

how not to get angry at girls
who want to be no more than friends
how to never leave mates drunk on their own
in case they start following strangers, force keys into hands
how to help friends not turn into men who attack

how not to turn into men who attack –
instead, we keep pushing this pattern of silence and shame
why were you walking that way?
why were you showing your skin to the night?

we said stick to the streetlights,
stick to the streetlights stick to the streetlights
and what if there aren't any streetlights?

and what if streetlights are not nearly enough?
and what if it's nothing to do with my hairstyle
or the way i am dressing; it was never to do
with the way we were dressed

do not ask why i smiled,
stop describing clothes as 'appropriate'
as if two inches more cotton to cover my knees
is any more likely to save me than a key clutched in hand

what are you telling the men
who just used to be boys –
the boy soon to be man?

cactus

boys are not born with bullets for brains
in the beginning, all babies cry

snug in the safety of womb
newborn boy-fingers clung tight to their carers

searching for nipples and guidance,
boys are not born with crosses in eyelids

as if army recruitment were easy, as if posters
aren't pinned in each dole queue, as if no men

have ever been drugged into carrying guns
hunted in pubs, woken up far out at sea

she put her hand on my belly,
said *boy* when you kicked

as if knuckles up, ready
to curl into black and blue imprints

pressured to impress in school playgrounds
onlookers circling excited for fights;

in the beginning, all babies scream
sleep when warm milk fills their bellies

how many times do you need to see beatings
before you might copy?

how many times do you need to be told
you are owed someone's body?

scolded that boys do not ask for chairs
 for their teddies on the back of a push bike

before you look back and there's no one to hug?
how many dolls must be ripped from boys' clutches

as if boy were an entity separate to father,
as if anger is the only emotion,

boys are not born dreaming of hurting
lust turned to raping, recoiling from loving

as if their faces ought not to smell
the sweetness of tulips in spring,

the choice between cactus or venus fly trap
for the little boys' bedrooms

how many times can your softness be mocked
before your whole body must harden?

the headlines label him a monster

by definition, a monster is imaginary
head of a hyena, hindquarters of a wolf
eyeballs forged from dragon eggs

give a man a fish, he will eat for a day
give the man the means to catch a fish
give the man a uniform and a gun

'it is unbelievable to think these offences
could have been committed by a serving police officer'
– detective chief inspector iain moor

by definition, unbelievable implies
not able to be believed; unlikely to be true
so extreme, so extraordinary

his friends said he wasn't called a bastard
in any sexual sense, just a cruel man in general.
oh, fine then, hand him the gun

his mother said he longed to join the army
to see the world. also, probably
excited by the weapons. finally, a truth

give a man a fish, he will eat for a day
give the man the means to catch a fish
give the man a uniform and a gun

a weapon and a status
power and importance
a uniform

and it is just a man
in uniform

just men in uniforms

just men

boy racer

blaring music from their cars
windows spilling violent lyrics
as if the singers are their bodyguards

buy the boy flowers

a single daffodil perhaps
one bunch of purple summer heather
don't let the daisy chains of childhood wilt
let the lilac whisper
this world belongs to him as well
let him see you at the doorway
a pot of yellow lilies
held out in your hands
watch him frown at first
as if you've got the wrong person
the scent filling his lungs

a belated thank you to my boy friends

to the boys who stopped the other boys for us;
shook their frightened fists, puffed up fearful teenage chests
to fend off other boys and men for us;

to the boys who called the other boys pricks for us
who scorned their friends who pressured us
pretended to be with us to ward off shame and strangers

to the boys who stood around us like salt circles
in nightclubs and moon-licked streets, their just-pubescent
muscles forging warnings best they could

to keep the older men away; the older men
who, quiet in the corners,
offered more expensive drinks, and confidence,

and us, excited by the savings and the power
our naked necks now seemingly possessed
freebies and flirting, god, how good it feels to feel attractive

until lights now up, those older men,
suddenly less friendly
come collect on their investment,

to the boys who stood in front of us then
unjudging, portcullis of unpractised punches
and in winter, when we were dressed

as if the frosted newbury high street
were a burning summer beachfront,
to the boys who lent us jackets

when clothes we hadn't worn to show our bodies
to a world which kept telling us we ought to,
began to freeze our bones;

and having danced until our high heels bled,
to the boys who picked us up, gave us piggy backs,
saved soles from broken bottles and shattered glass;

who walked us safely to our homes, then away
less safely to their own, or who, crashing in our beds
or on our sofas or our floors, slept beside us

and in the morning, us apologising over breakfast
for the trouble, to the boys who, stuffing toast
into their gobs, told us it was fine, as if it was

at the shop, they did not ask about you

for danny

just packed the toothpaste and the loo rolls
into the bag, handed me the change
as if it were possible i'd see your face again
perhaps tomorrow, or next month

and on the street, no one sobbed,
just walked by me, not saying your name to one another
and the sparrows in the sycamores
chirruped no less noisily than before

as if you haven't gone anywhere, as if
your laughter were not needed for seas to rise and rain
as if you might still get the second round in next month
when we meet, remember, like we planned?

THE OPTIONAL PAPERS

I was a very sexist teenager. Even into my twenties I was fairly sexist.

In college, when I was seventeen years old, the English teacher set up a class debate. It's the only debate I remember doing at school. I didn't realise until I went to Cambridge University that a lot of schools had regular debating classes and debating clubs, and that so many of those politicians smiling and laughing while debating everyone's wages and human rights are probably just reminded of their schooldays.

On that note, I also didn't realise that different schools offered different subjects. I just assumed that the A levels I could choose from at my school were those that were part of the A-level curriculum that the government decided on. When one of my university friends told me they'd done Spanish A level, and another did Law A level, I was totally confused. I just assumed all options were available to all schools. As if.

Anyway, back to my sexist school days. The debate was:

Group A: Men are better than Women
Group B: Women are better than Men

We were given the opportunity to choose sides. Mainly, the girls chose B, the boys A, but I got in quite early, putting up my hand to join Group A.

The reason; honestly, I chose to argue that men were better than women because I wanted the easy option and, for that reason, I genuinely could not understand why anyone would choose side B.

From what I had studied, men had discovered everything, invented everything, written almost everything, had the most money and led most countries. Even if I liked boys and men in general a bit less than most of the girls and women I was surrounded by, still, from a more factual, historic point of view, as far as I could fathom, it just seemed so much easier to argue that men were 'better' because, and I think I truly believed this, they must be better at everything to have done all that.

I don't remember most of the debate, but I do remember one thing. One of the girls on the opposite side, my friend Sophie, quoted all the work of the suffragettes and other women's rights organisations as part of their argument. That same year, Sophie also led the entire sixth form into a protest about the school uniform. She almost single-handedly changed the policy, which allowed girls to wear trousers to our school for evermore. She was amazing.

Suffice to say, I knew fuck all about the suffragettes.

For my parents' sake, I would like to add here that it is highly possible they'd tried to engage me in various conversations about things like this, but I hadn't listened. At school, we had for sure studied very little about this. Nothing, I think.

When Group B finished their suffragettes argument, I didn't really get it. I didn't get why that was an argument for women being better. If anything, in my head, it was the opposite; if women were better than men, they wouldn't have needed all those organisations to help them become equal. Surely, the only reason women had needed to fight was because men were better in the first place.

I don't remember which side eventually won this debate and I realise now that it is obviously a ridiculously simplified idea. We studied Alice Walker's *The Color Purple* and William Shakespeare's *The Tempest* later that year, which opened up my brain a tad more, but it seems not enough.

By my second year of university, I was still fairly anti-women. On paper.

I was studying Modern and Medieval Languages, which included a lot of literary and philosophical texts. In the first year of my university course, all our reading was set.

In the second year, it was more flexible and we were allowed to choose different options, if we wanted. One of these options was to study books written by women. Women's Literature.

I did not choose it. In fact, I almost grimaced at the idea. No chance.

In my head, if these writers were as good as the men, they'd just be in the main literature course, which wasn't called 'Male White Literature' and therefore, duh, would include whoever was the best. Why would I choose a sub-section to study? Why would I specifically choose to read books by women if they weren't good enough to just be set texts? Sub. On the bench. Not playing. Also, it was only really the female students that were choosing to study female writers and if they were that good surely everyone would read these books, not just the girls?

It was only in my fourth year really, when I was studying German philosophy – Nietzsche, Hegel, Marx and Freud – that I started to question this ridiculously engrained belief.

I wanted to study Freud at first because he wrote a lot about interpreting dreams and I found that very exciting. Also, he talked about sex a lot, which I was also interested in reading about. After studying him for a while, however, I realised how much I disagreed with him and I started to realise I could disagree with people, even men on my reading list at a prestigious university.

After reading his theory about female orgasms being immature if they involved the clitoris and not their husband's penises, I realised in that moment I'd read about one hundred books by men and about five by women, of which three – Shirley Hughes, Bel Mooney and Judith Kerr – were kids' books my mum had chosen to read to me.

I realised why my grandma had always asked my brother and

father and uncle for their opinions about things that my mother and aunties and myself often knew more or at least as much about. I remember my male cousin saying at one point, 'Gran, Hollie's literally studying that. I don't know, ask her!' She didn't. My gran absolutely did not hate women either: she'd just been taught all her life to believe in the genius of man over all others.

Perhaps if I hadn't started university at eighteen but had taken a gap year, I would have realised these things in my first year because I'd have been well-travelled and would have lots of photographs of me saving poor people's lives by repainting schools in villages I'd paid £5,000 to visit.

I really only wrote that paragraph out of bitterness, sorry. Those photographs were all over so many white students' walls at my university, it was like I was in a white missionary camp for a while.

Gap year or no gap year, from Freud onwards, the world of words was forever changed. I started to unpick some of my own prejudices, looking back on all the times I'd been thinking about this imbalance but hadn't quite grasped what was annoying me so much.

Times like at primary school, when my best friend Jodie and I decided to change the words of the Christian hymn from 'He's Got the Whole World in His Hands' to a more inclusive 'We've Got the Whole World in Our Hands' because I guess it must have annoyed us in some way that the boys' hands were getting all the attention. We were told off by the teacher for getting the words wrong and being 'cheeky'.

Or in French, aged about fourteen, when we were all shocked by the words for 'they'. In French, these words are gendered. There is the male they, 'ils', and the female they, 'elles'. When it comes to mixed groups, even if there is only one male in that group, and all the rest female, you use the male they, 'ils'.

In class, we asked our poor teacher for ages, confused about it all.
But miss, what if there's like five hundred girls and one guy?
Ils.

109

All right, but what if there's like ten million girls and one guy but he's late?

Ils.

But miss, that's not fair! we (girls) shouted, as our boy friends sat smug as fuck, seemingly unperturbed, the teacher apologising that it's just how it is.

Ah, just how it is. Let's move on.

How many people have been told to just move on, that that's just how it is, to not become a bore, to get a sense of humour, to keep calm and carry on? A lot of people get really angry when you question stuff. Like him having the whole world in his hands.

I wasn't being cheeky, I realise that now, almost thirty years later.

role play

ok, you can be galadriel and hermione
it was sexist of me to say you couldn't;
i'll be frodo then, and gandalf and god

It is a big deal that in many religions we are told God is He. I've had family members (male) get really pissed off with me for not using 'He' to talk about God to my daughter, as if I'm making an unnecessary fuss or just being a pain in the arse. Which I am, but only in their arse; it's alleviating the pain in mine. It's so fucking hard not to believe that you are a killjoy or worry that you're a killjoy and need to shut the fuck up when talking about these things, which often, individually, seem fairly irrelevant, especially when you're continuously told they are.

Whenever I start to question whether I'm losing my fucking mind over these sorts of differences, I flip it, whatever *it* is.

Like the word 'guys'. I use it all the time. We are OK with it mostly; 'we' being the non-guys. No, it won't ruin my life. No, I don't generally give a shit, on an everyday basis, but to claim it has no effect on people is absurd.

I can't imagine what it would have been like if we'd grown up with everyone shouting 'hey girls' to groups made up of mixed genders, or people referring to God as a she and praising the mother, daughter and holy goat (that was the other word we changed in the song), or having to opt for the 'male literature' or 'white poetry' course if we wanted to read anything by a white person or a man.

The question of statues is currently at the forefront of these sorts of people-getting-very-angry-about-change discussions, triggered by the dragging through the streets and dumping into the Bristol waters of a statue of a Bristol-born transatlantic slave trader and merchant.

It's not so much the question of what to do about statues such as this that fascinates me; personally, I'd verge on them being taken down and melted and remade into one thousand statues not of warmongers or murderers, sort of the opposite of what we did with spoons and saucepans into bullets during wartime.

What amazes me most is how few people are willing to accept that this shit makes a difference; that a child growing up walking around streets, staring up at these huge statues, learning the names and stories of these people because of a random walk to school or through a park or to the library, would be totally unaffected by who they see above them, towering over, held up by history. It's a ludicrous idea, like us white people being the only ones ever to claim not to see colour. Yes we do, you know it and I know it, so stop fucking pretending.

raised

written beneath the Melville Monument in St Andrew Square, Edinburgh

god, it makes the neck ache
looking up to guys like this
carved into our cityscape
backlit by a lashing reign

how many undeserved names
eternalised in stone
still stain our sullied sky
haloed by the sun

~~some say~~ plaques are not enough
plasters to a septic wound
~~some say that~~ we should fell these faces
replant our forest floors for good

feed the rubble to the roots
history ignores
until history reblooms

six hundred thousand humans
this man enslaved
yet still we let him stride the stars
whilst they remain unnamed

~~some say~~ it's gone too far
ripping artworks from their plots

~~some say~~ it makes a difference
which figures children spot
as they skip across the city
searching heroes to adopt

there are more animals
than women here
more rich than poor
more white and gold

i know this killer's name now
by accident, in passing
on a simple city stroll

as if he's someone to look up to
as if he's someone we should know

us, shadowed by his glory
down below

In 2021 a new statue was erected in Cardiff of a person called Betty Campbell, sculpted by Eve Shepherd and chosen via public vote. Betty Campbell was the first black headteacher in Wales. I think it is only after walking past it, and stopping in my tracks, that it made me realise how rare it was to see any tribute such as this.

In 2022, new research by Art UK revealed that just 2 per cent of named public statues in Britain commemorate people of colour.

In Edinburgh, at a similar time, a campaign group found there were more statues in the city of named animals than named women. In Scotland as a whole there were twenty public statues of women, five of which were of Queen Victoria. Queen Victoria is the most statued person in the UK, if statued can be a word. When researching why she, over other monarchs or immensely rich imperialists, is the most statued person, most suggested it was mainly because Victoria ruled for ages and also because the Victorians were really 'into statues', alongside jigsaws, talking to friends whilst walking, and spreading syphilis.

just a nurse

the women in my family are the stupid ones
not a label i invented, invented by the older men
as all inventions were when they were young

my grandmother was 'chatty', my aunty, 'kind'
but the older men, the older men
were 'business minds'; 'intelligent'; 'wise'
did not take kindly to be being beaten
at trivial pursuit
my mum was stupid too; *just* a nurse,
a pocket money job
and none of us spoke up for her
as far as i remember it

when he was sick, my grandad
the water in his feet swollen as a womb
his daughter at his bedside
my mother called for frequently
to dab his frightened skin

i still remember that shift in him
streams of admiration pouring from his lips
as he sipped ever slowly
from the water glass again

the softness of her hands
massaging his pain

just a nurse
he did not ever say again

it's people like you, tracy

who make it all happen, bring out the decorations
pin up the paper chains, lick stamps to letters
and actually post them, wrap ribbons around gifts,
hang fairy lights measured in sections from fences,
fill pumpkins with sweeties and chocolates
for the evenings when small monsters and witches
and goblins stand smiling at doorsteps, people like
you, tracy, who fill bowls with crisps, and keep on refilling,
whose fridge is full of diluting juice already diluted
just waiting in jugs as if water were born fully dressed,
like you, tracy, who run school fêtes and street fairs,
get funding for playground repairs and end of term discos,
put christmas trees up in your living room window
meticulously covered in tinsel and slaloming santas
to turn cold winter streets into glittering galleries
without people like you there'd be no family gatherings,
no point trick or treating, no birthday cards landing
on door mats, no children's first discos, no end of year proms
no plates full of cakes on arrival, no magic diluting juice
ready and cool to grab when you're suddenly parched,
people like you who stage celebrations, make children believe
their teeth are worth gold and that elves might cause havoc,
seasons don't just greet themselves, there are people
like tracy, hidden and humble, exhausted all over this earth
pulling the rigging, building the sets, setting the spotlights,
seating the guests, clearing the stage when curtains are drawn
and we are all partied out from the music and feasts
as people like tracy refill the jug with the perfect amounts
of water and sweetness, as if it's always just there in the fridge.

116

HAVING A DOOR NUMBER

When I started at Cambridge University, I didn't know Tory and Conservative were the same political party. I was not a politically engaged teenager in the obvious sense. I got very annoyed when my dad would force me to watch the starting summary on the six o'clock news every night. Only after watching this snippet of world politics were we allowed to switch over to the six o'clock comedies – *Fresh Prince, The Simpsons, Blossom, My So-Called Life* – each time pissed off that I'd missed the start again.

What is the point of watching the news? I'd complain. *It just makes me feel shit and I can't do anything about it anyway.*

I found out about Tory and Conservative being the same when I realised the boy I fancied at university was only interested in girls who knew about politics. My friends spent weeks teaching me about the set-up of parliament and helping me to learn the names and jobs of those in the current Labour cabinet. I made up rhyming poems to remember who was minister of what. Yes, the reason I began learning about how the UK parliamentary system works was to impress a boy.

And then, just as I had learnt it all by heart, the cabinet reshuffled.

I did not know that cabinets could shuffle. I did not know that the health minister could suddenly become the transport minister. I had assumed that these people were specialists in the departments that they were leading. I'm not sure what pissed me off the most; that, or the fact that all of my learning, just so I could chat to this boy, was now down the fucking pipe.

He fancied my mate anyway. Seems he was interested in girls *actually* interested in politics, not just, you know, swotting up for a snog.

In my third year, the government proposed a new system of university fees we called top-up fees, to raise the yearly fee for university admission, as well as proposing to allow variable fees across different universities, meaning universities like Cambridge would be able to, and likely would, charge way more in tuition fees. My interest in politics re-emerged, this time because I finally realised changes such as this would actually have affected me were I in my first rather than last year at university, and that politics wasn't just guys from Eton banging their fists and guffawing.

I heard that more Cambridge students went to protest the potential closing down of a late-night kebab shop than to protest this possible increased inequality in access to education, possibly because many of the students around me were paying less for their university than their school fees had been. I say paying, I mean making money by putting their student loan into an ISA.

In the King's College canteen – if you can call a room that looks like Hogwarts hall a canteen – one of the wealthier boys, without even a fiddle of his cufflinks, declared how positive these new top-up fees would be because it would finally once again sort out who should and should not be at universities like Cambridge.

His conviction was fascinating. There was no question to him that a wealthy background was a symbol of higher intelligence, that charging higher fees would sort out who 'should' and 'should not' be able to study for longer, that intelligence and money, no, not money, wealth, were intrinsically linked.

snob | American Dictionary
snob. noun [C] us. /snɑb/ a person who judges the importance of people mainly by their social position or wealth, and who believes social position or wealth makes one person better than others.

My gran was a bit of a snob. She was the first person in my family to go to university and her first boyfriend, a fellow university student, dumped her when he saw where she lived. She told me this story many times. He also demanded her father give him the fiver back that he'd coughed up to buy her a handbag, as she was now not marriage material and it apparently wasn't fair he didn't know that when he purchased the bag. She was that sort of snob. A 'putting on her National Trust voice [as we called it] when talking to the doctor because she'd grown up poor' sort of snob. Not a real one.

This boy at university was the first dictionary-definition snob I'd met in real life. It was a bit like being at a zoo. I just stared at him.

I rarely joined in political discussions with other students at Cambridge because I always felt like I knew nothing and would just look stupid. Also, because a lot of the more confident students didn't shy away from ripping the piss out of others for not knowing as much as they did. They often spoke really fucking loudly in your face and I'd heard enough shouting in my life to not want it as a hobby in the bar when taking a break from studying.

So I just stared into this very wealthy boy's face as he spoke, the way I would later stare into the faces of certain politicians, politicians of similar backgrounds and schooling to this boy, wondering if they were also so certain of being better.

Going to Cambridge was amazing, difficult in many ways, much less for me than many others from less represented backgrounds, but it did open my eyes to another world of people; those who seemed delusionally confident, even as teenagers, about their worth in the world.

I had also never met so many teenagers who had never worked. Not weekends, not summers, never. And who then didn't work during university and graduated with no experience whatsoever of anyone leaving a five-pence piece on the table and laughing because you forgot to bring the mayonnaise they asked for at the end of a five-hour shift. I guess you can't work so easily when you go to boarding school. I'm not sure how that sort of stuff works.

waitress

written after reading Jack Monroe's phrase
'always. punch. upward'

between the tables and the kitchen, we shimmered
flustered and smiling, trying to ease between
the anger of angry customers and angry chefs

it wasn't our fault the ribeye was not to your liking, sir
it wasn't our fault, chef, the table is complaining
yet here we are again, all fists facing downwards

us waving waitress peace flags,
such easy punch bags for every tired tongue
smile, the customer is never wrong

shocking, how easily adults found it to shout
at us, one five-pence piece left on the table
to ensure we knew our worth

In my first translation class – I studied French and German – we were given a French text entitled 'Grand Cru'. I knew 'grand' meant large or big and 'cru' was the past tense of 'to believe'. I wrote something like 'A Strong or Vast Belief'.

The teacher, seemingly finding my translation absolutely hilarious, read it out to everyone. The class laughed. Here's the joke, if you don't get it: 'grand cru' is in fact the name given to 'a wine of the most superior grade' and it would therefore just be left in its original form in the translated text. How hilarious that this eighteen-year-old did not know that. If the article had been entitled 'WKD Blue', I'd have been fine.

A few other memories in this respect:

A conversation at a party of people studying medicine where they were discussing *what people without A levels even do* and coming up with some 'hilarious' ideas of jobs like shop work and plumbing. *Can they even spell?* My friends and I left at that point. I wish I'd have said something, but I didn't want to cause a fuss.

A dinner during which someone asked me if we got checked for guns going into our state school each day, *state school* said in the sort of disgusted way my grandma used to say *sanitary products*.

Being asked if it was hard going to a state school with all those, and I quote, *you know, common people*.

A dinner at which I was asked if it was difficult being at Cambridge with such a *common accent*.

Being asked if I was watching *Blind Date* ironically. It was my favourite programme at the time.

Being told 'God no, that's my bodyguard's house!' when I stupidly mistook the detached house in front of the mansion for the student's own home.

A crowd of people, as I wrote down my address for sports kit to be sent to my family home, getting very excited about the fact that I had a house number, because they'd always wanted to meet someone with a house number. They were being nice and genuinely excited, but it was still fucking annoying. To be fair, I had assumed they all had summer houses in Italy and it turned out three of them didn't.

Being told it was really cute my mum was a nurse. Cute. She loved that.

Being asked what I meant by 'free' when talking about what school I went to. 'Like, totally free?' the girl replied. She looked so puzzled. I still don't know if it was because she didn't know anyone who went to one of these exotic free schools or because she didn't know there was such a thing as free education. I hope the former.

Being asked by someone I thought a friend did I mind if we didn't walk together in public outside the college. She was on the verge of being invited to a dinner with Cambridge's equivalent of Oxford's Bullingdon Club and had to be wary who she was seen with. This time I said *yes, I do mind*. Thinking back, maybe I should have just done it. She was in no way from a wealthy background so I guess the idea of being able to mix with these Eton boys may have offered opportunities she'd worked desperately hard for.

When I started at Cambridge, there was a lot of talk about schools. I kept getting asked what school I had attended. I didn't understand why.

Where I lived, we used to ask this question sometimes, but that was because there were about four state schools in my town and we wanted to know if people we'd met were at one of our enemy schools or not.

We knew which people went to the local private schools because the girls had messy buns and tans from actually going skiing in winter and the boys wore polo shirts with the collar turned up. Yes, I genuinely thought I could spot someone who went to private school by the style of their ponytail. Yes, I was also very prejudiced. Yes, I still sometimes think I can.

When I replied each time 'St Bartholomew's in Newbury' with a sort of awkward expression across my face, I was met with a befuddled look or an 'oh, I don't know that school' and I would think, *yeah, why would you know it unless you're also from Newbury?*

I didn't realise, until I was in a group of students asking this question to one another, how many of the students had all attended a network of about ten public or very wealthy private schools. Not just private schools, but certain specific private schools.

Where did you school?

Oh me too.

Oh yes, my sister went there.

Oh Winchester, nice.

Rugby, sure sure.

That sort of thing.

A lovely friend who'd come from Belfast said it was even more unnerving to her because in Northern Ireland that question has more of an *are you Catholic or Protestant?* vibe.

One of my favourite moments was when I was asked what my grandparents did for a living. Yes, I also thought it was a strange teenage topic of conversation until realising that some people's grandparents wrote the books we were studying or started revolutions.

On my mum's side my grandad was a sort of clothing agent and my grandma trained then worked as a primary school teacher from her thirties; on the other side my grandparents owned a Spar grocery store and post office within it. As other students approached our group, the girl I'd told this to kindly introduced me, having assumed that is what I meant, as the heir to the entire Spar chain of grocery shops.

I am not saying this to mock. My mum quickly argued the inverted snobbery out of me when I began taking the piss out of eight-year-old kids.

King's School is a private school founded to educate the choristers in the King's College choir, part of the same historic foundation as Eton College, situated at the back of the college I went to in Cambridge.

Some of these little boys who sang in the King's College choir would walk through the grounds of the college, wearing their uniform. This uniform consisted of tiny top hats and tailcoats. The first time I saw them, I burst out laughing. I winced at their voices, already speaking like the Queen, like mini politicians. I'd never heard children talking like that, only adults on TV. It hadn't crossed my mind that this accent could also come out of tiny mouths. When I told my mum, she didn't laugh back.

They did not choose where they were born or what school they would be sent to any more than you did, Hollie.

Personally, I went to a private school for two years; for the last two years of primary school, around nine to eleven years old, I got a scholarship to a mixed local boarding school where I didn't board, but desperately wanted to, mainly because of whispers during the morning classes about my friends jumping in the bath in pyjamas at midnight. I didn't think about the missing your family stuff at that age. I guess I was lucky enough not to be able to imagine it.

From a small local state primary, suddenly there were proper science labs and a forest and children from all over the world sharing sweets and noodle snacks I'd never seen before, and loved, and there were doughnuts at the tuck shop every day at four.

Less exciting, the egg-and-spoon and three-legged races of my previous primary sports days were replaced with actual athletics, and the parents' race, always one of the funniest, now seemed to be less of a laugh and more of a crucial competition between ripped army-captain dads desperate to prove their exceptional speed to nine-year-olds, and each other.

My favourite memory from this two-year glimpse into the world of private education, apart from my friend's Sandy and Hatty and John, is a story my mum recently recalled.

At these sports days, parents were asked to bring a picnic. My parents turned up with some sandwiches and strawberries and biscuits my mum had packed. All the other parents turned up with full-on fold-out tables and chairs and proper expensive picnic hampers with plates and cutlery tied with ribbons inside.

My gran was with us, and because of the luxuriousness of these other families' picnics, she assumed that they were food stalls offered by the school, and started to walk around accidentally stealing other people's lunch.

The reverse happened to me at the first corporate gig I ever did. It was for a legal firm, I think, though the main thing I remember was paying £14 for one thin pizza at the very fancy venue to share with my friend Nicola. I was a deep pan person at the time and the thinness of the crust added to the insult.

The pizza was cut into small squares. Nicola and I stood at one of those high-up tables, really hungry, plate in front of us. Immediately, older members of the law firm walked up to our table, stopped, smiled, thanked us and stole our pizza, tiny square by tiny square, assuming we were standing to serve it to them. We were too shocked to say anything.

Despite the divides of Cambridge, the grants available to help those students who had not experienced the world of 'grand cru' dining before the age of eighteen, were various. I say this so as not to put off anyone from applying. These universities, more than many others, have money to give you and are amazing places to study.

I often hear people complain that so many politicians have been educated at Oxbridge. (This word is an amalgamation of Oxford and Cambridge. I didn't know that when I looked at applying to these universities and thought it was a place in England.)

Fair enough, we don't want parliament full of Oxbridge graduates.

Class-based inequality is dire in politics and working-class representation at the majority of universities is shite, something only Scotland seems to be tackling in the UK.

But having studied at Cambridge University, and having seen the levels of embubblement, as I'll call it, the extent to which many of these much wealthier students, mainly from those public or well-known private schools, did not mix with other students who had not attended their school or schools they felt comfortable showing an interest in, had often never mixed with young people outside this school circuit, neither before Cambridge nor at Cambridge, nor, I assume, after Cambridge, was incredible.

From childhoods in detached houses with secluded private drives where you will never bump into neighbours, to private buses to private schools away from the local kids, to holidays in second houses away from the local area and so on and so on; having seen this, I no longer believe it's so much the specific university that is the central issue or even the fact that these politicians so often went to Oxford, but rather that so many of them, those who have been making decisions for centuries on public health and education and housing and, well, every single thing affecting our everyday lives, have been so disassociated from the actual public sphere at almost every stage of their upbringing, that there is simply no chance, or very little, they can relate to even the average citizen, let alone those in the least privileged economic situations.

So yes, there needs to be a much larger class diversity in politics, but I'm not having the lazy 'all politicians are the same' line spouted out to excuse you from getting off your arse to vote, or certain university attendance used as full-throttle evidence of this. It's inaccurate and it also shits on those people I met at university who went through the absolute runners to get there, and to compare those people to the likes of Rishi or Boris simply because they share a degree, is pure laziness.

There are two things I'm certain of in life. One is that I will never run a marathon. The other, particularly after attending Cambridge University, is that I will never vote Conservative. This is not through hate or annoyance or being called common by ignorant teenagers. It is not because of Boris Johnson's hair or the way Jacob Rees-Mogg stretches out over the parliament benches as if he's sunning himself on a tax-haven beachfront. As much as I can't stand these folk, I don't know them and I don't think it's helpful to pick apart their appearances. Trump included. He's not dangerous because of his tan.

please, sir

two hundred years later
oliver is still standing
with a bowl in his hand
and a hole in his belly
as jacob rees-mogg
describes as 'rather uplifting'
the increasing work of foodbanks
to feed this country's children

I will never vote Conservative because at the basis of the Conservative mindset is this idea of meritocracy, the idea that anyone can be anything if you just work hard and are determined enough, an idea that has been disproven so many times throughout history it's like buying a house knowing that the foundations are built on slime; an idea I saw disproven so starkly by so many of those I was forced to sit at dinners with at Cambridge. Of course, there are other moral objections I have to Conservative Party policy, but even without those, I do not think this supposed socio-economic foundation on which they base the majority of their policies works.

Deep down, I think we all know that no one gets where they are by hard work alone, perhaps especially the folk pushing this as a concept on which to base government policy.

It must be so lovely to truly believe, if you actually believe it, that hard work is all that counts; that people are where they are because of the effort they have put in and little more; that people are poorer because they are lazier or stupider and richer because they are cleverer and worked harder for it and deserve everything they have earned.

That I got my degree because I worked really hard at school and got good grades and was just, you know, smart is a cool idea. I *did* work really hard at school. I worked really, really hard, every single night in my bedroom till the early hours. I did every piece of homework ever set since homework was handed out. Others things were fairly helpful too though:

Having my own room. Having a brain well suited to sitting in a classroom for hours at a time. A quiet home environment. Being in a family with money. My parents' free education. My free education. Being in a family with money. Museums being free. A mum who would knock on my door and bring me snacks every two hours while I was sticking Post-it notes covered in physics equations to my walls. Plenty of food. Being in a family with money. Free asthma treatment. The free local library. Holidays to other countries. Being read to every night as a kid. Love. A detached house in which I could not hear my neighbours through thin walls. Being in a family with money. A computer I shared with my brother to do homework on. No one I had to care for during my childhood. Being cared for by my parents. Being in a family with money. No addictions. Encouragement. Parents helping me with homework. No one needing me to work long hours as well as doing school work to bring in money because we already had ... money. Money. My family had money.

What a get-out-of-jail-free card belief in meritocracy is. How much less guilt-ridden you'd feel walking past a person sleeping on the street. How brilliant you must think you are if you truly believe you did everything all off your own bat. Self-made is the most bullshit phrase I have ever heard, especially when applied to those born into so much privilege. *Really Alan, are you? Did you push yourself out your own vagina, Alan? Did you build the transport systems all your workers take to get to work for you, Alan? Do you dispose of your own shite in your own back garden, Alan?*

During a 2005 election, Boris Johnson once said: 'Voting Tory will cause your wife to have bigger breasts and increase your chances of owning a BMW M3.'

Big tits joke aside, I think this is exactly the draw of the Conservatives for those who are not super rich already; this idea of aspiration, as if voting Conservative will more easily acquire you the same level of wealth as those who lead the party, a party which forwards this idea of the hard-working wealthy person who made their own fortune, and can now reap the benefits. In reality most were born into golden babygros and the policies they push absolutely will not have the same financial impact on those not born drinking 'grand cru' from their nanny's breasts. I mean paid nanny here, not gran, which would be another story altogether.

self-made

self-made, you declare, as if you strolled confidently
from your own vag, already fully dressed in a bowler hat
and three-piece suit, bank notes in the babygro,
baby-neck long enough to reach your own lactating tits,
self-made, self-made, you wail again,
self-swaddled in self-assurance, spouting stories of success,
how well you learnt to read and write by reading books

you wrote yourself on paper forged from the felled stumps
of your own self-serving bones, *self-made, self-made*
you moan, as if no midwife and no mother
as if no nurses and no doctors, no teachers, no tutors,
no factories, no farmers, no friend's father's contacts,
as if no hand ever held your own till traffic slowed
and green men glowed, as if you never once lay helpless
in a nappy full of shite, desperately screaming for a change

Looking up the word meritocracy in the *Oxford English Dictionary*, the example sentence is telling: 'Britain is a meritocracy, and everyone with skill and imagination may aspire to reach the highest level.'

If this were true, the fact that so many prime ministers have come from one single school would be a mind-boggling mathematical coincidence.

My daughter asked me if I think we will ever invent hoverboards. We had just watched *Back to the Future*. I said it's being looked into. And maybe we would have invented them long ago if we hadn't spent the last thousand years educating inbred royalty over all other human beings on the planet.

Perhaps the person who could have invented hoverboards fifty years ago was never taught to read. Perhaps the people with the capacity to cure dementia are currently being thrown out of primary school by extremist governments. Perhaps you're really, really good at something you've never had the opportunity to learn. Maybe I'd have been a world champion equestrian if I'd had a horse; an expert composer if my school music teacher hadn't spent every lesson pissed in his car or perving over sixth-form students. What wonders could be achieved if every brain in the world had been given access to equal education and opportunity is baffling. What an absolute waste of talent and possibility inequality and poverty bring to the world.

Of course, as well as the extreme examples of snobbery and

ignorance, there were also plenty of wonderful people at university, from a variety of both much more privileged and less privileged backgrounds than myself. Not everyone who went to Eton was a wanker. Not every state school student wasn't. Not everyone who was sent to private boarding school has become an arrogant tosser. Many, it seems, found it pretty traumatic.

At my graduation, my dad, just to make sure the louder of the tweed-suited public school parents knew that our family were, in his lovingly repeated words, *just as good as them*, ordered champagne at the bar to celebrate, insisting the bartender pour our champagne into pint glasses not flutes.

the queen was not your grandma

grey curls do not a grandmother make
is an ancient english proverb i made up
to stop my friends losing their fucking minds
about the death of a monarch

it wasn't an easy life for her, you say
cool, neither was my actual grandma's
or the other people who died that day
we did not cry for either

did she ever send you pocket money, the queen?
sellotape five twenty-pence coins to cards
send them every week with a letter that said
'i love you' and 'keep working hard at school, my darling'

did she ever warm your towel
after showers or bring cherry almond cake,
freshly baked when she visited
because she knew it was your favourite?

did she ever visit you?
were you even allowed inside her house?
did she ever tell you stories
about her younger days,

like when your grandad,
the first time he met her parents
pulled off the entire tablecloth
thinking it was a napkin

or that time her husband,
inspecting the electrical equipment
in a factory in scotland, said it looked so crude
it was likely done by an immigrant?

oh sorry, that was the actual queen
not your grandma
it's difficult to remember which is which
seeing as they both have grey hair

sweet little woman that she was
running a global empire
head of a billion-pound business
unlike your actual grandma, who didn't

whose funeral was so much smaller than the queen's
because fewer people loved her
despite how much lovelier she was

in the modern art gallery with my dad

the reason i do not like this painting, i thought,
is because i am art-stupid. if i were art-clever,
i would see something in the painting
or on the painting or around the painting or inside it
or however art-clever people read paintings
and i would stand and be amazed
and a stranger would pass me a glass of something vintage
and nod beside me in silence
and we would both know why we were nodding
and we would move on to the next painting
which i also do not think i like, but would like, i think
if i were art-clever, and i'd say to the stranger
how i'm really fascinated by the way
that single green dot on the plain black background
alludes to the eighteenth-century tradition
of questioning scientific purity
and the stranger would smile and say, *yes
i think you may be onto something there!*
and we'd laugh in that way art-clever people laugh
when they says things like that;
instead, i stand back from the painting
and say *i don't really get it*
and my dad says *that's cos it's shite*

lobster

for the first time i saw people point to an animal in a tank,
then eat it

it was difficult to work out which i found more revolting –
the skeletal bodies of the lobsters shuffling silent in the tank
or the humans salivating at the grotesque through the glass,
until finger pointing grinning at which poor git
they had decided best to feast upon that evening;
elated, or at least contented that the chosen beady eyes
would soon be dropped into a boiling pool of salted suffocation,
placed by smiling waiters onto polished silver trays

is it because they're so damn ugly we can look at them so soon
before we rip their flesh apart, call it romantic, as if a pick n mix
of breathing beastie sweeties, swipe left
on a cannibal's dating app,
treat our lovers to a limb for a special valentine's dinner,
match their seasoned brains to a crisp white chardonnay
to get us in the mood for fucking later on

my eyes flicker between the creatures in the tank
and the creatures at the table sucking muscle out of pincer,
licking oily buttered lips,
cracking jokes across ironed cotton covers
now spotted with spit and juices i am unsure what to make of
you really must try it, hollie, it's delicious,
a little claw debris stuck to the corners of their mouths

i saw a lobster once, suddenly, in a rockpool in dunbar,
paddling with my daughter – i screamed, splashed away,
blamed a sudden sharp shell on my sole, did not want her

to hate these creatures as i'd hated them,
i do not know exactly why they frighten me so much,
i did not look in the rock pools all summer,
so disgusted by the thought of these monsters

is it because they look alien to human? each feature
the enemy opposite of what most consider beautiful
that we will place the tanks next to the dinner tables,
call it classy; are cows too cute when they're alive
to be kept in cages outside burger bars? *mummy*
i want the black and white one, it's got such a pretty face

in the newspapers, when a person we deem pretty dies
the headlines always mention how sad it was
such a pretty person died; what if someone we deem ugly dies?
is it still a waste of beauty? lobsters versus bunny rabbits

around the world, people have stopped eating octopus
after a netflix documentary deemed them highly intelligent;
did you know they have thousands of colour-changing cells
under their skin? did you know they change colour
when they sleep? there has not been
a popular netflix documentary about lobsters
if there were, perhaps we'd all know how they regenerate limbs,
that they piss from their faces, die mainly from exhaustion,
or boiling water in pots in upmarket restaurant kitchens
do not age the way we age; do not weaken, do not wrinkle
– they are everything we long for

if i changed colour as i slept, would you love me more?
i'd probably love you more

glass

seven hundred and sixty windows
in buckingham palace
and still they do not notice
what's going on outside

strike

a scented candle will not calm you if you can't afford to eat
and foodbanks at your work are not a treat,
nor a substitute for wages
the matchstick girl died in the end, remember
so do not tell me *all politicians are the same*
it doesn't matter who you vote for no one listens any way
the word weekend is as man-made as billionaire, bankrupt
shareholder, credit card, pension, sick leave
laws have and will change constantly, that's the entire point
of politics; don't believe you are not part of this,
your daily life is forged by endless choices
other people made; do you remember when your grandad
could legally rape after smiling down the aisle?
when rapunzel was exiled for a baby in her belly?
do you remember when kings had divine right to rule?
when oliver asked kindly for another bowl of gruel
and working-class children worked illiterate in factories?
when junk food was advertised between cartoons on tv?
when no one without property could vote for their futures
and landlords could openly discriminate on race?
life is what you make it says scrooge to bob cratchit
your fate is in your hands and postcode and health service
and transport and childcare and neighbours and leaders
as headlines point their fingers, distracting us
with the same stories they've tried to tell for centuries;
blame the workers, blame the migrants, blame the mothers,
the double* ones especially, blame the addicts,
blame the poor, blame the boats full of people

---

* I wrote 'single mothers' here at first but decided this is a rubbish phrase and
from now on I'm referring to them as 'double mothers' because they do double the
work and their relationship status is irrelevant.

fleeing fear you cannot fathom,
blame mary and jesus knocking at the fucking inn again
as suella proudly shouts *go back to where you came from,*
hails an airplane to rwanda then stands up smug
in parliament to sing the favourite tory chant:
anything is possible for those who just work hard
anything is possible for those who just work hard
as if migrating for your future is not an excellent example;
as if most richest in this country were not born into wealth;
as if most poorest in this country have been sitting
on their arses; as if letting people drown in the moat
around this castle will make more homes affordable,
landlords accountable, your brother employable,
enough staff in hospitals – once upon a time
we stopped a refugee from syria coming here to live
and suddenly all billionaires
said how silly they were being avoiding paying taxes
so they gave back all their stolen wealth
and divvied up the profits; instead the nurses
are on strike and we're still blaming the nurses
the teachers are on strike and we're still blaming the teachers
now the greedy railway staff now the greedy junior doctors
as if their lives are not devoted to putting other people first,
as if a day stood at the picket-line is a day out at the park
anything is possible for those who just work hard
anything is possible for those who just work hard
it doesn't matter who you vote for, all politicians are the same
light the scented candle, burn your fingers in the flame

things i didn't question

architects of important buildings are named on the plaque but not the builders. public statues are of royalty or war. trains have quiet carriages but not loud carriages. people who present documentaries don't have regional accents. characters with big boobs on tv aren't as intelligent as characters with small boobs on tv. people presenting the news do not show emotion about the news. men are not as good as women at cooking in houses. men are better than women at cooking in restaurants. men have one ear pierced. women have two ears pierced. if you wear an anklet on the left ankle, you're a lesbian. if you wear an anklet on the right ankle, you're a slag. the word slag. the word virgin. eton college. people who can't afford to buy things in full pay more for those things. people in russia are naturally better at ballet. some people live in palaces. people in china are naturally better at maths. some people are royal, other people are not royal. santa claus brings rich children more presents than poor children. white men are better at swimming and polo and golf and mass shootings in the usa. life expectancy is related to how healthily you've been eating. if you work hard, you can achieve anything. people in prison are bad. homeless people didn't work hard. god helped famous christian people in the usa become really good pop singers. god is a he. god starts with a capital letter. businesses and brands and people's names and countries and the word i start with a capital letter. the words we and love and grandma do not start with a capital letter. school is free. university is not. seatbelts. eating cows and pigs is fine but eating horses and frogs is gross. eating hash browns for breakfast is normal. eating jacket potato for breakfast is not normal. two women can never have proper sex. dog shit can't stay on the road but horse shit can. pretty characters are kinder. people with warts and scars on their faces are mean and scary. little boys cry a lot but men don't. teenage girls make fewer jokes to teenage boys than teenage boys make to teenage girls. boarding schools for five-year-olds. homework. first-class sections. eating with forks and knives. weeding. weddings. taps. renting. passports.

WORDS

Moist Velvet Volvos

Warning:

There is a lot about the word vulva in this chapter.
If you do not find it at all difficult to say this word, well done,
you can probably just skip the first two sections and go on to page 177.

If you hate this word and think
'I don't want to read this section because gross',
I think you should read it.

What is not named does not exist.

HARRIET LERNER

sunrise on venus

so slow to turn, this roly-poly planet
venus, visible tonight,
where each day lasts two hundred and forty-three of ours;
one year shorter than one day

what luck here on earth to spin so fast
on our axis as we orbit; only twelve short hours to wait
between each sunset sunrise sunset sunrise
splashed across our skies

if born mid-night on venus, the sun
might never rise in your lifetime
as you, growing older, listen in awe
to your parents' tales of colour, of dawn

or else, born into the dawn,
beneath the scorching venus sky
your whole life
in an endless wake of day

BALD EAGLE AND THE MISSING WILLIES

The English language has the second largest vocabulary of any language in the world. There are so many words there's even a word to describe something when it is 'slightly or partially open': ajar.

When my daughter learnt the word 'ajar' she thought it was totally weird. Our conversation went like this:

> *Me:* Goodnight, lovely.
> *Her:* Goodnight, Mum.
> *Me:* Do you want me to leave your door ajar?
> *Her:* What?
> *Me:* It means a little bit open.
> *Her:* Why don't you just say 'a little bit open' then?
> *Me:* Well, because ajar means a little bit open so I used that word.
> *Her:* Why is there a word for that?
> *(She starts laughing)*
> Is there a word for a lot open?
> *(I think for a sec)*
> *Me:* I don't think so. Just for 'a little bit open'.
> *(She carries on laughing about it as I leave the door ajar)*

The English language is a phenomenal language. It has so many, a plethora, a real glut, a superfluity, an overabundant excess of words.

There aren't many languages you can be as specific in as we can in English.

In English, you can laugh in loads of different ways: you can chuckle, chortle, snort, giggle, snigger, guffaw, tittle, hoot, cackle. You can also, in more idiomatic terms, piss your pants, fall about, crack up, roll around, split your sides. In some languages, you just laugh.

In every single sentence we speak, the history of humanity hides. Say anything in English and you are exhaling centuries of the mingling and movement of people, of international trading and invention, trauma, exploration, conquest, conflict and censorship; the ancient and unending path of those migrating across the surface of the Earth is uncovered in each sentence we utter.

Like: *Can I borrow your mascara?*

Can – from the old English *cunnan* (know), related to the Dutch *kunnen* and the German *können*, from an Indo-European root shared by Latin *gnosere* (know) and Greek *gignōskein* (know).

Borrow – from the Old English *borgian*, from Proto-West Germanic *burgōna* (to pledge, take care of), from Proto-Indo-European -*bhergh** (to take care).

Mascara – from the Italian *mascara*, which comes from the Arabic *maskara*.

One simple question and we span centuries and continents. Also, no, you can't, because I once got conjunctivitis from using a tester mascara and had yellow shit all over my eyelashes, sticking them together while I was sleeping.

We have so many words in English, taken and translated and mistranslated and gargled together from other languages. All our words really.

A few other favourites, origins simplified: karaoke from Japanese (though in Finland I was told it was actually Finnish so I'm not sure now); ballet from French; paparazzi from Italian; penguin from Welsh; and yes, tea from Chinese, no matter how many other words we love to ram before it like 'English Breakfast' or 'Yorkshire' or 'Scottish Blend' or 'Lady Grey' as if desperately trying to smudge the place of birth on its passport. How different it would sound, how differently our island minds might have opened up all these years if the comfort of a good cup of tea hadn't had their birthplaces so arrogantly erased.

Don't cry love, I'll pop the kettle on and make you a lovely Rwandan cuppa. Feeling sad? Oh there's nothing a lovely Indian-Kenyan blend won't sort out.

There's a section entitled *Why is it called 'Yorkshire Tea'?* on the Taylors of Harrogate website that supposedly answers this question. The tea is named after the place it is blended, or sold. The section suggests: 'blends from multiple origins need to be named more creatively'. Referring to the blend 'Russian caravan' it jokes that 'it wasn't very practical (or catchy) to call it Oolong Keemun Lapsang Souchong, so instead it was named by its trade route'. Yeah, make it more catchy. Sure, sure. Also, if it's about creativity, the name 'Yorkshire Tea' is hardly a creative fucking masterpiece. It's like calling a piña colada a Scottish cocktail because you pulsed the fruit with the rum in the blender in your kitchen in Muirhead. For info, the piña colada was born in Puerto Rico.

I think there ought to be a rule that says that those people shouting about getting 'Britain Back' to some sort of fictionalised past of white people whose families come only and forever from Kent are no longer allowed to use any words that originated in other countries to make their point.

As well as the words that travelled here from all corners of the world, we have also had and have words continuously invented by politicians and scientists, writers, cool kids and money-makers.

The word cellulite, for example, invented by a guy who then made a lot of money selling treatments to help rid us of what was previously just called 'skin'.

The word Brexit, a cleverly light-hearted-sounding pun to represent a huge political decision.

The word frappuccino, invented in Eastern Massachusetts, USA. Do not try to order this in Italy; they will either cry or throw you out of the country.

Despite this huge variety of English words, despite having words to specifically describe the bastardising of Italian coffee culture with US diabetes levels (studies show many frappuccinos contain up to sixteen teaspoons of sugar, twice the entire daily recommended maximum adult intake); words to specifically describe in English someone who is sexually attracted to corpses (necrophiliac, mostly men), or the tingly feeling of cold in your fingers (gwenders), or the very tip of your middle finger (dactylion), or the process of covering a vulva in itchy diamanté stickers (vajazzle, a portmanteau of the word vajayjay and bedazzle, popularised in the 2000s), there are also missing words, words which exist in other languages, many other languages, but not in English.

Enter the conversation had by parents and carers all over the English language-speaking world about what the fuck they will call their daughters' ... *you know, err, well, ummm, lady's front bottom intimate area, err, wanny, err, private part V-Zone fanny flower.*

What is the female equivalent of the word willy?

Silence.

In French, one of our closest linguistic neighbours, the word for penis is *le pénis* and testicle is *le testicule*. The word for vulva is *la vulve* and vagina is *le vagin*.

For children, in English, penis becomes willy, a word all kids know and hear and understand. In French the equivalent is *zizi*. In French, vulva and vagina become merged into the kiddy word *zézette*. In English, nothing. It literally doesn't exist. Necrophiliac, yes, *zézette*, no.

The confusion that the lack of a willy equivalent in English pulled me into as both a child and a parent is extraordinary. Everyone used a different word. Personally, the most common word I heard for vulva was front bottom, as if I were some sort of double-arseholed child monster. I learned that boys had willies and then wondered what I had, as every adult and child and book and doctor used an array of flowers and noonoos and fluffadoofs and fandangles to describe my genitalia, or else just ignored it altogether, too awkward or embarrassed to even speak its name, whatever name that might be.

If I'd grown up French, I would most likely have thought there were oranges and lemons and *zizis* and *zézettes* and gone out to play.

Of course, there's shame and embarrassment towards discussing genitalia in most languages, and even with the existence of these words in French, there's still a lot of bawking among adults as to which words they will and will not use, but that missing word in English, that missing unifying term still causes so many parents and carers and nursery workers and teachers to ummm and ahh and panic and flit to extraordinary levels over how to label the vulva for a child.

I typed '*zézette*' into wordreference.com, my favourite online translation service, to see what it would come up with as an English equivalent. The search yielded no direct results but a confused chatroom of native French speakers. One user was asking for help translating the word *zézette* and the conversation that followed was amazing to read.

> *on a bien zizi, willy, pour les garçons. Et pour les filles?*
> ('so we have *zizi*, willy, for the boys. And for the girls?')

The 'top response' from this discussion came from Pyan, who tried to help the baffled French student find this missing English translation:

> This thread suggests fanny (British English only) is the most common in Britain and I think it is probably right. I've heard china (childish pronunciation of vagina), minnie, front bottom and toosh but not most of the others listed below.

Pyan then cites a *Guardian* article talking about the long list of names for the vulva in *The Vagina Monologues*:

There are the pretty Blue-Peter-kitten names (minnie, fairy, fluff) and terms with an affectionate nod to nature (butterfly, daisy, flower), nonsense words (cootchie, poontang, fuzzy, toosh). Many of us grew up with a front bottom, others with in-betweens, down there, pink parts and lady-bits.

Pyan then suggests *The answers will probably be different for American English* and closes with a cheery *I hope this helps*.

The fact that we never invented, or didn't deem it necessary to invent, or censored the terminology for this female body part for children's ears means that we now have this plethora of different and fairly ridiculous nicknames for the vulva and vagina combo that we use with children, most of which either refer to sugary edible treats or are entirely made up words. From my own experience, these include: front bottom, minny (which always made *The Beano* even funnier), wanny, fanny, cookie, private parts, baby hole, special area, muff, muffin, lady parts, nonny, fandango or, post-puberty, lady garden and beef curtains (I think this is my least favourite of all).

English is not the only language in the world to have this missing-word issue. Swedish had it too, but in Sweden they did something about it. They literally invented a new word.

Pre-2006, Swedish had the same linguistic gap as English did. There was a word like willy, *snopp*, but no universal kiddy word for vulva or vagina. After a campaign begun by a social worker, Anna Kosztovics, to highlight the dangers of this linguistic vortex, Anna invented a new word: *snippa*. The Swedish government and the education and healthcare system were like, we get you Anna, good point, let's protect kids, so they got on board and, within a couple of years, the word *snippa* was in everyday use, taught in all schools, said by all carers and kids, many now not even aware it was such a modern invention.

There are debates about whether *snippa* is the most appropriate word – mainly because it was formed from the male word *snopp* – as well as whether it was really necessary to invent a kiddy word. However, I still think it's a fairly incredible linguistic feat to see a problem caused by a gap in the language and to invent a solution, everybody on board.

Despite this Swedish success story, I have no doubt that this wouldn't work in English.

Most practically, because English is spoken by a lot more people in a lot more places than Swedish is. Any campaign to invent a new word in English would have to be agreed upon by various countries' leaderships and spread across continents.

Also, it's not necessary. We already have words for these body parts and so even if we could follow Sweden's model, which we can't, experts don't actually think we should. According to child-protection experts, it is much better to just teach kids the correct names.

We don't have kiddy words for the majority of body parts. We never invented kiddy words for shoulder or arm or neck or nose or fingers or tongue. Just the genitals. Oh, and the womb, pointing out most often that 'Mummy has a baby in her tummy', a word we also use for the stomach, as if babies swim around in our stomach acid until they are ready to pop out our foofoofs.

By using kiddy words for genitals specifically, we act as if those body parts, correctly named, are not for children, too adult, different, or too shameful to name, despite them literally being on children's bodies from birth. Yes, even the clitoris.

I am going to admit here, I actually checked this online because I still had it engrained in my head that maybe this was wrong. I then looked up facts about the foreskin after learning that both the clitoral hood and foreskin can get kind of sorely stuck during first clitoral or penile erections. I then fell into a foreskin tunnel and through

The Blindboy Podcast discovered that at one point in the history of Christianity, twelve churches claimed to have Jesus's holy foreskin in their possession and people travelled to see it, while other serious theologians refuted this, forwarding instead the belief that Jesus's foreskin was in fact what Saturn's rings were forged from.

Anyway. Instead of inventing a new word as was done in Swedish, there are a number of current campaigns, stemming primarily from child-protection and women's or sexual health organisations, such as the Eve Appeal in the UK, NHS sexual health services and EnoughAbuse.org, urging adults, from parents and carers to doctors, nurses and teachers, to please, please, for the love of children's and young's people's health and safety, just use the words vulva and vagina when teaching children the name of these body parts.

No more fluffy minny wanny front-bottom fuckery, please just tell them what their body parts are called.

This sounds easy. Just use the words vulva and vagina. Cool. All good. Just words. Not harming anyone. Eleven letters in total. Easy to say. Helpful to know. What's all the fuss?

The fuss is, we've been indoctrinated over hundreds of years to vomit over the word vulva and run screaming from the word vagina as if it's a newly steaming volcano.

I never knew how indoctrinated my own language was until I was in my late twenties, potty-training a young daughter, trying to teach her about wiping and washing and trying to name the vulva, which was a pretty important part of both of those processes. Five letters and I just could not get the fucking word out of my mouth. The first time I said it, I almost vomited.

The power of culture never ceases to fascinate me. I started to question how much control I actually had over my own mind, and mouth. Why could I not say this word? Why did it feel so weird to say? *Come on, Hollie, say it. I wipe my vulva like this. I have a vulva too.* Fuck, why is this so fucking difficult?

I hid my disgust from my kid, like my fear of spiders, determined to say the word as casually as possible so I would not pass this ridiculousness onto her, but inside, each time I said the word vulva, it was like I was alone in a shop changing room with a dress too small to get off stuck around my shoulders.

It's such a weird feeling knowing your brain has been so affected by outside influences that it struggles to literally string letters together to form a word that is in no way harmful to anyone, not an insult nor slur, no reason not to be said other than years of cultural censorship and shaming.

That night, I started to test myself, to say words out loud. What other words does my mind rebel against? The hardest for me to say were: vulva, vagina, moist and wet. Not hard to see what these have in common.

Murder. No, that was easy to say.

I started to pit words against each other. Whichever makes me cringe more as I speak it out loud wins. Like:

say *murder*

say *vulva*

Vulva easily wins.

say *vulva*

say *testicles*

Vulva's still worse for me to say, though both are tricky.

say *vulva*

say *vagina*

Vulva again. Why does my body hate this word so much?

Which of the below do you find harder to say?

Gunshot wound

Wet vulva

Gunshot wound

Wet vulva

What a ridiculous language we live in. I started to practise saying vulva, literally practising these five letters out loud as if reciting a very dull one-word poem, over and over again. I once went to a poetry gig where someone did read a three-word poem for five minutes, simply repeating the words peanut butter jellyfish over and over again. That was also pretty boring.

Vulva vulva vulva. Vulva vulva vulva. You can do it.

I began training, determined that, at some point in my future, naming this body part would not make my body shake in disgust.

PS: The language with the most words in the world is Arabic. Apparently, the poetry is totally gorgeous.

'beef curtains'

is the most disgusting metaphor
for a body part i have ever heard

curtains, maybe, fine, drawn back by hand
when the body longs for light,

teased apart at night-time
strip of moon on sleeping cheek

but beef? really? beef curtains?
huge drapes of cut off flesh?

dangling blood-drained, dead; how heavy
heaving labia like these onto curtain hooks

the stench of decaying fabric
as they rotted in your bedroom

and what other furnishings to match?
beef cushions? beef table cloth?

a beef valance, perhaps?
who started this?

what did you see, you poor sod
to turn this wishing well of pleasure

into a nightmare of interior design?
fucking in a burger van?

fingering a butcher?
cunnilingus in an abattoir –

the shadow of a lover's vulva
projected massive in the moonlight

onto the ribcage of a gutted cow
skin stripped, hanging at the window

your tongue trying desperately
to carry on licking; eyes flicking
between the carcass and the clit

there's no wet rose, i've checked

no apple blossom blooms no fern unfurls
those soft folds either side aren't dewy petals
fondled kindly between index and thumb;
my scent is not of marigold or lily

how comfortable the tongue sits
huddled behind poetry –
lips tiptoe past in slippers; shhh
compare it to an orchard of oysters
bible bellyful of figs, but still can't even name it

how absurd this bitter taste is
how can five split-second letters
rest so heavy on the tongue

the first time i was touched
no bud was plucked from shallow earth
i was not plucked from anywhere
no garden patch deflowered
cherry still on cherry branch;

i did not wither after opening
i did not die nor did i bud

whisper, and it blushes rushing blood
keep singing those sweet songs my love,
see the way it swells

not unlike a tipping ocean wave
nor a daisy to the yawning sun
not unlike a mussel slurped in cream

160

nor a genie gently rubbed
not unlike the bulge of candyfloss
freshly spun from sugar, melting sticky
gloss across an eager, greedy face

but more just like a vulva
at least eleven points in scrabble
though i've never seen it played

100 REASONS NOT TO SAY

Hollie: Hello, I'm Hollie and I've managed to say the word vulva for over five years now.
Carole: Oh well done, Hollie. *[Everyone claps]* Nicole, would you like a go?
Nicole: I don't think I can, Carole, sorry.
Carole: That's OK, don't worry, take your time, Nicole, it's difficult for all of us. Start with the V.
[Nicole tries, but can't. She sits down, defeated. Everyone claps again.]

Unfortunately, there is no vulvas anonymous support group to help us all say this dreaded word.

Since making the grand decision to use it in my life and my poems (when, you know, it's relevant), I have been approached by some of the groups campaigning for the rest of us to do this.

Every time I share a post from one of these campaigns I get loads of positive responses from people about when they first said this word, how long it took them to say it, why they started, how hard they found it, and so on. It really is like a fucking support network. I also get annoying responses from smug fuckers who never vomited over this word and are like 'grow up, it's just a word'. They don't understand the pain.

The most fascinating thing, though, is the negative backlash. The lengths us adults are willing to go to just to not say this word are breath-taking. Myself previously included.

First of all, for anyone still umming and ahhing about whether they can cope with saying it to their kids or students, here are the reasons why I do, and why you should join the club too.

Oh Hollie, do we have to? Why can't we just carry on awkwardly pointing or just choose our own favourite words from 'privates' or 'minnies' or 'tuppences'? Why are you forcing us to say these dreadful V words, Hollie? Why do you hate us so much?

I don't hate you or your floofadoof. I have just read far too much on the topic to go back now. The evidence is overwhelming. Briefly . . .

Shame: there is a much higher likelihood of feeling bodily shame growing up if there are parts of the body we are taught to either ignore the existence of or lock up in secret shhhh boxes labelled with a variety of nicknames. Like if people just pretended you didn't exist or refused to say your name or just called you Bob, cos that's the name of someone who looks a bit like you. Well, that's how the vulva has felt for centuries.

Pain: if people do not know the proper name of, or are too ashamed or embarrassed to name certain body parts that are causing them pain or discomfort, there is a much lower likelihood of people describing this pain, seeking help for this pain, going to the doctor's to check this pain and so on.

Pleasure: if we are ashamed or embarrassed or silent about the body parts we want touched, again we will find it so much more difficult to talk about them, for good or for bad. It's pretty difficult to ask someone to touch your clitoris or massage your labia with some coconut oil if you either don't know these body parts exist or can't bring yourself to say the words or are too embarrassed to mention you have a vulva at all.

These next reasons broke my fucking heart and of all of them are the main things that have convinced me, especially as a parent, to use these words.

Child protection: according to a child-protection officer who messaged me, as well as the many currently campaigning who haven't messaged me directly, abusers are manipulative and they prey on ignorance and shame. A child or young person (or adult, anyone really) who knows about their bodies, who can unashamedly name their vagina and vulva, penis or testicles, is more likely to tell someone what has happened, and where. Abusers will know this.

Teaching children the correct words for genitals has been encouraged for years by those in child protection. I think it's about time we listened to them and not the parents writing letters about how they don't like little Sammy knowing the word vulva in case it gives him nightmares about hairy vultures coming to destroy his toys.

From a legal perspective, explained to me by a criminologist specialising in child protection who commented below a post I put on Instagram, even if a child – or adult, but it's most problematic with children – does tell someone about abuse, it is much harder to prosecute an abuser if the person who has suffered abuse cannot clearly and correctly label the body part that was touched.

There is no turning back. Normalise these words and they will be normal to your children or pupils forever and ever amen. Your child will lose absolutely nothing by knowing them, they will not suddenly turn into adults or sex-obsessed monsters; yes, they might say it in public not knowing that the generations above them are still trembling with shame, but by knowing these words and being comfortable in using them they will be more protected from abuse, pain, embarrassment, fear and so on and so on.

So no, let's not keep calling it a fucking floofadoof just cos it's less likely to make us cringe.

As I said, despite all of these reasons, there is still so much backlash from people to these campaigns. The more I think about it, the more I can't believe I live in a world where campaigns to literally name a part of the body are necessary. We are so fucking weird.

The most vehement backlash I get is this: Why would you even need to say this word *to children*?

One reply I had on Twitter (notice the use of the word 'bits') stated: *Why on earth would you speak about your child's bits with them?? Find it a bit weird, in fact very weird, might need to be reported to the police!*

I thought it was sarcastic at first. It was not. Others agreed.

Why would you ever talk to a kid about their vulva?

Uh, the same reasons you need to talk to a boy about his penis – toilet training, washing, not to mention any medical issues that might affect that area of the body; plus, repeat till I go blue in the fucking face, child protection.

Also, children ask. Children are very curious about their bodies before we indoctrinate them (or don't, let's not any more) into the shameful world of what they can and cannot discuss. Kids ask about bodies all the time, genitals included. Kids fucking love talking about genitals almost as much as they love talking about their own shit and who the fuck are we to not tell them what parts of their bodies are actually called?

Imagine your kid pointing to their arm and asking what it was called and us being like 'erm, well, err, I'll tell you when you're eleven' because you know that an arm, as well as being good for hugs, can be used for punching and you don't want your kid to punch anyone.

Another consistent worry is that these are adult words, and it's weird to use them with children.

So, willy is OK but vulva and vagina, penis and testicles are adult words. They are 'too much' for children. It is 'weird' to use these words with children. Therefore, because we have willy, we need to think of a 'child-friendly' word for vulva instead.

Well, we're not Swedish and we can't, and also shouldn't, because see above. Also, I've now spoken to ten families who use the word vulva with their children and no one exploded or turned into slime. I get it – a baby with a 'penis' immediately also makes me imagine a small human born with massive adult genitals. But that image will lessen if we get used to using these words.

165

Another very common response is this: I'll say vagina but not vulva.

What the fuck are we like? Seriously. How are such harmless words this powerful?

I have had so many conversations with people who agree to say vagina but not vulva, cos that's just 'too much'. I've had emails from parents and carers saying that their children's nurseries and pre-schools and primary schools will teach vagina but not vulva too. It's just too much. It's hard enough getting the first v word out, let alone having another one to contend with.

According to the Eve Appeal's 2020 study, only 1 per cent of people are willing to say the word vulva. According to research by Bodyform, 73 per cent of women don't technically know what a vulva is. And that won't change if we keep fucking teaching it incorrectly.

When I was pregnant, I had a chat with a fellow pregnant friend, also expecting a girl, about what we would call our daughters' vulvas once we, gulp, had to start naming it. During the conversation neither of us could actually say the word vulva. If we were pregnant with sons it's very unlikely this conversation would have happened. I imagined two dads discussing what to call a baby boy's 'bits' the way we were discussing what to call a girl's.

Dad 1: What are you going to call his, erm, you know?
Dad 2: Oh god, we've been talking about that! I just don't know yet. We were thinking maybe front tail?
Dad 1: Yeah, that's what my dad used to call mine.
Dad 2: Yeah, or maybe baby spurter or mini sword or baby corn or maybe flower-stemmy stem. I'm not sure really. Ah!
Dad 1: I might just use the adult word. I read somewhere it's good to do that.
Dad 2: What – testicle? You can't say testicle to a kid!
Dad 1: No, penis. I think the testicle is the bit below the penis, isn't it?

166

Dad 2: The lower external pee area? Isn't that where they wee from?

Dad 1: No, I think the penis is the oblong bit and we wee from there and then the testicles are below, aren't they? Or is that just the lower penis? Yeah, I think the penis is the thin, wiggly bit and the testicles are the bit below. Oh, I don't know!!

[both men giggle about the fact they have no clue what the words for their own anatomy are]

Dad 1: I might try to use penis and testicles then.

Dad 2: Really! Urgh, I think that's going a bit far. I couldn't make myself say penis to a child. I'll maybe just say testicles for all of it.

Dad 1: Yeah, I'll probably just stick with front tail or mini corn.

Again, I get it: we don't know what the vulva is, so keep saying vagina. We feel weird saying vulva, so just call it all a vagina. But that's not the solution. Apart from the fact that this is totally incorrect, and lazy, and really, really unhelpful to all the little girls especially, it's also weirder surely to highlight the vagina so much because, of these two body parts, it's the vulva that children with one actually use daily. Though again, just teach both; it's not difficult and we need to. Here's the difference:

The vulva is external. It includes the urethra (where you wee), the clitoris, the labia – inner and outer, and the mons pubis.

The vagina is internal. It includes the vagina, which goes from the vaginal opening to the cervix.

If you feel you need backup for this, the best book I've found in this respect is called *Your Whole Body* by Arctic Flower Publishing. It's amazing and covers all body parts, including the ears and toes and the scary, scary genitals. It's aimed at very young children, but I learnt a few new words from it in my thirties. About my ears.

I don't deny it's difficult – it *is* bloody difficult. It's difficult to be the first parent in the playground who teaches their kid the word vulva, especially when other parents stare aghast after your toddler then comes up and uses it in public.

And it *is* very difficult when your kid says to their ninety-year-old grandmother that she wiped her vulva by herself and your grandmother looks at you like you have just taught your five-year-old daughter how to worship Satan.

It is difficult to use and say these words, because we have been taught for so long that they are sinful, or disgusting, or weird, or non-existent. The vulva did not have to be labelled on the UK curriculum until 2021, most educational resources spoke only of the vagina, the Collins Online Dictionary definition of the word vulva still states 'vagina' as a synonym; our culture is still saturated by its mistaken identity. Even now, it is consistently used incorrectly. It's no wonder we're still so confused.

Even the most famous theatre play about the vulva is called *The Vagina Monologues*, I imagine because *The Vulva Monologues* wouldn't sell in the same way, either because people would deem it 'too much' or because a lot of people wouldn't know what the fuck it meant.

The last response I get is pure denial. I find this one the most fascinating.

No, they insist, there is no problem with 'this word', no need to talk about it, they're totally happy to use 'this word', they have absolutely no problem with 'this word', they just don't, you know, like it. The sound of it. Totally nothing else. Just the sound. They don't like the 'v' or the 'ulv', or, you know, words ending in the letter 'a', and they don't fancy using it for that reason.

I've been given such an abundance of reasons for this apparent phonetic dislike of the word vulva. In reply to one post about this, the responses were:

I just don't like volvos so it probably reminds me of that type of car. *(Yes, this was a real response.)*
I think maybe it's because it sounds like vulgar that I don't like it.
I don't mind the word vagina because I think the sound of it is a bit more powerful, but not vulva, I just don't like the sound of the word.
I just don't like the word vulva.
I don't have a problem with the word vulva, I just don't use it.
I don't have a problem with the word vulva, I just prefer to say vagina.
I don't like words beginning with v. I just don't like the sound of that letter.
I think it sounds like Vulcan, the ancient Roman God of the fire of volcanoes and deserts and metalworking, and fire is dangerous.

I made up that last one up because I discovered the god Vulcan while looking up words which sound like vulva.

I'm not saying that these aren't valid reasons why people might wince at this word. People *can* have dislikes of certain sounds and noises and words. Phonophobia or misophonia is the fear of certain sounds. Verbophobia is the fear of certain words, but generally because of the way they have been used in a person's upbringing.

I have always felt sick when people use the words *clump* and *cluster*. For me, I am certain my mum's nursing stories are to blame. Say those words and I immediately think of boils or the tentacles of a verruca, that sort of stuff. I cannot eat Clusters cereal for this reason. The reason I wince at these words is pretty obvious. I hate when a beautiful poem is ruined with a cluster of stars. Urgh.

So verbophobia with vulva, in our culture, is understandable too, annoyingly. But again, this isn't about the specific sound of the word, but the connotations, social or personal significance or stigma. When I hear people say, 'I just don't like that word', when it is about a word that has been maligned or silenced for centuries, I'm dubious. Would we rather convince ourselves we hate the letter 'v' or volvos, than actually admit we've been indoctrinated against our own juicy bodies for centuries?

love, ulverston

if you don't mind the word volvo but can't stand to say vulva
don't vomit at velvet but shudder and splutter, disgusted
to just utter vulva; perhaps it is time you venture to ulverston
stumble up over some cumbrian cobbles, uncover a vug
or a volva, adventure up valleys perhaps with a lover
or other such buddy, conversing about volcanic eruptions
or the roman god vulcan, lover to venus, till, utterly famished
you plunge like underfed vultures to stuff rumbling valves
with some lovely pavlovas or pulverised halva,
mumbling between mouthfuls how utterly lovely ulverston is;
how you didn't expect to love ulverston quite as much
as you do but you do, you really love ulverston now

I say vulva all the time now. Not, like, shouting it in the street or in the middle of conversations that have nothing to do with it, but in context. When I need to.

I still find it sticking in my mouth every single time, like too much peanut butter on a spoon. Culture still clamps my tongue after a good five years of using it. I mean saying and writing it – I've been physically using it all my life!

Since my vulva revolution (like vodka revolution but less sugary shots), I have been introduced on several occasions as Hollie, who loves writing poems about the word vulva, or Hollie, who is obsessed with vaginas. This chapter of the book likely won't help with this.

But I'm not. I'm really, really not.

I just want us to have vulvas and vaginas and penises and testicles and know what they are and for every child and young person to be as protected as possible and every person in pain to seek help and every horny person to be able to tell their sexual partners where they like being touched and for that to all begin by us normalising these tiny words for tiny children in our tiny homes and tiny classrooms so that we can be sure that the next generations are not going to have this ridiculous fucking issue, and then I want to walk away and get on with eating my mint choc-chip ice cream in the park.

buying a volvo

*A seven-point role play to ease you into saying the word vulva
until it doesn't make you vomit in your mouth each time you try*

1. Pretend you are a car enthusiast.
   Say: *I'm a car enthusiast. (I'm a car enthusiast.)*
Not like Jeremy Clarkson. You're not an arsehole, you just love
your car. You have one car by the way.
   Say: *I have one car and I love my car.*
   (I have one car and I love my car.)

2. Now pretend that the car you have is a Volvo.
   Say: *I have a volvo. (I have a volvo.)*

3. Pretend you think your volvo is the dog's bollocks/cat's labia.
   Say: *I love my volvo. (I love my volvo.)*

4. Now pretend someone is standing next to you who doesn't
know about cars.
   They ask you: *What's that?*
   You say: *Oh, that. That's my volvo. (Oh, that. That's my volvo.)*

5. Pretend:
   a) they think your volvo is really cool
   Wow, they say, it's lovely, that volvo. Is it velvet interior?
   Smile at them and take the compliment.
   Say: *Thanks a lot. I like my volvo too. And yes, it is a velvet
   interiored volvo.*
   *(Thanks a lot. I like my volvo too. And yes, it is a velvet inte-
   riored volvo.)*
   or
   b) they are not impressed with your volvo. They are an

arsehole who thinks volvos are all shit even though they've
never had one

Pretend they say: *What a shit volvo.*

Pretend they say: *Your volvo is really ugly.*

Pretend they say: *Your volvo looks cheap.*

Pretend they say: *Your volvo doors are a bit of a weird shape.*

Pretend they say: *You should paint your volvo another colour.*

Pretend they say: *You should get alloy wheels on your volvo.*

Pretend they say: *I think your volvo seats are slightly lopsided
and you should pay someone a lot of money to cut them into a
more attractive style.*

Look at them. Pretend this doesn't bother you at all.

Say: *Fuck you. My volvo is fucking lush and I know how to
drive it just fine. The interior is soft and warm. It's lined with
velvet and it has five different gears and I know how to drive
using them all because I have a manual licence.*

6. Now pretend the person who appreciated your volvo wants
a lift in it. Look at them. Think about your volvo. Try to work
out if they are:

a) the sort of person who would appreciate your volvo once
inside as well, who would not just put on the radio station
they want on the radio and listen to their own songs, but
someone who would ask you which radio station you want
to listen to and would fiddle with all the buttons inside
your volvo while you drive, until your favourite tune is
blasting out and they'd learnt all the words and you'd sing
it together in your volvo with the windows down and the
air rushing past your faces and it would be so, so much fun
in your volvo, or

b) the sort of person who would try to secretly pick their
nose and wipe the bogey under the left side of your velvet

volvo seat where it would harden over the years until it lost its stick and dropped to the floor

Practise your replies.
Yes, you can have a ride in my volvo. (Open door for them.)
Yes, you can sit on the velvet interior of my volvo.
Yes, you can try to tune the radio of my volvo.
Yes, all right, you can lick the dashboard of my volvo.
Maybe if you spend a while learning how to polish this volvo properly on the outside I might let you in one day.
Yes, you can come into my volvo and stay there all day.
No, you are absolutely not getting anywhere near my volvo, get your hands off.
Sorry, there's not enough space, there's already someone in my volvo

7. Finally, pretend one day you see a scratch on your volvo. A crack in the windscreen. It might just stay like that or it might get bigger and bigger until it shatters the windscreen. You just DON'T KNOW because research into cracks on volvos is so much less funded than research into cracks on porsches. What do you do? You go to the garage. It is free. You pay your taxes, your volvo can be checked ANY TIME YOU NEED because you live in the UK with a free VHS (Volvo Health Service).
The mechanic says: *Hi, can I help?*
Do not be scared. Everyone has problems with their volvos sometimes.
Say: *Yes, I have a problem with my volvo. (Yes, I have a problem with my volvo.)*
Do not worry about the mechanic looking at your volvo. Mechanics see volvos every day, they're so used to it.
Say: *could you have a look at my volvo, please? (Could you*

have a look at my volvo, please?)

Describe where it is. The problem I mean. Not the volvo. A volvo mechanic should know where your volvo is although even mechanics sometimes get this wrong because sometimes mechanic school doesn't even teach mechanics what volvos are, which is fucking unbelievable really.

Be specific.

Say: *There's a problem on the inside of the left-hand door of my volvo.*

Say: *There's a slight scratch on the windscreen of my volvo.*

Say: *There seems to be some leakage from the exhaust pipe of my volvo.*

If the mechanic doesn't look at the volvo but instead tries to diagnose the problem with closed eyes and just offers you thrush cream for the five-hundredth time instead

Say: *Could you actually look at my volvo please? (Could you actually look at my volvo please?)*

If the mechanic says they're not actually enough of a volvo specialist for this matter, ask where the volvo specialist is and if you can get referred to one and go and see the volvo specialist instead to get your volvo windscreen crack looked at. Do not worry about making a fuss. Your volvo is very important and leaving cracks unchecked might mean that one day the windscreen just suddenly shatters or the exhaust smokes on the motorway.

Thank the mechanic for their help with your volvo.

(Thank you for your help with my volvo.)

Go home. Relax. Pour yourself a drink. Have a look at your volvo closely again otherwise you won't notice other scratches if they come. Give it a polish if you fancy (only water is needed for volvos, remember). Give it a hoover inside if you want (this is only for actual volvos). Dust the seats. Sit in it by yourself for a while revving the engine. It's yours to do what you want with.

After all, it is your volvo.

Now, imagine you live in a country where all of the mechanics' fees for your volvo are included in your tax payments and the only thing which keeps volvo drivers like you driving around in volvos which keep breaking down or causing damage to their drivers or just not driving quite as smoothly and comfortably as you know they can, is because volvo drivers like you have been taught to be too embarrassed to say the word volvo or made to think their volvo is such a shit car that they don't want anyone looking at it, even themselves, even volvo mechanics.

Drive safely in your volvo. Get a cup holder.

NIBBLING ON THE LABIA MAJORA

almost

i watch you stop yourself sometimes
almost speaking; i am almost speaking too
you kiss my neck. the room silent except lips
desires tiptoe in whispers; *what did you say?*
and i wonder, blushing, might you somehow
search inside my mouth for all those secret treats
i almost said; i try again: can you hear me?
almost speaking i can hear you, almost speaking too

Biologically correct terms are really important for knowing your body, protecting children and guarding us from unnecessary shame, but when it comes to sexy talk, they don't cut it for most folk.

I love the lightness and lust and play of language and I think we have slang words for this reason as well, to separate the official and the formal from the fun; the anatomy classes from the sensual massages. A happy ending for all.

Will you kiss my neck for five minutes and then nibble my labia minora, then rub my clitoral hood on the left-hand side with oil in a slow, light and circular motion in exactly the same place for nine and a half minutes while kissing my neck nape until my clitoris becomes fully erect and my nipples harden and then keep doing that while

177

pressing lightly on my perineum with your other palm and licking my right nipple until my muscles contract into an orgasm, please? is not something I'd find very sexy to say despite it being a fairly accurate representation of one of my most likely ways to orgasm. Though actually, writing this, I'm imagining a biology laboratory and a white coat and might be changing my mind.

When I was applying to university, my teacher at school advised me, if asked in the interview what book I was reading, I should say *Ulysses* by James Joyce. I didn't do this because I hadn't read it.

Since then, the book *Ulysses* has been in my head as the pinnacle of what I should read if I want to be considered 'clever'. A lot of people seem to think this about this book. It is one of the most started and never finished books ever written. I still haven't read it. There's an audio version produced by the very beautiful Parisian bookshop Shakespeare and Company, if you fancy trying it that way.

What I *have read* by James Joyce are the love letters that he wrote to his lover Nora Barnacle and the letters she wrote back to him.

'... then I will lick the lips of my darling's cunt. You will begin to groan and grunt and sigh and fart with lust ...'

This is one quote from Joyce's side of the lovers' scribbles. Here are a few more:

'I felt your fat, sweaty buttocks under my belly and saw your flushed face and mad eyes.'

'You must have given that naughty little cunt of yours a most ferocious frigging to write me such a disjointed letter.'

And finally, the simply worded: 'Fuck me in your dressing gown.' Excellent.

I liked this last one because I was taught for years that feeling 'sexy' mainly meant wearing lace underwear, most often stuck up my arse uncomfortably, and stockings and pretending to be stupid, and I liked the idea that Nora's dressing gown was what really turned James on. I love a dressing gown.

I also liked that Joyce was excited that Nora masturbated rather than seeing it as an insult to him, which I find a very weird thing in some relationships – the *I caught my husband masturbating!* sort of outcry, as if now you're in a relationship, you're no longer allowed to drive the car by yourself, and must always wait until your partner also fancies it/is available to take the wheel. Imagine if we did that with eating, and not just orgasming, waiting for each other to always be hungry at the same time in order to have a snack.

I also wondered if the 'fart with lust' was referring to fanny farts or bum farts (wasn't sure what to call these here) and have decided that it was probably the fanny variety, otherwise known as queefing.

For anyone worried about the bum sort of farting (this is the most ridiculous phrase I think I've ever written) in front of a sexual partner, eproctophilia is a sexual arousal from flatulence.

When I read these lovers' letters, I was like 'fair play to you, you horny beasts'. I was also in slight awe of their confidence at talking 'dirty', as we call it, so well to one another.

It seems that most people find 'sexy' or 'dirty' talk pretty tricky. There are thousands of articles online supporting people to build up the confidence to get these words from your brain to your lover's eardrums. So many words and so much want and so much worry. It is daunting. What if you try it but your lover actually hates the dressing gown you got them?

I also wondered what these famous lovers, later husband and wife, would have been like face to face. So confident in ink, but would James Joyce have been as strident in his 'fuck me' request if he was saying it directly to Nora as she walked into the room, dressing gown in full throttle. Writing this is really making me want to put on my dressing gown. I think I'm with Joyce on this one. It's so fucking sexy feeling warm and cosy and comforted.

I also wonder if these lovers' communications would have moved with the love-letter times; how many aubergine emojis Nora might have sent today; how many quick snaps of his helicoptering cock Joyce might have beckoned her with before receiving photos in return of her said sweaty buttocks. I wonder if Joyce ever said 'fart with lust' in person. Who knows.

The first time I had a lovely sexual experience in person I had little fear of 'sexy talk' because it was in French. I found it much easier to talk about things in another language. I didn't realise how much easier I found it until I then tried in English.

Maybe because in French it didn't quite feel like my own voice. Like a masked ball but instead of your eyes, it's your speech all dressed up in glitter and feathers. Maybe because I wasn't that good at the language, and the boy's English was almost non-existent, so I just had to be more blunt about things.

I also don't like my own voice much. Sexy characters in films do not have accents from the outskirts of Reading, and hearing my voice out loud is about as much of an anti-aphrodisiac to me as being told to smile more by passing men. The first time I was told this by a guy on the street was about four hours after my grandad had died and I'd gone for a walk. I said 'my grandad just died' and walked away.

I have also said 'my grandad just died' on other occasions when men implied I'd be prettier with a smile on my face, because my grandad said I could use his death as an excuse to get out of things whenever I wanted. Have a go if it happens to you. Just stare back and say: 'Hollie's grandad just died.' I'm sure my grandad would be happy to help.

When I spoke in French, it wasn't a dull Reading accent I was hearing; it was French spoken with a foreign accent, a totally different audio experience.

Thinking back, I think it helped that the words I was saying, in French, had no past. I'd not learnt to find them weird or cringy or gross or been brought up ashamed of them or overheard them said in derogatory or disgusting ways by some guy on a screen or a lechy older man in a club. They were just words in another language, which were really thrilling to say and even more thrilling to hear.

I think lechy guys have ruined quite a lot of words that could have sounded sexy to me if I'd not heard them come out their slimy mouths for the first time. Breasts is definitely one of those words, first heard said by a friend's father and for years I just couldn't hear it without the creepy feeling, which is a shame because breasts are fucking amazing. I have tried really hard not to let words be taken from me for this reason because it's not fair and hearing them in my boyfriend's tones has definitely helped to break that sleazy barrier.

It's annoying when people ruin words, extra annoying when they ruin sexy words, because for females especially, we don't seem to have many in the first place.

Don't get me wrong, English has a lot of words to do with sex and pleasure. Words to describe the most intricate and specific of sexual preferences or acts.

Some of these words, I love. Like edging, shallowing.

When my book *Slug* was translated into French, I had a few meetings where I had to explain to Clément, the lovely editor at Le Castor Astral, certain phrases the translation team had questioned.

One of these was tea-bagging. I explained.

So it's not about actual tea bags, it's an, umm, sexual term in English, tea-bagging?

I'm sorry, I still don't understand, he said, politely as ever across the Zoom.

So, well, it's a phrase to describe dipping your testicles into a lover's mouth, like the way you dip a tea bag into a cup of warm water over and over again.

Ah, he replied, much more swiftly this time. *No, we don't have this in French.*

Yes, French may be seen as a sexier language in many ways but does it have a metaphorical phrase for the dipping of testicles into a mouth? No, it does not. You're welcome.

There is also no direct French translation of dogging. I found out, once the French translation of *Slug* was out, that Le Castor Astral, the name of my lovely publishers, translates as 'The Astral Beaver', astral as in related to the stars, which is so weirdly fitting for this book, seeing as there's so much about both space and fannies.

English is undoubtedly a rich and ridiculous sexual language, constantly budding and blooming, a garden full of all of the linguistic flavours of our desires and dislikes. It's just that some of the very basics, particularly for women, still seem to be sorely lacking or despised to almost unimaginable heights.

Like cunt, the linguistic origins of which are debated but which most scholars agree used to be a word we could unashamedly use for the vulva and vagina. It is now one of the most taboo words in the English language, and without a doubt the most harmless of the taboos. Literally, a word that means vulva and it is one of our most notorious profanities of the entire English language.

Or moist. Another word that we could and have used to describe a female state of arousal and which, for its sins, has been claimed as the single most hated word in the English language. Not only that, it seems that it is hated primarily when attached to female pleasure.

When the *New Yorker* asked readers to nominate a word to scrub from the English language in 2012, the overwhelming consensus was to ditch *moist*.

A group from Oberlin College in Ohio and Trinity University in San Antonio, Texas, ran three different experiments to try to find out what the disgust for this word was based on and, despite a large number of participants insisting it was just the sound of the word they didn't like (seems we do this a lot with these sorts of words), the participants did not show the same disgust for any similar-sounding words.

They did, however, show most disgust when the word moist 'was accompanied by unrelated, positive words like *paradise*, or when it was accompanied by sexual words'. The younger the participants, the more disgust they had for the word and the positive sexual associations.

Personally, it holds up. Almost every woman I know hates this word.

The thing I found saddest about our hatred of moist is that the positive associations were what we seem to hate; in most practical states, moistness is a positive thing, both in terms of baking and sexual desire.

What do vulva and cunt and moist have in common? They are all extremely hated words. Anything else? Hmmm, let me think.

Some other things I noticed that were missing from my basic womanly sexy-word options in English:

Nouns. Penises get nouns for their arousal. Vulvas don't. As in, penises have an actual state of arousal in the English language. Like, erections. Penises and nipples and clitorises all get erect, according to the dictionary, but only penises really then get the noun form: erections.

Penises also get:

Hard-on
slang (orig. *US*).
A. *adj.*
Of a man: having an erect penis; sexually aroused. Cf. hard *adj.* 1i. *rare.*
1893 J. S. Farmer & W. E. Henley Slang III. 270/1 *Hard-on* adj. phr., prick-proud.
1961 C. Cooper Weed i. 18 Fresh home and hard-on, he'd found the street and apartment.

Stiffy
slang. An erection. Cf. hard-on *n.*
1983 M. Gee Sole Survivor vi. 60 Pretty hot stuff. Ha, saying it's given you a stiffy. Put a cushion over it, that's right.
1987 A. Maupin Significant Others ii. 17 Me hot Cuban lover with the permanent stiffie.

2002   Time Out 2 Jan. 135/3   It comes in praise of all things penile,... extending through the problems of unwanted stiffies in the gym changing room.

Boner
4. *slang* (orig. *US*). An erection of the penis. Hence *figurative*: a strong attraction to or state of excitement about something specified.
1936   *Psychoanalytic Rev.* 23 72   In his dream he had a feeling that he was 'pulling a boner'.
1962   C. Sigal Going Away 68   The little dog used to raise a boner every time it walked into a room where Rickie was present.
1991   Village Voice (NY) 26 Feb. 36/3   I had all the access an English major with a boner for rock could hope for.

I'm not saying we're all comfortable saying these words, but at least they were there, at least it was like you had something, like your arousal existed, all fairly normalised, or at least known by the time I'd started secondary school. In my sexy situations, vulva pumped with blood, clit hard, wet, labia puffed up and throbbing beneath my jeans like a horny hot-air balloon, what could I say: I've got a what? Nothing, I had nothing. Where's my noun?

This was especially annoying because as well as having a multitude of common words to describe their arousal, guys could also just point, or move your hand over their trousers and silently, often shyly, show you; that first step of visual proof wasn't available for us, our arousals being a subtler creature of sensual delights. So we had to talk. With almost no words to use.

Perhaps it is a bit crap that all male arousal, vocab-wise, seems to be limited to the hardness of a dick, which does diminish the more nuanced side to sexual pleasure and undoubtedly puts fuck loads of unnecessary pressure on young guys, lapped up by the Viagra industry.

Still, it would be cool for our aroused fannies to have a few nouns too.

Recently the nouns 'lady boner' and 'cliterection' have been bandied around, which is cool but, again, I'd quite like to get our own nouns rather than borrowing Adam's ribs all over again.

As well as having nouns for their arousal, penises also get verbs that have an ending. Happy-ever-after sort of thing.

As in, a lot of the verbs about pleasuring a penis finish with the word 'off' as if the plane will definitely not remain on the runway.

Penises get 'wanked off' and they get 'sucked off' and they 'pull' or 'tear the head off'. I do not get 'fingered off' or 'licked out off' in our language, even when I do in real life.

This isn't because women don't orgasm or want to orgasm, but it is maybe because female orgasm isn't given as much importance.

The words 'blow job' and 'hand job' work along similar lines. They are an activity with an end point. A job that implies a completion. Lick job or finger job there is not.

Perhaps it's nice, not having all these end goals to our vocabulary, not limiting sexual enjoyment to this one 'orgasm' ending, not putting the pressure on too much. Maybe it's a good thing that vulvas don't 'off' so much in our language; that their pleasuring is not seen as a 'job', not defined by historic employment practices. Maybe it means that our sexual vocabulary isn't limited to this ticked-off mindset.

Or maybe all of this unfinished language around our sexual acts adds to the notion that women just don't need to orgasm as much as guys do, or that their orgasms are super complicated or less necessary.

Thing is, when alone, most women do 'finish'; they do 'wank themselves off', even if they don't use that phrase. And I'm almost sure most want that when with a partner too, no matter how many articles we read about it not being as important for women as it is for men. The fuck it isn't.

Dr Laurie Mintz says it best when describing the pleasure of hook-ups.

> When masturbating, 95% of women orgasm. In 1st time hookups with other women, they orgasm 64% of the time. In 1st time hookups with men, they orgasm 7% of the time. This tells us that the problem isn't women's ability to orgasm. It's our cultural scripts for heterosexual sex.[*]

Yes, when alone, 95 per cent of women do leave the runway. The difference between this percentage and the dismal 7 per cent is what? Fear of asking for what you actually want because it differs so much from the standards set? Lack of communication, lack of confidence, expectations, the boredom of teaching, not being believed anyway?

I've spoken before about the word wank more generally.

When I began my sexual life, there really was no all-known girl's word for masturbating, so we either stayed silent about it or used wank as well, which at the time was defined in the dictionary as 'for males' and doesn't really describe the action very well.

I was overjoyed recently, on rechecking the *Oxford English Dictionary*, that the 'for males' has now been shifted to 'chiefly males' in the definition of 'to wank' and that an example of female 'wanking' in literature has been added from the brilliant book *The Panopticon* by the delight of a Scottish author Jenni Fagan.

No wonder it was a struggle to talk sexily as a young woman in English, when not only our actual pleasure was often shamed, including pleasuring ourselves, but when so many words and endings and states of arousal seemed to be missing from our specific sexual vocabulary or just borrowed or refashioned from a male history, or if they did exist, viewed with disgust and horror by the whole of

---

[*] Dr Laurie Mintz. *Twitter*, 20 May 2021. https://twitter.com/DrLaurieMintz/status/1395344031924817923

society, or else ruined by some slimeball. Tea-bagging, yes, an aroused vulva, not so much.

Perhaps it's also quite an exciting place to be, in a time of linguistic invention. We need more colloquial words for the basics of much female arousal; for the taking off of the clitoral cockpit. Yes, I'm very pleased with that last sentence.

A swell?

A puff?

A licking off?

A roundabout (for those who enjoy the circular sort of fingering motion)?

I'll keep thinking. Those are terrible. If only Nora was still around to help us.

drizzle

seventeen years old, and i am silent
it is drizzling outside and we are touching
above a blanket still fully dressed
on someone's bed in someone's bedroom
whose address i don't remember
whose parents were away or out for dinner
or didn't care – my god,
the excitement of being wanted

if i'd needed to tell him about the rain
spitting intermittently outside the window
that would have been easy
– english is excellent at wetness when it rains

he is hard with all the kissing we've been doing
puts my hand onto his jeans to signal his erection
as if a silent movie mime, as if our tongues are just
too busy. he blushes, swallows a speech
that never comes; this isn't easy for anyone

still, all the words he has

if i'd needed to tell him about the rain
i could have; raindrops fattened from a drizzle
now batter at the window
clouds burst open in a downpour;
english is excellent at wetness when it rains

in lithuanian, there is a word
for the beginning of autumn
the moment leaves turn rust,

as tree trunks hold in breath
to stop post-spring shivers
turning into winter's death;
so many gorgeous, gorgeous words

i want to tell him where to touch me
tell him i am hard as well,
erection wettened swelling puff
blood rushing; i want to tell him
to finger me or lick me off until i too
have an ending; i want to take off
into air with him; english is so excellent
at wetness when it rains

in italian, abbiocco is a drowsiness
that embraces your whole body, gently,
full after a lunchtime feast,
eyelids reclining comfortably
so many gorgeous, gorgeous words

we keep kissing, half from passion,
half to avoid communication; embarrassed
some couples after thirty years of marriage
still struggle to tell each other
what they want –
this isn't easy for anyone

in scots, sitooterie describes a corner
snuck into by lovers
made romantic by its shadows:
so many gorgeous, gorgeous words
no wonder we talk about
the weather all the time

he cums into my palm, i do not cum
we giggle, a little awkward, i do not ask
to carry on; this isn't easy for anyone
still, all the words he has

often, i re-imagine
sex scenes from my past
my dictionary overflowing

glimpsing his erection
you've made me hard please make me soft
i'd reply *i have a swell*
please could you lick me off

he'd say that his erection was hard as seaside rock
– needed lips around it
i'd say that my clit was swollen sweet as candyfloss
– needed tongue to melt it

seventeen years old, and i am silent
body desperate, cursing language
english is so brilliant at wetness
when it rains

love language

disappointingly, life is not perfect
but the plums in the park are in season;
their branches heaving and free

and just as i realise the juiciest one
is out of my reach, you stretch up
and grasp it for me

the young boys are buying viagra

poem written after being told that a lot of the people buying viagra are young guys who don't physically need it but are totally paranoid about not being able to 'get it up'/'keep it up' if they hook up with someone, unaware that a rock-hard cock is not the only interest a lover will have

the young boys are buying viagra
anxious of not getting up on demand
as if dicks must be more akin to a scaffold than skin
unaffected by nerves or a cold or a drink
a mind drifting dreamwards, a shock of storm weather

so the young boys are buying viagra in hordes
have to be hard, have to be hard
walking round nightclubs with drug-ready dicks
scared shitless of first date 'failings'; of teasing

if only the fluffers were left on the screens
sat at the side of the stage, ready with mastermind massage
preventing the actor's professional postures
from falling from grace

if only those pop-ups preaching each day
at young boys just learning to touch
about how to be biggest and how to be hardest
and how to keep fucking so long
their dick turns more hammer than heart

if only the adverts admitted
how hands can learn tricks
no dick can compete with; how fingers

and lips are an equal; how the world is awash
with lovers thrilled by a softness of touch

how in this vast solar system of sex
their dicks are just one
of many potentially magnificent planets
– not the whole sweating sun

love letters

i send screenshots of my battery
at sixty-nine per cent,

you reply with three plump aubergines
a snapshot of your waking skin

requests beset with heart and fire
for photos of my *cherry tits*

face to face, we blush –
hands fidget when we kiss

i think love letters
have always worked like this

LIGHT RED
(NOTHING ABOUT VULVAS HERE)

Sometimes I'm jealous of babies. Babies just gazing around, before we yell excitedly *look, a daisy* in their faces, look, a duck, ducks, say ducks, look tree, say tree, tree, tree, look clouds, look sky, look, look, sunset, say sunset, say purple, say purple sunset.

I will never be able to look at the world and not see it in words, in groups and hierarchies, constantly labelling everything my eyes land on.

I never realised how much my view of the world was shaped by words until my teacher in primary school revealed to me the horrific truth that the sun was in fact a star. Just our word for the star at the heart of our solar system. A star, like many of the other millions of stars out there with solar systems spinning around them, not even the biggest. In fact, smaller and less bright than many other stars we see when we stare up at night.

It broke my little six-year-old brain.

I just kept staring up at the sky, trying to think of the sun and the stars and the stars and the sun as the same thing. It was so difficult, because words had duped me into thinking they were totally different entities. Like all those are stars, but this is a sun. Very different. Very important. I still have to remind myself now. The sun is just one star. Fuck.

The second time my brain was bent out of all known shape was by my beautiful friend Tammy at university. By this time, I was pretty obsessed with language, and with trying to learn other languages, or at least the two languages that had been offered by my secondary school – French and German.

I met Tammy in the first week we arrived and I'm very thankful for that. Tammy spoke more bluntly of her love for learning than anyone I'd ever met and from that month on till today and I'm sure far into the future has taught me almost everything I know about Russian history, growing your own vegetables, sex, forgiveness and swimming in lakes in Derby.

In our first year of university, Tammy informed me that the word for pink in Russian is 'light red'. Or rather, that there is no word for pink in Russian, because pink is light red.

I frowned, the way you often do at first when you learn something that fucks up the way you think of the world.

Russian is weird, I said.

No, English is weird, Tammy informed me.

I tried to do that thing where you work out, like with the stars and the sun, if everything you ever took for granted was based on nothing but words.

I imagined a paint palette. The three primary colours dolloped on it.

Yellow paint plus white paint = light yellow. Still a shade of yellow.

Blue paint plus white paint = light blue. Still a shade of blue.

Red paint plus white paint = fuck. Tammy's right.

All my life, I saw pink things as a separate colour to red things. I questioned whether things were pink or red. My lips, my lipstick. Cherries are red (except the black ones). Apples are red (except the green ones). Tomatoes are red (except the yellow, green and black ones). My tongue is pink.

I didn't see lighter blue or lighter yellow things as a separate colour to darker blue or darker yellow things. The daffodil had a light yellow trunk and darker yellow petals but the roses lining the neighbours' garden were some pink some red.

Even shades of orange, green, purple. Add more white, they just become lighter orange, lighter green, lighter purple.

But this word pink, this deceptive fuck of a word had made me fairly certain that at some point, as you add white paint to red paint, it becomes an entirely new colour. No, no it does not. Ask the Russian kids. They're not duped by this shit.

While Russian kids are not fooled by pink, however, they're not entirely immune to this linguistic bullying, or in more official and less opinionated terms, the distinct evolution of colexification in different languages.

Colexification is the use of a single cover term to express something, i.e. in English we colexify blue and green. We colexify pink. I just learnt the word colexify while writing this so I'm going to keep repeating it till I actually understand what it means which right now, I don't totally.

In Russian, as well as in Italian and Hebrew I'm told, there is a separate word for light blue, just as in English there's this separate word pink for light red. So where I see light blue as a shade of blue not a distinct colour, other children I assume see light blue in the same way I see pink, I mean light red, I mean, *ahhhh*.

I looked into the mirror that night, pouting my lips like I always have, and still do almost unconsciously now, to make my face look more sexy-trout cheekboned.

I looked at my pouty lips more closely. I tried to remove the word pink from my brain. *My lips are light red*, I tried to think. I looked at my pink top.[*] *My top is light red*, I tried to think. I looked down at my pink trousers and pink shoes. *My trousers and my shoes are light red*, I tried to think.[†]

My brain screamed back: *No, idiot, they are pink. Pink pink pink. There's no such thing as fucking pink*, I screamed in response.

---

[*]   I doubt I was wearing a pink top but it makes this flow better as a memory when discussing the colour pink so I'm going to pretend I definitely was.

[†]   I definitely wasn't wearing pink trousers or shoes, but you get the idea.

Yes there is dumbass, my brain yelled back.

And what about grey? It continued, even louder now, laughing like Chucky in the movie *Child's Play*, which I would urge you never to watch because you will constantly imagine being attacked by a doll when you drive for the rest of your life.

Is grey just light black?
Or is it dark white?
Or is black different because black and white
are like all colour and no colour
not colour colours
so perhaps grey is midway
between everything and nothing
are my lips pink or light red
are my eyes light blue or are they russian?
and what about my face?

Why do I see my nose and mouth as different and my cheeks and eyes and chin, as if my chin is somehow its own being, different to the bit of skin between it and my lips, and what the fuck is that called? Where does my face finish and my neck begin? What about all the bits in between? Why don't they get their own words too? And where is my breath and your breath and where does anything begin and end if not just in words and is anything real any more and where do my cheeks even start and are they pink or light fucking red when I blush?

I walked around for a while desperately trying to unsee pink but I couldn't, I could not see this colour as light red no matter how many times I said it. So I came to terms with this and started using pink again soon after because saying light red in conversation and then explaining you are saying light red because your friend Tammy informed you about Russian words makes you sound like a total fucking cock in every social situation I can think of.

While writing this, I remembered that Tammy also told me that, in Russian, the word for eleven is like ten-one, and the word for twelve is like ten-two and that the words eleven and twelve are actually pretty odd and that teenagers, in many, many languages, are called teenagers at age eleven because really, mathematically, this is when you become a teen, which means 'plus ten'.

After a while, I came to terms with the fact that my stupid brain would never unsee pink separately from red and all was calm until it came back to me over a decade later when I received a message on Instagram from a woman who loved poetry and was blind. She told me that she enjoyed my work but that every time I posted a poem on Instagram she couldn't read it.

She uses technology that reads people's Instagram posts (and everything else she scrolls online) to her. She sent me a video of what she hears described when I make my poems into lovely little colourful squares. What she gets is this:

Image blank.

Literally the robot reads the words: image blank. Nothing.

I thanked her and read up on image descriptions, trawled through other people's profiles who I'd been told were good at these.

It was easy with the poems.

As well as making them into colourful squares, I just post the poem in words in the caption. Then the computer system with which she and many more partially sighted or blind people read, reads this description out, albeit in a computerised and not-very-good-for-poetry sort of voice. At least it doesn't read it in a really forced overly dramatic poetry voice, though, which would possibly be more irritating.

A week later, I was staring out of a train window and the sunset was what I would describe in my normal best descriptive vocabulary for a sunset as 'absolutely fucking incredible'.

I snapped a quick photo of it, sent it to some friends and said 'absolutely fucking incredible – sending love'.

I looked at the sunset again and at my photograph and decided I'd post it online – for what reason I'm not a hundred per cent sure but in my head it's because I thought it was beautiful and uplifting and I wanted to share that in case anyone was feeling like the world was underwhelming.

Probably it was also because for some weird reason I felt like it was a really good photo of a sunset because, well, the sunset looked incredible in it, and somehow I felt like that reflected my photography or observation skills, when in reality it was the world that was beautiful and fuck all to do with me aiming a cracked iPhone screen at it.

So I posted the photo online and wrote something like 'cracking or gorgeous or absolutely fucking incredible sunset'. I can't remember exactly. What I did then remember was the woman's message the week before.

Image blank.

My first reaction, in all honesty, was 'for fuck's sake'. As in, *this is all good for poems but posting an image description for everything is a bit of a pain in the arse*. A pain in my arse. In my fast-food-picture-posting-world-of-social-media arse. I started trying to write the image description, almost annoyed at the time it was taking me.

I wrote:

[image description: a photo of a beautiful pink and purple sunset taken from the train window as I zoom past Doncaster.]

I re-read the image description. I didn't click post.

What does beautiful mean if I can't see the sunset? And does anyone need to know that the photo of the sunset is taken from a train window? And does anyone need to know that the train at the moment the photograph was taken was zooming through, into or out of Doncaster?

I decided yes, Doncaster was important because if anyone lived near Doncaster who hadn't seen how beautiful the sunset was maybe they'd feel some sort of pride in that, even though that's a bit weird because it's literally the sky which in no way belongs to Doncaster.

So I left Doncaster in the description, despite it not really being part of the 'image' as such. I removed beautiful because I wasn't sure what that meant any more.

So now it read:

[image description: a photo of a pink and purple sunset taken from the train window as I zoom past Doncaster.]

With beautiful removed it didn't really work because it wasn't just the colours that made it so incredible. I thought about it. What better words could I use that you didn't necessarily need to have visuals to feel?

Gorgeous. Exquisite. Stunning. Striking. Breath-taking.

I decided on breath-taking, because things that have made me gasp on regular occasions have not just been visual; the first sense of a milk stream flowing inside my body out of my breasts into a baby's mouth; my partner kissing my neck softly as I fry mushrooms; the first time I slid down a really long waterslide?

Tingling perhaps too, I thought. Or delicious? A tingling sunset. No. A delicious sunset? Breath-taking it was.

So now it read:

[image description: a photo of a breath-taking pink and purple sunset taken from the train window as I zoom past Doncaster.]

The fact that it now had 'taking' and 'taken' in the same sentence annoyed me, but I got over it. It's not a poem, I thought, it's an image description.

I didn't post it. *Pink and purple*, I thought. *A pink and purple sunset.*

These image descriptions are used by partially sighted people, and by blind people. In the case of the latter, if you've never seen colours, let alone the mess of shifting shades of colour that a 'Doncaster' sunset brings, then is there any point me describing the sunset as 'pink' or 'purple' in a description written for this very reason?

Then I thought of my friend Tammy. Fucking pink. *How the fuck do I describe this fucking sunset if pink doesn't even fucking exist?*

After about an hour trying to describe the sunset, the sky outside now almost invisible in its blackness, I never re-posted the photo with an image description because I was too confused and worried that it would be pointless to describe it.

I have since enjoyed learning more about image descriptions and I've stopped lamenting the ten minutes of time it takes my selfish ass to write them.

About a month later, I posted a photo of my own face. I don't post many photos of my own face, but I sometimes do. It was a gig poster made by a venue I was performing at. They'd used my face and some words describing the show.

At first I wrote, almost automatically:

[image description: a bloody awful photo of me staring gormlessly into the air surround by the words . . .]

Then I wrote:

[image description: a photo of me taken by a photographer I didn't really know well who made me stare into the air like I had no thoughts in my brain which is why my face looks so bloody awkward and I'm not sure how this photo will help convince people to come to my gig.]

Then I wrote:

[image description: a photo of me wearing a cardigan that I love because it used to be my grandma's. It's so soft, I love the feel of it on my skin and the black colour reminds me of liquorice which I like chewing on. I'm gazing up a bit awkwardly at the wall because I'm not that comfortable having my photo taken but my eyes look very fresh and sparkly, which they are.]

I know the point of image descriptions is not this but since this woman wrote to me so kindly it has made me realise that every photo I have ever shared could be described in thousands of different ways and I've decided to take the positive route.

I don't want to slag myself off in photos any more, and when I write more positive image descriptions, picking out the things that make me happy, of which there are many in every photograph I share, I feel better.

I'm not sure if this is selfish, or if this is giving an impression of myself, particularly to partially sighted and blind people, that I'm some sort of smug twat who sees the entire world in rainbows. Rainbows. How to describe a rainbow. Would I describe it differently if I spoke in another language? What are rainbows called around the world? How could I do an image description of all of those colours? Perhaps image descriptions are poems. Perhaps all poems are just image descriptions.

**[image description never posted:
sunset from the train window in doncaster**

the sunset has made a mess of its plate again;
undecided between dinnertimes, both night
and day in sight, heckling each other from the
far sides of my eye-line; the sharpened fists of
cliff shifting to dusk-smudged silhouette as
thick strati of storm threaten the backdrop blue
to ashen rust, some purple cirrus wisps like
crocuses in uncut spring, one lonesome puff
of candyfloss still clinging light red outlined
as final strikes of sun spotlight a patch of
distant hilltop with fading yellow gasps, till
nighttime licks the whole plate spotless black]

MOTHERLAND

Flags and Fiction

We laughed, – knowing that better men
would come,
And greater wars: when each proud
fighter brags
He wars on Death, for lives; not men,
for flags.

WILFRED OWEN, 'The Next War'

mother/land

when was the first flag drawn and coloured in?
printed onto tea-towels?
spat from open windows during football matches?
fashioned into swim trunks and bikinis,
announcing english skin on spanish sands?

our first stab at the moon, a flag
as if the universe gives a shit
could have been a peace sign

enter someone else's local
eyes turn
bare-fisted as a fact

meanwhile, beneath a streetlamp lit
glittered with befuddled moths
tiny kings in tiny kingdoms
fling postcode gauntlets, as if codes of dna

as mothers praying, screaming
four babies born each second
lungs sprung open in a gasp

bloody, blind and desperate
fingers clinging to a motherland
still so much less protected
than any make-believe map

spring baby

for mine and any other buds born in springtime

your birthday is marked
by cherry tree blossoms
unfurling their toes
turning winter to pink

i think, as i pass
each new petal in bloom

that was you
that was you
that was you

if not for belfast

where my grandad learnt to dance
the way the lads taught him to dance
the way my grandma saw him dance
the way they danced that night together
back in glasgow

if not for all those belfast boys
for all their belfast hips,

he might not have caught her eye, then her hand,
then her rhythm; she might not have had a baby
one year later, then another, then my mother,

because she saw my grandad dance
the way the lads taught him to dance
as the songs came crashing past, in belfast

butter knife

my heart has pumped for forty years
without me even asking
and you tell me to keep my elbows off the table
use a different knife for butter

caterpillars don't grow wings
they disintegrate completely
re-emerge with hieroglyphics at their backs –
meet me there, in this world

where caterpillars disappear themselves
and teardrops can be conjured out of thought
we are all magicians here,
so lay your head upon my shoulder

tears do not run out any more than kisses do
so kiss me,
the body is a wizard
and rain today is pounding on the streets

and there is air inside our lungs
as ancient as the first oak, and fireflies
make light inside their abdomens,

and you,
you once fed through your belly button
so do not tell me not to laugh
one teaspoon of a neutron star
could balance the entire human population

and once upon a time, inside my savage skin
in a room made of blood and luck
i grew a whole human child from compliments and kisses,
who now stands as tall as me, gigantic,
and everyday chameleons are changing colour

and flowers, stronger than cement
burst through cracks in pavements
where man-made explosions once obliterated
every living thing, so do not tell me
to stop dreaming, as if it's too late,

our eyes, from the very second we are born,
know exactly how to form water out of hope

JUST LIKE US

Being born in and growing up in England within a loving all-Scottish family is both a blessing and the most loving nip in the arse.

A blessing, because my family are totally gorgeous, and I love them, and also because I got so many lovely gifts sent to me from Scotland as I grew up.

A loving pain because a huge number of those gifts were Scottish-themed reminders of my motherland: tartan tea towels, tartan scarves, teddies in blue woollen Scotland jumpers; the most recent, a mug with the very subtle message: I Love Scotland, which I received last Christmas from my dad.

One of my most memorable pieces of family love/Scottish propaganda was a postcard my gran sent me. I was studying French and German at university, and it was obligatory to work for a year in either a French- or German-speaking country. I worked as an assistant teacher with the British Council for a year in Guadeloupe, an island in the French-speaking Caribbean. My job was to help students with their spoken English and to teach them about 'English-speaking countries and cultures'.

Within a week of my arrival, I had received a postcard from my gran. The postcard image was a close-up map of Scotland. On the back, she had written four words only:

Remember Scotland. Love Gran

When I was pregnant, my dad requested just one thing of me. When I go into labour, could I just drive across the border into Scotland to give birth? From my house that would have been a five-hour drive, I imagine slightly longer if done simultaneously to a small child making its way from my uterus, down and out of my flaming, stretched vagina. So let's say seven hours depending on traffic and speed of dilation.

The request, half in jest, made me question two things.

One, how much my father knows about labour.

Two, what difference (apart from the amazing free baby box of essentials you get given in Scotland after birth) it would actually make if I did that; if I drove over the border, popped out a child (as I've heard people who have never given birth refer to giving birth), got the Scotland birthplace tick and then drove back to my home in England to raise her.

I like tartan tea towels and there are lots of things that are really exciting about having a slightly different heritage to my parents; it's just slightly awkward when your heritage is that of their historically hated enemy.

The only time I ever got my 'bikini line' waxed, before going on holiday with a boyfriend for the first time and thinking it necessary to rip out all my fanny hairs, I was in Stepps, Scotland, staying with my gran. Before I went, my gran joked, 'Mind you don't talk too much, they might rip everything off.'

I walked into the beautician wondering whether my gran might actually be right and whether, after my accent revealed me as an English, I might get a less sympathetic approach.

Stepping anxiously into the reception area, I spotted my cousin Tracy waiting for an eyebrow threading. I was genuinely ecstatic that she was there. My cousin, proof of my Scottishness. It was as if I was looking at a guardian angel, my fanny now protected. Tracy is brilliant in general, not just when I'm scared of getting my clitoris accidentally ripped off.

Of course, it is ridiculous to think that this local beautician would be so bigoted or unprofessional but anti-English sentiment has been drummed into my mind all my life because, well, it exists.

The experience *was* horrendous but not because of my accent or the beautician's handiwork.

Firstly, when asked what I wanted done, I had no idea and was too embarrassed to describe any of the parts of my vulva so sort of stammered and pointed. I'd heard that the most painful bit of a waxing was the bit at the top of the vulva where the outside fanny lips (labia majora, I later learned) meet but where the hair still sort of grows under it. I didn't want that touched, please.

She told me to get on the bed thing and pull up my skirt. I asked if I needed to take my pants off and she said *no, it's fine* and smiled. She then looked at my pants and said *oh, actually, your pants are bigger than normal, I'll get you some paper ones.* They were bikini pants; what the fuck's everyone wearing in Scotland?

In that moment I simultaneously discovered that I apparently wear bigger pants than the waxing population, and that paper pants exist. When handed them, one side of the pants was really thin, like the width of a piece of rope, the other baguette wide. I assumed that the thinner side was for the front because more people I imagine were getting their vulvas than their arse cracks done. I took off my pants and put on the paper pants with the thin bit at the front.

The beautician came back in again and I lifted my skirt and she told me I'd put the pants on back to front but *not to worry it was fine* so I lay there red-faced with what was essentially a paper thong stuck up my labia.

In terms of the actual process, it was so fucking sore I wrote a poem about it.

vulva wax in stepps

as the woman i didn't know
ripped out my unassuming pubic hairs
stuck to cooling molten lava strips
from the crevice of my labia
where the lips meet at the top
like the most delicate of prayers
i wondered about existence
and whether, in these paper knickers,
which at first i wore the wrong way round
as my fingernails indented my wrists
with a bracelet of tiny crescent moons
enforcing a second numbing pain
to distract me from the possibility
that, vulnerable as foreskin
or that faint stitching round a testicle
that my vulva lips might split apart
like wish bones snapped for luck
and i breathed like giving birth
and sobbed secretly inside
remembering that not only had i
paid for this experience
and taken time out of my life
to champ on my own tongue
believing for some reason
that my grieving, balding fanny
now red raw with pointless pain
were essential summer packing
for a one week trip to spain

Please note: my friend Becky got her vulva waxed regularly and says it stops hurting so much. I believe her, but not enough to ever try it again. Saying that, she has also recently swapped to laser. I sometimes wish there were professional barbers for vulvas. So like if you do fancy a trim one day, you can get one without having to balance like an inelegant erotic gymnastics trick over the bathtub yanking your labia in all directions to reach round as your backbone breaks. Maybe there are. I've actually never checked.

I saw a sign outside a waxing parlour recently advertising *vagina waxes* with the phrase: *Don't shave your vagina, wax it!* That was more worrying to me than anything. Even a place specialising in removing hair from this body area still gets it wrong. There is no hair on the vagina. To get a vagina wax would be both pointless and extremely dangerous, as warm wax is poured into your hole and an ambulance swiftly called.

Part of me, after having my daughter, did wish I had driven over the border. It annoys me that I felt this way.

One of the reasons I so wanted to appeal to this Scottish side of my upbringing, aside from fitting in with the family I loved, is because the reaction to saying you're English compared to saying you're Scottish is almost diametrically opposed.

Oh, you're Scottish! The stranger's face lifts, eyebrows welcome the benevolent hilarious underdog, companion to the world. *Such friendly people, the Scottish. Good whisky!* On the other hand, tell them your English and it's more like: *Oh, right. Fuck the English.*

At first, I played on this. Ignored the English hate side of things, embraced the Scottish love whenever I could.

It worked best when abroad, my accent now unplaceable to a foreign speaker's ear, the freedom to finally take on this identity with no one able to hear the falseness of my accent, was joyous. I could finally be seen as Scottish.

While working in Guadeloupe, I went on a half-term trip to Dominica. At the end of the trip, as I was waiting for the ferry, there was a delay. An older man and I were the only two white people in the queue. He was annoyed about the delay and, in full khaki suit and hat, like something I'd seen only in *Indiana Jones*, he left the queue to complain loudly to the person checking the tickets.

Having been unsuccessful, he stormed back to the queue, came directly up to me and said very loudly: *Unbelievable isn't it, it doesn't even help to tell them you're English any more.*

I'm not English, I replied with a slight Glasgow-lull, and it felt so fucking great to say but it was stupid. It wasn't not being English that made me find him repulsive.

Over time, I got a bit a bored of all the stereotyping. I started to feel guilty towards all the friends I loved dearly, all the lovely people I knew born and raised around me in England as I laughed, united against the fucking English. I felt a bit of a fraud, playing on all of these national stereotypes, acting like Scotland was a holy paradise of people ready to befriend any stranger they happened to come across in whisky bars globally.

I prefer Scottish politics. I prefer the way Scottish leadership does not scapegoat immigration and opens its arms much more lovingly and gratefully to those who have chosen to settle in the country. I am proud of many things Scotland leads on, most recently: beginning the global push to provide free sanitary products in all schools; free university access; the baby boxes; scrapping the ridiculous leasehold laws; the rights to roam.

But I didn't help make those things happen and, seriously, Scottish people are not all friendly. Scottish history is not all benign. No history is all benign. There are loads of bigoted bastards in Scotland.

Yes, Scotland, politically, has been shat on extensively by Westminster, and remains locked in a ridiculous relationship with very opposing UK politics, but the individual people are no nicer than those from England, Malawi, Brazil, Bishop's Stortford. And many, many parts of England, and many people in England, are also shat on extensively by Westminster, and are also very fuck-ing friendly.

About three months after meeting the colonialist-dreaming rep-robate in Dominica, I was chatting to a guy in a bar in the south of France. We got onto my background and I replied that I was Scottish.

Oh Scottish! So friendly! he began.

He was just being nice, but caught me at the wrong time. I couldn't be bothered with it any more.

Not really, I replied, stony and straight-faced. *No friendlier than anywhere else.*

What a miserable cow I must've sounded. But the world is as full of brilliantly friendly kind people as much as it is full of arrogant tosspots, sometimes the two residing in one body on different days or times of day. This idea of Scotland that I so desperately wanted to be part of is bollocks, I thought. I feel like a complete traitor to my family saying this, but I believe it.

I love my family with all my bloody human heart and I love going to Scotland to visit them all and when I pass people in the street with accents from Glasgow and Dunblane and Kirkintilloch and Muirhead, I feel like I am floating in a warm bath of home.

But growing up between two geographically cuddling, histori-cally punching countries has made me slightly embittered with ideas of nationalism and national pride and national stereotypes, coming mainly to the conclusion that they are in general a load of shite.

I used to love hearing my gran say things like *that's the Scottish in you, love*, but when I think about it now, it's like really? Is the fact I was friendly to the man at the local post office really a Scottish thing? Is that fact I cracked a joke you found funny a sign of Scottish wit? Unsurprisingly, the Scottishness in me was responsible for a lot of the positive traits; the English upbringing a side note to be mainly ignored in these compliments.

I toured Ireland in 2023 and was told by four different people in the audiences, after enquiring about my background and learning my parents were from Glasgow, that yes, they could tell, that they knew I had something else in me; that Scottish bite; that Scottish down-to-earthness.

It's always meant lovingly, and I used to soak it up proudly, but it does increasingly feel a bit of a fraud.

I get it. In Ireland especially. Or, well, lots of countries that England has historical fucked over. I always tell people my parents' background for exactly that reason. But it's a bit lazy and a bit of a piss-take when people who liked me or my poems or my chatting are almost relieved when I tell them my family are Scottish, or rather, that I'm not totally English. Like yeah, I thought you couldn't be fully English seeing as you're not a total cunt. That sort of thing.

it's a scottish thing, love

it was difficult to know what was actually *a scottish thing*,
and what was just the way my dad liked cooking omelettes,
thick as bricks, chip and burger filling;
on the french exchange i ordered one, runny, unexpected,
explained confidently to the interested french family
how omelettes, *in scotland*, are thicker, cooked for longer,
filled with chopped up chips and burgers; and they nodded,
ah oui? interested in our cultural differences; listened
as i regaled them with some other culinary scottish trends;
how the cheddar cheese is orange, and macaroni
the only pasta dish traditionally served, *in scotland*,
with a side of baked potato or inside a pastry case
and how people, on saturdays, *in scotland*, the posh ones,
dine in garden centre cafés, eat tatty scones served inside
a buttered roll specifically for mornings besides shelves
full of chutneys you only buy at christmas
and how women's necks in scotland, circled in *perils*

221

are constantly in danger of royals on holiday
in the highlands mistaking them for deer, and my dad said
that's a scottish thing; like kindness, like humour,
not needing to drink water; like calling coca-cola 'juice',
like not being a prick; at work, in her first month
in england, after my mother's consultation,
a patient dropped his trousers and his boxers, penis fully out
as the english nurse, on reading my mother's scottish notes,
mistook 'a skelf on the pinkie' for a knife wound on his cock;
she stood, searching his befuddled foreskin, finding nothing;
he stood still, wondering why he had to get his dick out
for a splinter on his little finger; at home, we didn't shop,
we got the messages, drank irn-bru, gave people phones,
said hello to the neighbours and to strangers on the street,
and gran said *that's a scottish thing,* smiling to people,
apparently, and sitting on yer mammie's knee, eating
coulter's candies, and my arms, freckled like my father's
and my aunty's, the pale skin below almost as obscured
as scotland's role in slavery, cherished as if skin could be
a signpost, as if veins were made of maps, as if tablet
were really so different from fudge

Of any line of poetry I've ever written, I'm most worried about my
dad's reaction to this last line. I do know tablet is a lot harder and
more crumbly than fudge. I'm sorry, Dad, it's just a metaphor. I also
still feel guilty I don't like tablet. Or fudge, so maybe that's OK.

It's a comfort, for sure, to laugh and tell jokes about how it's
so Scottish to do certain things. Thing is, I hear exactly the same
traits told by my friends whose families come from other coun-
tries or parts of the country. That it's so Polish, so Portuguese, so
northern, so London, so east London and so on to make too much
food or to always welcome guests; how many stories I've heard

about Polish grandmas who always have a big pot of soup ready or that's Lithuanian aunties for you, a constant cake on the go, or how Brazilian men really know how to dance. Go to any Italian's house and they'll have three lasagnes waiting in the oven just in case friends pop by!

Will they though? Even the stingy bastards that can't cook lasagne?

I really love feeling like I'm a bit Scottish, and that feeling Scottish means something, something specific, something special, especially, I think, because I've never lived there and sometimes wish I had. It's so good to feel rooted; to belong; to share something in common with people you love. The entirety of my family are there. We're not spread around the world. Almost everyone was in Scotland, within about an hour radius of everyone else, and then a few England stragglers. Oh, and that third cousin in Canada.

But perhaps enjoying a dance, or making big pots of soup, or bringing out cakes for visitors is just part of being human, and that's also lovely. Maybe it's just that your grandma's a good host or felt guilty if she didn't always have some soup ready. My Aunt June brings out a three-tier tray of millionaires shortbread and pastries filled with cream and mini sausage rolls each time we pop in to say hello. Is she a typical Scottish aunty or is she just fucking lovely? Was it her Scottish rhythm that made my grandma a gorgeous dancer, or did she just go to Scottish dancing lessons as a child and love to dance? Does my mum smile and say hello to everyone passing in the street because she was born in Glasgow or does she just know everyone in our town because she was a nurse there for forty years? Did my grandad love telling dirty jokes cos he was Scottish or because our family are all filthy-minded?

One of my friends, watching me wash up by filling the bowl half full of bubbly water and, well, washing and rinsing the dishes, took the sponge and said, *I'll show you how to wash up the French way.*

She put washing up liquid on the sponge instead of in the water.

That was the difference. I'm pretty sure those are the main or only two ways most people wash up in the world of washing-up liquid, not an English versus French cultural conundrum and certainly not connected to some sort of soil-based bloodline. Sometimes, I wash up like that too.

My favourite result of stereotyping is Paris syndrome.

I learnt about this via my boyfriend via The Blindboy Podcast. In brief, Paris syndrome, coined in the 1980s by Hiroaki Ota, a Japanese psychiatrist, is the label given to a sense of extreme disappointment exhibited when visiting Paris. Romanticised to such an extent by literature and film, 'the syndrome is characterized by a number of psychiatric symptoms such as acute delusional states, hallucinations, feelings of persecution (perceptions of being a victim of prejudice, aggression, hostility from others), derealization, depersonalization, anxiety, as well as psychosomatic manifestations such as dizziness, tachycardia, sweating most notably, but also others, such as vomiting.'[*]

I think I have the opposite. No matter how much dog shit I stand in in that city, and there is a lot of dog shit, I'd still rather stink of shit in Paris than of roses in most other cities on Earth. I don't want to ruin this myth by ever moving there. I think new motherhood is a bit like Paris syndrome. It's sold as such a rose-tinted glory, and so every cigarette butt, every stitch not healed, every piece of dog shit on the street, every bleeding, weeping, sleepless reality hits all the harder.

What frightens me about this sort of comforting patriotic praise and national pride is likely obvious; that for every positive slant, the flipside comes full force; how easy xenophobic and racist fingers and fists come slipping into the equation, reliant on a similar lumping of human beings into single syllables. Like the English all being cunts, for example.

---

* Chelsea Fagan, 'Paris Syndrome: A First-Class Problem for a First-Class Vacation', *The Atlantic,* 18 October 2011, theatlantic.com [accessed 20 February 2020].

It amazes me how people are so willing to blend the personalities of people from certain cultures or countries or classes together in one foul attack but would still swear blind they are nothing like their blood parents or siblings – the closest to their own DNA they will ever come across. Ah right, so all Romanian people are the same, but you and your brother David are absolutely nothing alike, right? This is perhaps the most evident in anti-immigration rhetoric.

One of the most memorable things a family member ever said to me about national identities and the dehumanising of people for political gain was my grandad in the scattering of times he ever mentioned war. He said the German soldiers were *young boys just like us*.

This sentiment has never left me; that someone can think like this despite all the national propaganda against it, despite all the friends he lost to 'their' bullets, to 'their' enemy fire, despite even his love for his country, he still did not believe in this us and them mentality. Not even as a teenager in the midst of war. Or maybe *because* of having been a teenager in the midst of war; boys *just like us*, who lost their best friends *just as we did*.

oh, perfectly content,

he nods, dozing in the day, cushion at his back,
handkerchief halo to hold the heat in through his bald patch

tv always on but muted, as we chatted about the neighbours
and he occasionally giggled, or smiled, then dozed again

twice, his squad was fired upon by bombers overhead
each pal left dead; momentary ceasefire reloading over him

on visits south, mum would take him anywhere for breakfast
you sure dad? the morrisons again? it has everything you need;

bacon brown sauce bap; grandchildren and daughters;
his wife, white toast, two fried eggs, free refill tea or coffee

the second time, swapping leave with a sympathetic friend
to attend his mother's birthday – the entire squad was killed

he shouldn't be here, he exhaled, so yes, old age
was welcome; each post-war hug a blessing;
what more could one man want?

when we hugged, his arthritic knuckle
stuck into my backbone; he signed up at sixteen;
took his teeth out at the table every time we asked

exam question for gcse english language:

**list seven rhetorical devices used in political speeches
to convince you to fear other people who have moved
from another country to the country you live in, without
knowing anything about them or their lives**

*for Suella Braverman's 'likely billions' eager to come to Britain,
and other perfect examples from British politicians*

one: exaggeration
there are billions of sand grains on every british shore
billions of raindrops in every british storm
but not billions of people trying to reach britain
on small boats across the channel

two: repetition
in the milky way, at least one hundred billion stars
almost a billion pounds we know of
in the sunaks' bank accounts
but not billions of people, not almost millions of people
trying to reach britain on small boats across the channel

three: metaphor
perhaps maths is not your strong point
nor geography it seems
you claim a hurricane of people are rushing to our streets
impossible, the uk is not warm enough for hurricanes

four: zoomorphism
what other slurs are your speech writers scribbling?
anything original? or just the same old tricks;
turn people into animals? insects? rodents?

any beasts we find revolting, or more subtly suggest it with

five: word association
describe immigrants as swarming
so that flies may fill our minds,
if that does not convince us

six: comparison
compare migration to invasion
make inflammatory statements
invoke imagery of immigrants as a battle we must fight

if that doesn't make us panic till we are utterly convinced
that immigration is to blame for every crisis in our lives

seven: lie

poem written one night when i was really missing some of my friends

You have been my friend, replied Charlotte. That in itself is a
tremendous thing.
– E.B. White, *Charlotte's Web*

my friends are scattered across cities now
across countries and countrysides
distant as aeroplanes watched at night from a window
wondering where those miniature people, strapped in
might be going

why did we scatter? were those studies and lovers
and money that broke us apart, birds migrating
confused by the bright lights of progress
were they worth it?

i can't tell if that light is a star or a wing-tip
either way, i just wish you were closer

either way, i just wish you would knock on my door
while i'm sleeping, throw a stone at my window and wake me
so we can sit on the pavement and talk about nothing
and everything, and throw balls at the curb
and never have left

the comfort of friends i can talk about anything to
i miss you like believing in fairies and god
like lone sheep in frosts, i am freezing and bored
of you not being around

i am so sick of dates in the diary
and i keep missing the timing of whatsapp chats
catching up on hundreds of lines of typed conversation
i'm now reading alone

fuck, where have you gone? i just want you here
your face, not emoji emotions
palpably sobbing or laughing
i want to stay up till midnight just to eat ice cream
wonder which one of us will fall asleep first
hear how it sounds when you yawn in the morning

i want us sat on the floor of my bedroom
excitedly laying out all of the duvets and blankets
and pillows and cushions
across this hard, uncertain surface of earth
till we are sure we'll be cosy enough

shit where you want, it's paris

it is raining in paris but the rain in paris
is much more attractive than the rain back home,
and my clothes are soaked but they are soaked in paris
so they cling to my breasts like a black and white film
and it is cold so cold but the cold in paris
makes my nipples perk up like cigarette butts
tossed on the pavements near the cafés in paris
where all the waiters are men and i can't work out why
and i am freezing and wet and everyone smokes
and the fumes from the traffic and the cigarette steam
make my eyeballs well up like life is a dream and the wine
is served in much daintier glasses with blackcurrant syrup
called kir so it's posh, and dogs shit on the streets,
so much dog shit in paris but it's just too romantic
to pick that shit up because all of the owners
are distracted in paris kissing in doorways of macaroon shops
that do not sell cupcakes because the women in paris
do not act like children and the coffee is black
and nobody smiles because everyone's wondering
if sartre was right or just had no friends
so if you need me tonight i'll be strolling through paris
with red lipstick on that never sticks to my teeth
as men piss in government-funded urinals
down alleys cos men just kept pissing in streets
and when i'm home in paris, lift broken in paris
after being heckled on the metro or the bus or the stairs
i'll stand on a balcony that's too small for a chair
because who needs to sit to see sun sets in paris
as the seine, like a postcard, saunters dirtily by
and cars below burning in the riots in paris
heat the night like a strike and i sip on my wine

two kisses of moonlight to wish me goodnight
and i lie back in paris, god i'm sexy in paris
having slipped into lingerie to sleep in in paris
as the blackness in paris makes love to the light
and i dream how one day i might live here in paris
high heels in the hallway, still smothered in shite

great britain

perhaps if we changed the name
from great to mediocre-britain
still-lots-to-learn-from-others-britain
trains-not-as-good-as-finland-britain
childcare-unaffordable-unlike-sweden-britain
middling-education-system-britain
healthcare-not-even-in-most-top-ten-lists-britain
but a lucky-hurricane-free-temperate-climate-britain
perhaps, if we hand-back-museum-treasures-britain
to the-countries-we-stole-them-from-a-while-ago-britain
and apologise and recompense those unpaid-enslaved-
underpaid-harmed-mistreated-workers-britain
we built-the-bricks-of-kings-and-queens-on-britain,
perhaps, if we-took-down-all-the-flags-and-bunting-britain
get-rid-of-the-ridiculous-leasehold-laws-other-countries-
scrapped-centuries-ago-britain
imprisoned-prince-andrew-britain
and admitted yes-it-is-quite-ridiculous-to-call-it-
english-breakfast-tea-when-not-one-of-the-ingredients
-is-made-or-originated-in-england-britain,
perhaps, if we hold up our hands and finally admit
we-are-not-the-greatest-in-the-world-britain
but-actually-fairly-mediocre-by-many-economic-
social-and-aesthetic-respects-britain,
perhaps, just perhaps if-we-do-that-britain
we might have another chance at eurovision

WHERE'S YOUR ACCENT FROM?

When I was fourteen my dad had a phone in his car, a very swanky phone that was voice activated. The Alexa of the nineties. It was programmed to respond only to my dad's voice. On many drives, Dad would casually say 'phone home' in his enviable Glasgow tone and the phone would ring our home number. For a while in my teen years, it was my life's mission to activate this.

Once we were home, I would sit for a while in the car, trying my best to perfect my dad's accent and get the voice activation to work for me, repeating 'phoonne hooome' over and over again, like a desperate deep-voiced Glaswegian ET, praying one day I would sound Glasgow enough to fool the robot. I managed it just once and the jubilation I felt was akin to winning at least 50p from the 2p machines. Clink clink clink.

The most annoying thing was that, in my head, my accent often sounded exactly like my parents and it was often quite disappointing when I realised that between my thinking voice and my speaking voice there was a tiny fairy sitting at a computer, reprogramming my vocal cords.

Still when I write poems, it's often in my parents' accent, or my cousin Tracy's, or whatever amalgamation of them exists in my brain. And then I read them out loud and it's like *who's that?*

If I'm touring in a different place, with a different accent, the accent I write in often morphs again.

The most disappointing was when I had a gig at the Seamus Heaney

HomePlace centre in Bellaghy, Northern Ireland, and had spent two days surrounded by these lovely tones. I spent one rainy afternoon in my B & B, chatting with the owner and writing poems in my bedroom, mainly about chatty taxi drivers and black butter. When I then read the poems out loud and did not in fact sound like Seamus Heaney, they didn't have quite the effect they had in my head.

Since I've been touring more, I've realised I find it more and more difficult not to mimic the accents around me. I often panic that I'll flip into a bad Hull or Liverpool or Sheffield tone on stage and sound like I'm taking the piss. This happens most prominently in Birmingham. When I'm drunk, I've been known to slip into a really terrible attempt at a Birmingham accent and I've no idea why.

Most people pick up accents; change the way they speak a little depending on who they're surrounded by, perhaps especially people who've been brought up in a mixed sea of voices. I've no proof of this last idea except my grandma suggested it; that because my accent was different to my parents', that I'd likely developed a musical ear and a less concrete accent of my own, and my grandma was really smart so I'll take it.

This happens with vocabulary a lot too. There are words I think with but will never speak with, or at least try not to. I often find myself censoring words that come naturally to me in thought, but which, once said in my accent, I feel a total arsehole using. Scottish vernacular. Like 'wee' instead of little. Like 'aye' for yes.

In my head, I say 'wee' about everything small. Sometimes I write it, and then delete and rewrite. Out loud, I gulp it back because I am personally prejudiced about posh English accents like mine using Scottish vernacular probably because I'll have heard a family member ripping that at some point.

The phrase I didn't do this with, because I didn't realise it was a Scottish thing, was 'give me a phone' not 'give me a call', until my friends in England burst out laughing and pretended to hand me a physical telephone every time I said it.

My English accent boomed most starkly when we went to Gino's, the local chippy near my gran's. We went there for a treat every time we visited her. As I got older, I was desperate to order my own fish supper. I asked for chips, a pineapple fritter (the vegetarian treat of the chippy – I was English and vegetarian, fuck's sake, I know, I know) and a pizza.

The guy behind the counter then asked if I wanted the pizza *plain or deep-fried* and I had no idea what he meant and I was trying really hard to be polite to this adult so I replied, my voice in our local family chippy now sounding more like the Queen than ever before: *Pardon, what do you mean deep-fried pizza?* My dad gave me a loving squeeze and quickly ordered the normal pizza for me.

The next time I went to Scotland, I was determined to have the pizza deep-fried. Again, I think in some bid to prove my Scottishness despite it being only me and my gran who would witness this. Again, the most crass stereotype of Scottishness, which is really just called eating deep-fried food, which people do all over the world, not only and not all Scottish people.

By the time I'd walked back to my gran's house the cardboard pizza box had given way in one of the corners from the weight of the grease. Undeterred, I took a slice, and loved it. I love fried bread so it makes sense that I'd love fried pizza.

After three slices I thought I was gonna vomit. I like eating shit food sometimes but, as a general rule, I much prefer eating meals that won't make my body more shit and death more inevitable after I've finished them. Saying this, I'm not into healthy versions of food that is intended to be shit. Don't give me a chip butty in brown bread. It's like asking me to go swimming without my goggles. There's no point.

For a different idea of Scottish food, check out the chef Owen Morrice. Also, my mum cooked really nice food too. I just didn't think of those dinners as being Scottish. Except the turnip mash, which I tried to feed to the dog a lot.

I started studying at Cambridge University at eighteen years old.

There, the lack of many accents other than received pronunciation was stark. Until I went to Cambridge I was the English cousin who sounds like the fucking Queen; at Cambridge, surrounded by people who actually sounded like her, I was the corgi.

For many reasons, I was desperate not to pick up this received pronunciation. I didn't want to lose my own voice to an accent that was, and still is, often described as 'better', 'well-spoken', 'proper', 'correct'. I guess I was privileged enough not to need to; my voice is pretty standard, traditional BBC Southern English. For those students from other backgrounds, especially those from working-class backgrounds, picking up received pronunciation could be life-changing.

I do still find it unnerving though, to listen to received pronunciation, because it strips voices of almost all information about a person's geographical background. Perhaps that's the point.

inverted snobbery

i find it hard to trust an accent
with no landscape attached
a voice that tells us nothing
of the foothills or the flat lands
which buds were cracking concrete
on streets you walked to school
how your neighbour took his tea
what you mostly ate on sundays
a voice that cannot whisper hints
of where you bought your sugar
what sat inside your pudding bowls
which birdsong might remind you
a little bit of home –
children do not choose their past
a bully is a bully no matter how they speak

it's just the only lips which scarred me
had accents weather-free
like the leaders banging fists
laughing on tv

By the time I left Cambridge, my voice seemed to have morphed, trying so hard to avoid the trap of 'posh', into sounding like some sort of *Mary Poppins* extra.

That mixed bag of voices seems to have relaxed into its own melting pot of place and blood and time, though sometimes, especially when recording radio or audiobooks, I'm still not one hundred per cent sure what's going to come out.

I had an epiphany once after a gig in Birmingham where I found myself slipping, despite not even being pissed, into the dulcet tones of this beautiful city. Perhaps, I thought, the weird drunk Birmingham in me is my voice's attempt to place itself somewhere in between my upbringing and my family.

Perhaps this is my accent homeland! Accent homeland being an entirely made up concept I had invented in that moment to mean the mid-point between my birth and my heritage.

I got the map up on my phone and drew a line between Reading, where I was born, and Glasgow, where my family mainly come from. No, Liverpool was in the centre, my exact halfway house. Fitting too perhaps, because for the last few years, my Liverpool gigs have sold out quicker than any others. Maybe they know they're special. Either way, I've no idea where the Birmingham comes in. Maybe I've just watched too much *Peaky Blinders*. Maybe I just love that city.

ordering chips in gino's

gaffer tape my mouth
at the chip shop down from gran's
in case the customers find out
i am a traitor

if you do not want
an english daughter, do not
move to england
before she is born – just a thought

and lord knows i love you, dad
but no i will not cross the border
when in labour just to birth my child
in scotland!

do not panic – i am already excited
to gift her just as many
tea towels, tartan dresses
squares of tablet

sing her songs
about crows that cannot fly
teach her ally bally bee
until the coulter's coats her teeth

but when i take her down for chips
by the crossroads near great gran's
i will hold her by the hand
and let her speak

kit

your eyeliner has been perfect since i was six
no, it's my cousin, but who's counting blood cells really
is that your sister? they asked, *god, you look so similar!*
and i beamed, proud; if i were brought up in scotland,
i used to think i'd share your hair as well, auburn and heavy
an autumn tree changed colour without shedding any leaves
as if redheads were handed out in hospital, with cheekbones
and a cutting scottish wit; oh teach me how to do it, kit,
that flick of music at each side of your eye;
oh teach me how to smoke chic; how to listen to an album
and remember all your favourites – you are the portrait
i would have painted if anyone had asked me what i look like
in scottish; poster of a popstar in my bedroom, you strolled
into every family gathering, kisses, called me *gorgeous*
and *honey* in a voice like rivers newly melted after winter
so the birds might splash again; then you left, to meet friends
in pubs i was too young to go to yet; you are the photograph
i show anyone who thinks i only have a brother
no, no, we have an older sister too

from home to home

from cambridge to glasgow

we cannot eat until the train leaves
that's the rule

her hand is in the bag
as soon as whistles signal movement
we start a game of snap
she pretends to take a biscuit
knows she has to eat the apple first

beneath the bridge at ely, we hold hands
on and off at peterborough, up and down
the stairs we dash, rucksacks on our backs
after another hour of chat and cards
the buffet cart comes past at last
two twixes bought, we bite the ends
important family tradition, suck the tea up
through the chocolate straws till the insides,
perfumed warm, melt into our mouths and hands

another game of snap

i used to have to bounce her on my lap
for hours on trains, walk up and down the aisles
back double bent in pain, hush her happy songs
for fear of angry strangers, carry her, carry the pram
carry all the bags together up and down the stairs,
pray we'd make the changes, pray she'd fall asleep
pray i wouldn't cry when tiredness got the worst of me
now i watch her colour pages, read a comic,

eat sandwiches and chat, as i stare out
at the passing years we've journeyed on these tracks,
she laughs when i start welling up – *for god's sake mum!*

she passes me a sympathetic biscuit
another game of snap

doncaster rattles past
durham castle winks at us
the train fills up with confidence
in rugby shirts with collars up

till newcastle, where, bridges at their sexiest,
the booze cart stops serving, girls get on
with rollers in, sing loudly with my kid –
hen dos are my favourite train companion;
an old man helps an older woman lift her suitcase up,
i reapply my lipstick for no real reason,
she slaps her hand on mine, two queens

berwick upon tweed, we stop and stare,
a postcard set to burst, i forever dreamt
of stopping there amongst that perfect
blur of bridge and beach

soon, static caravans squat like sheep upon the cliffs
a lonesome bench where walkers sit
gazing out to sea, *one day we will stop there*
share a sandwich

she agrees, beats me with two sevens
one heart one diamond

fruit is finished, biscuits open, hills now mimic mountains
fields sliced by dry stone walls, she twitches on her seat,
feels the shift in scenery, stones turn small and red
on cottage driveways, she feels we're getting close,
between each bite of buttered roll
begins the constant repetition: *are we in scotland yet?*

i pretend to check by looking out for tartan sheep
(she no longer believes in these) sees the flag, and screams

swift past portobello beaches, we pull into the capital
run to see the castle view,
through princes street gardens
return, sweating, for the final change

final train –
this is when the cake comes out
stuff it in our eager mouths
we've waited seven hours for this

i beat her with two fours, though she insists
her hand is under mine – it definitely isn't

too impatient for another game
we watch city turn to hill
until city sneaks back in again

and noses to the glass, we look out
for the tower blocks, she sees them first
and screams, leaps from seat
packs her crayons in her rucksack
i collect the crumbs of cards and snacks
we get ready with our hats and coats –

queen street station, glasgow

where, waving in a line, they wait,
mum and dad and grandma
to welcome us back home

kirkie

between chryston and the campsies, kirkintilloch
underdog of local towns, the sort of place
comedians refer to to look edgy

like they've never seen the high street, the hilltop park,
the river walk, laden with the sort of views
americans buy a passport for

over two ice-cream parlours now, charity-shop haven,
five cafés with extensive breakfast menus, *even vegan*
an italian, fairylit for christmas all year round

even when the daffodils, so many daffodils, are out;
and as sun sets down each evening, my aunty
with her slant-roofed attic, holds out open arms,
window above our double bed to picture-frame the clouds

oblivious

beneath us
earthworms churn soil
swallow one country's graveyards
to shit into another

above us
birds hover
easy over barbed wires
seeds falling from their beaks

in between
we stamp passports
wonder where those flowers grew from –
proudly back our teams

MALUSDOMESTICAPHOBIA

My elderly neighbour once came knocking on my door begging for help. I panicked and let her in, thinking something horrendous had happened. She showed me a new keyring that one of her family members had put on a new set of keys they'd cut for her.

It was yellow.

She was breathless and shaking, asking if by any chance I please, please had another keyring I could swap with hers, as the colour was making her feel so sick.

I've never seen someone so affected by a colour before.

Xanthophobia relates to the colour yellow, one of a set of colour-related phobias, collectively grouped as chromophobia or chromatophobia.

I used to be fairly sceptical of phobias, likely because, as far as I know, I don't have one. So, you know, if I don't have it, it must be a load of bollocks. That sort of sceptical; the no knowledge and no research sort of scepticism.

A brilliant friend, one of the most 'outdoorsy' people I know, has a deep phobia of apples, so much so that she did not buy a house she loved after looking for almost a year, because of an apple tree in the garden. She couldn't bear to cut it down because she's a lovely person, but she also couldn't bear to sleep in that house, head on the pillow, knowing all those apples were out there, just outside the window, dangling from the branches by such a thin cord, ready to fall and rot, the ground a graveyard of slowly decomposing apple gunk.

One of the positive things about her phobia was that it was very easy to please her kids when they came to my house just by offering them apple-related treats – Appletiser, apple crumble, apple slices even. Maybe she faked the phobia to make her kids want apples. If so, clever.

An apple phobia is called malusdomesticaphobia. I have since found out one of my family members also has it. I think Eve probably did after the fall of Eden, but that one's easier to explain. A phobia I can understand more is arachibutyrophobia, which is the fear of peanut butter sticking to the roof of your mouth.

I love peanut butter to almost sexual levels, but I remember my mum telling me, when I asked her if it's possible to eat poo, that it wasn't because it would stick to the roof of your mouth and throat as it is too mucilaginous to swallow. She compared it to thick peanut butter, which put me off peanut butter for a while but I love the taste too much for that association to have lasted.

Also, my mum didn't use the word mucilaginous. I just looked up the word 'sticky' in a thesaurus because I'd used the word sticking and then stick and wanted to vary my language a bit, and the word mucilaginous was given. It means: having a viscous or gelatinous consistency.

Ephebiphobia is the fear of teenagers, thought to be brought about mainly by the negative portrayal of teenagers in the media. Strange, sad, to have a society where we've created a fear of young people going through what I'd suggest is the most tricky time in life. How many other phobias the media has undoubtedly created I don't know. Phobia of your own face without a filter coming soon. Phobia of going outside without make-up on in case someone calls you brave for just having, you know, your face on show.

A more recently coined term is nomophobia, which is not yet fully defined but refers to a fear of being detached from mobile phone connectivity.

Perhaps the most unfortunately named phobia is hippopotomonstrosesquippedaliophobia, which is a fear of long words.

People are so fascinating, and phobias remind me how different everyone is, even people living in the same country, even people living in the same household, even twins.

The flipside to phobias are philias, a fondness or abnormal love for a specified thing, and perhaps also fetishes, described by Collins Online Dictionary as 'an unusually strong liking or need for a particular object or activity, as a way of getting sexual pleasure' but which can include inanimate objects, body parts, or situations not commonly viewed as being sexual in nature.

I googled 'optician fetish', because I used to get so excited getting my eyes tested and I haven't gone to the opticians since I was fifteen and I now think it's because I quite enjoyed the feeling; that close, close breath on my cheek as the optician (I have no recollection of the actual person, just the feelings) stared closely into my eyes through some sort of small robot telescope contraption.

The memory of a slow, low voice whispering 'now look over my left shoulder', eye patch over my right eye, my skin twitching half tickled half wanting to laugh hysterically as I read PEZOLCFTD and he said *very good* and now look over my right shoulder. Oof.

You are not alone, the internet replied, dishing me out vast fictions of optician fantasies.

As well as those who also fantasise about opticians' tests, I discovered some other eye-related excitements: glasses fetishes, many of them, most commonly fetishes for women wearing glasses. Also, oculolinctus. This is also known as 'worming', and refers to the paraphilic practice of licking eyeballs for erotic gratification.

Apparently, this has 'trended' among young people in certain areas after it went viral on TikTok. In Japan, doctors were having to issue warnings about long-term eye damage and, according to teachers, some classes had around half the students turning up with eye patches due to infections.

Ironic that for centuries many religious and political leaders attempted to claim that masturbating could turn people blind, and now there's an actual sexualised activity that could. So stop licking each other's eyeballs, kids, go have a wank.

The more I read about all this stuff, the more and more it seems that the world is just mainly full of people, full of phobias and fantasies, spanning every border line drawn on any map.

Aside from what TikTok tells you you should enjoy, and for the love of your eyesight, please don't just do what TikTok tells you to do, people are turned on by so many different things. Imagine if the only standards of adult sexual relationships were consent, safety, communication and loving it. It's so sad that this isn't the case.

Some people love sucking toes, some love pretending to be your doctor or elfin queen; some love dressing gowns, some love rubber. There are people who are turned on by fog and people who are turned on by eye tests. Unfortunately, my friend says it's all done by computers now anyway. There's very little whispering any more.

Weirdly, I did have a spare keyring in my kitchen drawer. A turquoise one. I swapped it with my neighbour's, and of all the helpful things I have tried to do for her over seven years of living next door, I have genuinely never felt someone so relieved or grateful as she was then. She thanked me for several months for 'saving her' from that horrendous colour yellow.

skimming summer stones

on a pile of sunburnt rubble
five stones left of a castle's gate
i watched you skimming pebbles
across the surface of loch awe

not knowing you could do that
i fell in love a little more

basically, i'm bored

*for becky and john, new neighbours and now friends who invited
me to their house for a drink 'but not to see john's cock', after i
posted this poem online, not knowing anyone in the village fol-
lowed me on instagram*

desperate for something different to occur:
an otter on the school run; a dad, cock-out
at the one-stop; post office selling lube;
even a thunderstorm would do

i was told that quiet villages
like the quiet village i am dying in
were full of secret sin;

i don't want to fuck the neighbours
and i'm fairly scared of thunder;
but an invite would be glorious now and then

philematophile

someone who is excessively fond of kissing

there is a new day every day
and the pebbles on this beach are warm
and nothing turns me on
as much as kissing you

on the sea, a path of light
leads to a full and patient moon
and nothing turns me on
as much as kissing you

so fetch a red rose every morning
feed me strawberries till i'm sick
a diamond on a silver chain
a dildo carved from amethyst

wrap gift bows round my ankles
rub oils into my aching feet
dress your lovely penis up
with every cock ring we can fit

half my life spent reading tips
of every top ten sex position
almost twenty years of testing
and still, nothing turns me on
like slow and solid kissing –

so swim your lips to mine again
my toes are treading water
lick the sun salt from my mouth

let our tongues whisper their stories

kiss my neck and breasts and legs
the sea is clear and bright and blue
and nothing turns me on
as much as kissing you

ORAL SEX

Politeness and Pomegranates

*the balls are always the most tickly, the penis
isn't tickly, it's just hungry for love*

ANONYMOUS FRIEND

*when it comes to pleasuring women and
conversing in the language of love, cunnilingus
should be every man's native tongue*

IAN KERNER, *She Comes First:
The Thinking Man's Guide to
Pleasuring a Woman*

not even a please

want to suck my cock? he asks
as if the pleasure would be mainly mine
as if, of all my body's cravings
within this fleeting glance at fleshy life

he's got a fair impression
crowded on this nightclub bus
that, rather than go home with friends
eat some chips with gravy on

bundle on the sofa
read a magazine in bed
fantasise in favourite knickers
till my cheeks turn infrared

that his dick in my mouth
no doubt still sweaty from the dancefloor lights
is that one thrill i'm missing
from this most glorious of friday nights

quite sure, as i stare at him
he'd be one of those guys
to shove my head down without asking
as soon as he's inside

no offer of a favour
he might give me in return
no – *would you like a lick, love?*
no – *i'd love to make you cum*

no thank you, i reply
in that balance we all learn
between firmness and politeness
lest we anger needy men

it's taken well this time
he informs me it's my loss
and i wonder if he knows
it's really not

the long-term effects of shame
or, *just let him stay down there*

if he tells you your butt is a chalice
cupped in his hands, and you know
he loves wine

that your scent feels like
supping on oysters, and you know
how he savours his seafood

if he tells you he lives to get messy
and you've seen him spill soup
many times down his chin

that he doesn't want air yet
can breathe underwater for longer
and you know how he smiles
sinking his skin into ocean

perhaps it is time you believe him
perhaps it is time you stop setting
a timer, tapping his shoulder:

are you sure?
are you sure?
are you sure?

SOLO SHOW

I learnt about cunnilingus at the age of twelve from the Outhere Brothers' song 'Boom Boom Boom'. It was the second single I ever purchased, which I bought purely for the non-radio-edit dirty version.

I can't quote the song here because I can't afford to – it's expensive to quote song lyrics and I'd rather spend the cash on train tickets – but I truly believe that if not for this song, which I listened to on repeat for a good few years, I would have had much less confidence in my own ideas sexually as I went into my teens, and I am eternally grateful for this.

To summarise the lyrics for anyone who isn't aware of this romantic ballad: the Outhere Brother, Keith, is extremely interested in having sexual intercourse with a woman whose bum he really likes the look of, specifically in the doggy-style position. He confirms that he will refrain from ejaculating until she is ready. I wasn't sure what that meant but it seemed like he was thinking of her.

However, and this is the bit I focused on as a teen, if the woman did not want to sleep with Keith, he suggested that perhaps she might sit on his face instead so that he could possibly have a taste of her delicious vulva. He was very polite about it all. Just possibly. If she fancied it.

Yes, the lyrics of this 'filthy' song pressured me less to go 'all the way' than my school sex education did.

If not for 'Boom Boom Boom', it may have been years until I

realised that the two-minute house-party blow jobs followed by being called a slag or half-wanted half-what-other-option-is-there-that's-not-embarrassing sexual intercourse was not the be all and end all of my possible sexual future.

By the age of twelve, I knew what sleeping with someone meant. I knew what intercourse was. I knew what taking someone from behind meant, and anal, and I also knew what blow jobs and sucking dick and giving head (to a guy) meant because those phrases were as common as cock-and-balls scribbles on secondary school toilet walls.

The only time I remember cunnilingus being discussed was during my later teens at a house party. A few blow jobs had been given in various rooms and boys had been high fived and cheered and well-done-for-fellatio bunting put up and congratulations and back slaps and confetti shaped like dicks thrown in joy as they returned from the bedrooms as heroes. No girl was high fived, or even thanked.

As we sat in the kitchen chatting, sipping delicately on our cider and blackcurrant mixes, the Kir royales* of the UK, one of my mates (male) asked the blow-job champions if any of them had 'returned the favour'. Love you Danny.

An immediate onslaught of girl and pussy shaming thus erupted. *I'm not doing that! Gross! Smells like fish! I'm not touching that slag.* That sort of mature response from the very guys whose dicks were at that point in time lulling in the dulcet sleep of post-blow-job joy.

No, none of them had 'returned the favour' because, if we were to believe them, the vulva is a disgusting bag of shit and they would never do something so gross.

Now, if not for the words of pussy-flavour enthusiast Outhere Brother Keith Mayberry, I may have believed from that day on that oral sex was the one-way blow-job road I was being told it was, and

---

* Kir royale is a French drink consisting of blackcurrant liqueur and champagne.

that the idea of licking mine or any other vulvas was utterly repulsive to all boys and men worldwide.

But no, I knew with the certainty of nineties dirty-version rap lyrics that there were many guys out there who loved this shit and who were both excited and honoured to have their face plunged into a tasty, tasty piece of fandango.

Even now, this insecurity about receiving cunnilingus lingers for many, because there are still many enemies out there. Of course, some folk, with all the confidence in the world, just don't enjoy oral sex. Fine. The whole point of doing these things is enjoyment and all bodies are different. But there are also swathes who can't, or at least find it tricky to, enjoy physically, because of mental barriers, which is a shame. Literally.

Historically, across a number of different cultures, cunnilingus has been shamed profusely, mainly for being unmanly, unmacho, demeaning to real men's mouths and minds.

From what evidence remains, there were loads of rules about sex in ancient Roman and Greek times, and cunnilingus really took the brunt of the bullying.

The sex hierarchy in general was not based on sexuality as such but, simplified greatly: penetration good, penetrated bad. Those at the top of the food chain did the penetrating, those below got penetrated, all of which still has many implications nowadays.

What's more, women were mainly seen as scum, and so cunnilingus, as well as involving no penetrating with your penis, also involved no specific physical male pleasure, and was thus akin to the shit on a shoe of the sex world: pleasing a scummy woman for pleasing a scummy woman's sake. It was shameful to do, degrading, and very, very unmanly.

Some even believed that giving oral sex in general fucked up your breath so bad, all vulva soaked or womany stinking, that it could turn even the most magnificent of feasts, if breathed on the food, into a putrid fish dish. A bit like King Midas with more rotten fish and less gold as the outcome.

Of course, human history did not just happen in ancient Rome and Greece, and not everyone would have agreed with that overarching hierarchy. A quick scan of the pagan beliefs of the sacred worship of the body and the divine feminine, including safe cunnilingus, reveals that people have indulged in, loved and lavished licking each other for fucking ages. PS: Be safe, you can't get pregnant, but you can still catch shit from oral.

While looking up all this oral sex history, I stumbled across the excellently titled article: Parents watch in horror as gorillas engage in oral sex in front of kids at zoo. I also discovered there is such a thing as an oral sex horoscope and that, according to some sources of astrological interest, Libras give lovely oral sex because of their people-pleasing sentiments, and Virgos give it well too because they like attention to detail, they are good communicators and like to finish a job.*

From the receiver side of the scales, the modern glittering feminine hygiene industry has undoubtedly been making its mark on the mental lode of attempting to enjoy cunnilingus, expert at pushing pink pretty products daily towards teenage girls in particular, with the message that our vulvas must be scrubbed with chemicals until they smell more akin to potpourri than pussy.

These companies know exactly what they're doing, adverts ringing with words and phrases like 'daily' and 'ultrafresh' and 'prevents odour' and 'protection' to hint just enough not to get sued that naturally our vulvas are stinking unfresh pieces of rotting ham.

One Vagisil product – Odor Block Daily Intimate Wash – claims 'triple odor protection', printed of course on to a cute pink girly background. Triple! How many fucking odours does our fanny need to hide? It comes in a range of scents including 'peach blossom', 'cucumber magnolia' and 'spring lilac'. Unfortunately it does not come in 'go fuck yourselves' scent.

---

* Amanda Chatel, https://www.yourtango.com/2017306232/horoscope-zodiac-signs-who-give-good-blowjobs

The companies never seem to actually use the words vulva or vagina on these products but refer to the 'intimate' areas, I imagine to avoid any possible legal repercussions to the impact that the daily use of chemicals might have if smeared over the vulva or, worse, up the self-cleaning magician known as the vagina. New slogan:

cleaning the vagina
is like cleaning the throat
– you don't

Obviously, there is no male hygiene section aimed at teenage boys' penises; no male equivalent to the 'Vagisil Ultra Fresh Intimate Powder for Daily Feminine Hygiene, Fresh Scent Deodorises & Prevents Odour'. Catchy.

No, there are no 'Dicksil Ultra Fresh Intimate Powder for Daily Masculine Hygiene, Fresh Scent Deodorises & Prevents Odour' or 'Intimate Pre-blow-job Lemon Everyday Knob Odour Triple Stink Block' wipes.

For the record, I don't want young penises preyed on too, I just want vulvas and vaginas not to be. I want the people running these companies to fuck off and leave our genitals alone and for everyone to use the one cleaning product that is best and free and won't fuck up our delicate bacterial balances: water.

As well as all the absolute unnecessary and harmful aspects of these products, licking a perfumed body tastes like shit. Or rather, like licking a deodorised armpit. I've done it; I can vouch for that.

intimate wipes

my vulva does not need to smell
of summer scented chemicals

blossom will not turn to fruit
in soil sick with pesticides

besides, anyone that close to me
tongue between my thighs

is there to taste a woman
not a washing line

Since discussing this particular house party more recently with friends, there were a few proposed reasons why oral sex was such a lopsided party game during those younger years:

1. The boys didn't give a shit about the girls' pleasure.
In my optimistic life outlook, I don't believe this to be true.

2. The girls didn't want it.
OR maybe they did but didn't feel like they could ask for it, because they'd not heard of it or because we'd possibly be called a slut if we did or because we were taught to be disgusted by our own bodies so much, especially our vulvas, and assumed that being licked there would be too disgusting for anyone to contemplate and therefore were entirely uncomfortable asking for it or enjoying if it was done, even if it was a good technique. It's hard to relax into a lick while thinking *this must be so gross for you* or *I'm disgusting* or *am I a filthy slag now and is everyone going to hate me?* and so on.

3. The boys were too scared to do it because they didn't know how to. This, to me, seems most optimistically likely. Oral sex is the solo show of the sex world. It's you standing singing on stage to an audience of one person's genitals. You cannot show someone how to do it by doing it in front of them. You can point roughly, explain, describe,

make 'mmm' noises while they try and all that, if you know yourself what you like, which many of us didn't, but you can't show them and fuck knows confident sexual communication is not a massive part of young (or adult) education.

So unless you are a cat who can lick its own privates or Prince or one of the apparently many men who took online courses in self-fellatio techniques during the 2020 Covid lockdown, oral sex is the solo of single-partnered sex; perhaps one of the most vulnerable forms of sex for this reason. This is also what makes it exciting. You (probably) can't do it to yourself.

But instead of saying *umm I don't know how to do this*, thus exposing themselves to possible ridicule mid-house party, the boys instead made jokes about girls' vulvas being fucking gross and smelling rancid (despite not having had their face actually close enough to confirm this), jokes which the girls then internalised and so didn't ask to receive oral sex as much as they might have and so the boys never got any good at it and so on, thus creating a vicious spiral of shame and insults and shit cunnilingus.

When one of my friends first gave cunnilingus, he told me how on finding himself face to face with his girlfriend's 'vagina', he was totally shocked by all the 'other stuff', as he had been taught that girls had a vagina aka tunnel between their legs, and nothing else.

What I'm saying is that cunnilingus is more complicated than fellatio. Not practically – practically it's the difference between eating an ice pop or a passionfruit. But, socially, cunnilingus was made complicated as fuck, at least in the heterosexual world I knew.

4. The girls didn't enjoy it cos the boys were terrible at it anyway.
See above. All part of the same spiral. A spiral I even believe DJ Khaled to be a part of.

If you don't know what I'm referring to, check out the 2018 *Breakfast Club* radio interview with DJ Khaled. DJ Khaled is a very famous and talented musician and during this interview, sex was discussed; Khaled writes a lot of extremely popular sexy songs.

After referring to his partner as his queen it then turned out he was very anti-cunnilingus within his personal life, with his response to whether he gives cunnilingus a clear 'Nahhh. Never!' and a repeated 'I don't do that, I don't do that, I don't do that.'

When questioned by the interviewer Angela Yee as to whether this means he doesn't expect oral sex, the Earth flipped on its axis to abusive levels.

In his own words: 'It's different rules for men ... You gotta understand, we the king. There's some things that y'all might not wanna do, but it got to get done. I just can't do what you want me to do. I just can't.'

The interview went viral on social media, with many insults and jokes thrown at Khaled. I get that. He sounds like a selfish, pushy prick. No one should be forced to indulge in oral sex if they don't want to, including famous musicians, but the predatory nature of phrases like 'but it gotta get done' in terms of women giving oral sex to men whether they want to or not can obviously fuck right off.

Perhaps he is just a selfish bully, or maybe he's exactly the modern incarnation of centuries of 'real men don't lick pussy' mentality. Maybe he's worried he'll be shit. Maybe the ancient Greeks were worried they'd be shit and created five hundred years of sexual hierarchies just to avoid saying, 'Erm, so what do I do here?'

Either way, apart from the Outhere Brothers, then later the explosion of the rapper Khia into my life, oral sex wasn't really ever talked about positively unless, of course, it was sucking dick. Even then, the messages were really, really confused.

I bet you love sucking dick.

What a statement. I remember being asked, or rather told this on the one bus which took us all to the one nightclub – Venom – just outside our small town, then back to the centre of town most Thursday nights in my late teens.

I bet you love sucking dick.

I looked at the young gentleman who said this to me. He did that half-nod thing boys do trying to be cool and hard while still, I imagine, dreaming of suckling at the comfort of a mother's milky breast and not having to fight to prove something about having a penis.

He repeated: *I bet you love sucking dick* as if I maybe hadn't heard the statement and was needing it repeated.

Was this an insult? A chat-up line? A threat? A genuine enquiry about whether I enjoy the delights of fellatio with a hint of a guess at the answer? A combination of all four? Do you even know what the fuck *you* mean? Do you actually want to know my response?

Well, young man, thank you for enquiring. How long have you got?

Let me begin by saying what an interesting statement that is. I do, as you suggest, sometimes enjoy indulging in the art of fellatio. I'm not so keen on doing it with a stranger who smells fairly pungently of Jägermeister shots, vomit and nightclub fag ends, but I do like it sometimes with my lover in the morning if I'm not desperate for a wee. Some days, I just don't fancy it at all and others it's the most exciting thing I can imagine doing with my Sunday afternoon off. I especially love when the sun is streaming through the window and the clean and eager body is all sleepy and warm from the sunlight and we can really take our time. I do like the feeling of being in control – it's rather invigorating isn't it, knowing you can please someone in a way they can't do to their own body? And you, sorry, how rude of me not to ask, do you – you didn't tell me your name – do you enjoy indulging in a little cunnilingus after a night out with your gentlemen friends, taking the labia slowly between your teeth like nibbling on a delicate piece of halloumi until the clitoris sings ready for your well-trained tongue? Do you love the pleasuring of the pussy? Do you really fucking love giving cunnilingus? Anytime? Anywhere? Every day? With anyone? I fucking bet you do, don't you?

I revisited these sorts of stupid conversations I was involved with or overheard about girls giving fellatio in my teens and twenties and flipped them just to hear what they would sound like if they were about boys giving cunnilingus to girls instead.

After a house party, age sixteen:

Oh my god, did you hear that three of the girls were queuing up last night at the party to get cunny off Max?

Oh my god, what a slag he is.

Yeah, he loves giving head. Apparently, he licked them all out one by one in the spare room.

Oh my god? Mandy got her pussy licked too? I thought she was really shy?

Well, dunno, apparently. I mean no one's gonna turn down a pussy licking. Not even Mandy!

Yeah. True. Can you believe, though, he asked one of them to give him a blow job afterwards?

Really? Gross. Did they do it?

No! Said his dick stank of onion.

Oh god, gross. I'd never let anyone suck my dick.

Me either. It's so weird.

After a night out at the local pub, age twenty:

Did you hear that Gary gave Marion a cunni at the back of the pub last night?

Seriously, where?

In the alley.

Oh my god, I thought they were gone a while!

Yeah, apparently, she said he'd made her clit all hard and wet and he needed to sort her out before she could come back in again cos she couldn't sit on the bar stool straight.

Did she do him?

No!

Tossed across the field like a strange insult, aged fifteen:

Do you wanna go on a date, Mike?

Erm, no thanks, Emma, I'm not really after any relationship right now.

Whatever! Well you're a pussy-licking slag anyway, I wouldn't wanna go near your mouth. I heard you've licked half the school's pussies. I heard your dad loves licking pussy too. Doesn't he? Your dad? Loves licking pussy? I bet your dad's a pussy-licker like you.

It wasn't until I was in my mid-twenties did I ever think that there was another, more nuanced response to the drunken bus statement/question: *I bet you love sucking dick.* Not once did I consider that this wasn't a question that required a yes or no answer. Or an answer at all, but I didn't see that as an option at the time. Also, silence was so often met with further cajoling that it didn't always seem safe not to answer guys. It still doesn't.

But oral sex is not Marmite. It's not a yes or no thing. Even Marmite isn't a yes or no thing for me. I sometimes quite like it with Cheddar at night, but not really on its own on toast in the morning. I like it thinly spread, but not if there are thick glugs of it.

Perhaps there should be a helpline for young people. An office full of staff trained and ready to respond to questions they were too shy or ignorant to reply to in earlier years:

Call 1: Katy wants to know what to say to a boy in her class who's just called her a dirty slag cos she admitted she masturbates.

Call 2: Brad doesn't have a clue how to give cunnilingus and Catherine's just called him a selfish jerk cos she's just gone down on him and he panicked cos he doesn't know how to so he said he found the thought of it gross.

Call 3: Juliet's on a night bus and Pete's just asked her if she loves sucking dick and she's not quite sure what the point of the question is.

It's not likely to get given charitable status anytime soon, but I could've done with it a few times.

age appropriate

typing blow job into pornhub is a roulette wheel;
anything is possible, the worst people are waiting
the kids in the playground make choking noises
gagging on mimicked dicks; oral sex reduced
to retching on penises before they've even kissed;
in my inbox, a letter from the school asks whether parents
think it's ok to teach the word vulva in the classroom;
in the park, children on their phones dare each other
to type porn in, pop-up photographs of women
you can hire, watch teenagers watch age unknown
watch rape upload watch anal ruptures on the increase
from pressure to mimic screens, watch men over twenty
father over one fifth of the babies birthed by mums aged
ten, eleven, twelve and thirteen; in my inbox
a letter from the school asks whether parents think it's ok
to teach the word vulva in the classroom, statistics rise
of first sex strangulation, in the blow jobs comments section
he says she'll probably just do it, don't worry
most girls are too shy or embarrassed to say no,
in my inbox from the school a response suggests waiting
till the children are eleven to teach the word vulva
some of the parents have complained

house party memories: high five

afterwards, the boys came skipping down the stairs, high fiving one another as if they'd just won at the pools, which in a way they had; her lips, they'd won around their skin, her tongue around the tips, the work she had to put in to make each of them enjoy it, and for a while they'd offered something in return; compliments, attention, admiration, some kisses on the neck in the living room, sighs of thankful pleasure, god it feels so good to give to other people, to be wanted for a moment, what a tonic to the blood; and so they came, skipping down the stairs, high fiving one another, some hard pats on the back, *nice ones* and *well dones* and *not bad, mate, not bad.* not one of them returned the favour, laughed it off when asked, as if disgusted by the thought, joked how pussy smelt of fish, implied uncleanliness, how they weren't getting their tongues close, and everybody laughed and we, the girls whose mouths their dicks had not just been inside nodded heads in unison, laughing at the insult, insulting our own skin, ready at that moment to never ask for any boy to go down on us again; looking back, likely none of them, those boys, all blow job loved and awkward brags, dicks now shrunk in winning smiles, likely none of them knew how to – lick a pussy, please a girl, locate the clit, nibble labia and nipple, ask what she would like, make her feel it was ok, dampen patterns in her skin the way she dampened them in theirs; insulted her instead; or perhaps just selfish pricks – i like to think the best of them; the boys, my friends, who i watched skipping down the stairs, who left her sitting on her own, as they would have left me too, as they would have left us all, waiting in the bedroom, throat swallowing their pride, high fiving one another as they waltzed into the kitchen where we waited for the gossip, muttered slag beneath our breath as well – at her, and at ourselves, mimicking the boyspeak;

perhaps we were jealous, i was jealous i am sure, though of what i'm still not certain; the attention, my empty mouth, desperate to please them and we laughed again and flirted, slagging off our stinking pussies and our friends; upstairs, she waited for a while, before plucking up the courage, god how much courage we girls needed, to come out of the bedroom, to tiptoe down the stairs into the staring, frowning crowd, palms tucked firmly in our pockets as we watched.

house party memories: high five: a re-imagining

this time we would be ready, lined up, palms open as a starfish as she steps from the bedroom, the scent of their semen still glistening on her lips like an oyster champagne breakfast; the boys, stepping aside, thank her once again, hug her gently, reassure her of their intentions, fingers massaging her jaw like circles in a turquoise pool of water around a fountain where shining copper coins are thrown by children making wishes beneath a mermaid made of marble whose nipples spill water-falls upon the warm and waiting water; she looks gorgeous, blushing, hair tied back in a ballerina bun, lips lit up like fire-flies, grin as wide as wings; smiling as she passes us, each one of us high fiving her like a slow motion love scene of reunited friends, our own bellies full of questions, excitement, the boys behind her in a line as if holding up her train, whispering apologies like prayers, begging her please let them try to try to please her, return the fragrant favour; *later*, she laughs, just let us dance now, and so we dance now, young legs and arms and heartbeats moving to the music, spinning round our handbags like stars around the cosmos as we chat over details and she giggles sweet giggles into the air of new experience and the record and the earth keep turning as we twerk until those boys, disappearing up the stairs, back into the bedroom, prepare for her return, shout nervously downstairs for another half an hour just to read once more the chapter from the bible of the body on how best to tease, with their yearning, learning lips, the mango flesh gently from the stone.

cover girl

in the girls' magazines, a sketched silhouette of lovers
looks awkward; reverse cowgirl rodeo, we studied,

stared, took notes like the diligent worriers we were.
him always inside her – tick – her fingers reaching down

into her own portrait flesh; explanations excitedly
declaring sex positions good for us

to get ourselves off simultaneous to pleasing him
leaning back might help, try to touch yourself as well

as if multi-tasking were the only way for us to cum
without making too much fuss about our lives

our own uncurriculumed clitorises waving frantic
from the layby, occasionally seen by passing traffic

every movie shows us all cumming together
one big happy family

meanwhile, fashion pages informed us what fruits we were,
what best to wear for apples, pears and fat slags, vomit at

our knee sag; begin skin routines at seven, comb eyebrows
and eyelashes; make face masks from unrequited cum

become a minus; replace school dinners with heroin
chic adverts filled with awkward anorexic adolescents

paid by adults to hold handbags looking 'fabulous' and 'sexy'
in lace underwear at seventeen they'd never buy themselves

we studied how to bag a boy; how to bag a man;
how to turn him on, how to gloss our lips; how to give

a twizzler blow job; how to let him know you like it;
how to moan when touched; how to act excited;

how not to knock his confidence
each time you do not cum

i practised on tennis racket handles,
played air penis in my bedroom

mouth open muscle ready for the jaw cramps
how to keep moaning with a mouth full of under-confidence

how to hold back our necks in case the penis made us gag
as if gagging were non-negotiable;

no one told us it was meant to be enjoyable
no one told us cunnilingus or consent

at school desks i prepared for the future,
staring between textbooks and the clocks;

skirts so short i distracted my own mind;
algebra and thigh gap on my mind,

trigonometry twizzler blow jobs on my mind
frantic cowgirl desperately rides below full moon

cowboy hat balanced on my busting throbbing head
trying desperate to remember all my lessons

all the top ten tips to flawless skin, top ten blow job tips
top ten sex positions, top ten ways to starve yourself

whilst giggling in shoes that cut your ankle bones
each time you simply tried to dance

whilst screaming do you love me?
do i look good? is my hair right?

am i pregnant? does my skin glow?
am i stinking? should i diet?

do you like it do you like it? yes i like it yes i like it
every magazine now read,

lips glossed and pout perfected
three years of research done

he pushed one finger inside me; asked me if i'd cum.
i nodded, moaned correctly, didn't want to hurt him;

wondered why my body wasn't working
why my body was so shit;

in the boys' magazines
there was football or tits

CUNNILINCTORS AND THE
QUIVERING KISS

after cunnilingus

so much mess around your mouth
you wiped a full arm swipe
across your lips, overly dramatic
tongue grabbing final licks of me
like children clearing pudding bowls,
brimful with ice cream

Art positively depicting oral sex has been found all over the world within a myriad of ancient cultures over thousands of years, from ancient Egypt to the murals of cunnilingus and fellatio uncovered but hidden from public view on the walls of Pompeii to, perhaps most famously, the very detailed instructions of oral sex techniques I have read, re-read and re-read within the Kama Sutra.

When I first bought the Kama Sutra, I thought I was going to uncover the most soul-enhancing freeing erotic texts I'd ever known. It was disappointingly tedious in places, with more instructions on marriage and musical instrument serenades and so much more judgement on the differences between married women, promiscuous women, loose women than I had ignorantly imagined.

That said, compared to the sort of either dull or violent language used to describe oral sex I was accustomed to in my teens – blow job, sucking dick, pussy licking and the atrocious skull fucking, almost traumatising to hear when you're a teenager just learning about your own pleasure – compared to all of that, the vocabulary was beautiful.

My favourite words relating to oral sex in the Kama Sutra are *Adhara-sphuritam* and *Amrachushita*. *Adhara-sphuritam* (the Quivering Kiss) describes a way in which the labia can be lightly pinched together and kissed as if kissing a lower lip of the mouth. This is just one of many ideas described in a lengthy step-by-step cunnilingus description. *Amrachushita* (Sucking a Mango) is used to describe a near-final stage of fellatio as stripping clean a mango stone.

I've read that a lot of the references in ancient biblical texts, mimicking the poetry of the time, to eating pomegranate seeds, or watching pomegranates on trees sweeten and so on, are alleged to be about giving and enjoying cunnilingus.

What poetry there could be in oral sex. How did we evolve into a culture that shames any teachings of actual passion or technique and devouring mangoes slowly as they melt in your mouth, yet normalises and in many ways aids a culture in which seventeen-year-old me is told I like sucking dick as some sort of half-threat half-terrible intimidating chat-up line by a stranger at the back of a bus and then called a fucking slag if I answer either yes or no or ignore him?

There is an excellent slang dictionary by Jonathon Green that charts the long and varied history of terms for oral sex acts, my favourite so far being: dickylicker, eating the seafood and cunnilingus, from the Latin *cunnus* – vulva/cunt – and *lingere* – lick – which as a word runs off the tongue pretty rhythmically.

Fellatio is similarly practical, deriving again from the Latin, *fellare* – to suck. I really love the sound of the word fellatio, like the name that a messenger might have in a Shakespearean tragedy – *What message do you bring, dear Fellatio?* That, or a really sweet and very buttery layered pastry.

The normalisation of cunnilingus in mainstream British films,

282

TV, pop music, is now making things a little more equal in hetero-sexual relationships, though it does sometimes seem that after years of depicting straight women coming in three seconds from three thrusts of a penis, we're now depicting straight women coming in two seconds from two licks of a vulva before the clitoris is even warmed up. The idea that cunnilingus is foreplay and therefore doesn't need foreplay is as unhelpful as the word foreplay itself.

quick scribble

rubbing the clitoris before it's aroused
and believing that's her done
is like waggling a penis when it's floppy and limp
and expecting him to cum

Discovering the word cunnilinctor has made all of the reading about oral-sex shaming and censorship worth it for me.

I'll say that word again – cunnilinctors. It means people who give cunnilingus, from the Latin for 'cunt-lickers', literally, though 'cunt-licker' sounds really rude now, whereas it sounds much more like an official job title or a new Transformer when said in Latin. I really just wrote that sentence above so I could use this word.

There's so much historical shaming, oral sex shaming, cunnilingus shaming. So much 'I don't know what I'm doing' shaming. So much giving and taking shaming. So much vulva shaming and clitoris shaming. So much penis too small or penis too big shaming. Such a long, long timeline that led to those boys' outbursts at that teenage house party. But at least I now know that the word cunnilinctor exists and that many people, not only Keith, are avid members of the cunnilinctor fan club.

Maybe the really incredible thing is how any one of us, in the face of so much opposing power, so many centuries of shaming and lawmaking, so many religious and political leaders citing so, so many stories to discourage us from enjoying our own bodies, so many awful depictions of sex and passion and pleasure in a media directed for years so often by these sorts of predatory men, now in prison, or dead, that despite all of this, maybe it's incredible that humans have still, in patches of flickering sunshine, managed to find sweet and harmless song in each other's skin.

Perhaps every harmless orgasm should be heralded as a success. Every sensual oral sex session. Mind and mouths and bodies united in friendship; like flowers growing tirelessly through the depths of demolition, somehow surviving, blooming despite all the odds, a battle cry, or rather a peace flag; let your cries of pleasure ring out like bells of hope; no, we are not listening any more, you are not having our bodies any more, we have made it through the swamps of shame and yes, we are still coming.

Perhaps this is the people's greatest achievement against the powers that be. Other than inventing the word cunnilinctor.

fellatio fellatio fellatio

sounds songbird *fellatio fellatio*

whispers of a kiss in snow
slush melting   mountain waterfalls
swallows sleeping soaring
a breeze beckons   wings gently open

fellatio draws back the morning curtain carefully
pushes toes below sun-scorched sands
till wet and cool

a feather lands
floats easy on a puddle

is not asked for angrily on buses
back from nightclubs, sweaty-dicked
and dribbling, *fellatio*

is given after bubble baths,
bath-bombs effervescing beneath balls
towel dried, laid out on silken bedclothes
served proud on gilded trays

a feast; spoonfed and relished
both guest and chef content

layers of *fellatio* beneath the cloche cloche
delicately buttered by pâtissiers
down song-warmed cobbled streets

fellatio is coming, they would cry
if an emperor, ancient, kind to his people
crowds smile, line the pavements

cherry trees toss confetti blossom as he waves
fellatio fellatio they chant,
smiling crying fainting

and when they dance, how they dance
the *fellatio,* a light-footed dance
partners swung across like laughter

till satisfied and sleepy, *fellatio*
is mixed with honey
is melted into camomile at bedtime

turns grown men into babies once again
fellatio he whispers *fellatio* you reply

lips heated on the radiator
genitals humming lullabies
snuggle into yawning skin

say *fellatio* three times
and all your sins will be forgiven
fellatio, fellatio, soft and hard and hot

awakens in the morning
sun warm across your flesh
is alive; dreaming; is the opposite of death

how to prepare rosehip syrup

once the first frost has thawed, close the curtains,
remove the battery from the back of every clock
lay a fleece across a sun patch to warm until golden
remove her clothing as if peeling back the layers of an onion
so that her skin may make you weep,
let your lips baste her newly naked body
oils upon your fingertips, canvas coloured in with kisses
syrup comes only once the rosehip bush has bloomed,
hold her hands in your hands
so she may trust enough to let her eyelids anchor
lay her gently on the blanket, pour a tea, let her drink it,
dip your fingers into music, and strum
the undulating surface of her sighs until all her limbs loosen
until her breath churns ocean
until her knees, fallen open like mangoes ripened slowly
eased messy with their sweetness, and her heartbeat,
quickening beneath the pulsing of your selfless thirst
ripples from your fingers like pebbles on the lake of her
set spirals in her skin until, rosehip hard and ready
a final kiss upon each nipple, you kneel at last between her knees
to lean in, and begin

but in heaven, they fed each other

watch me eat this banana
i'll watch you eat that fig

watch me lick the bitter sweet
from inside this lemon tart
i will watch you tongue the jam
from the jammy dodger's heart

put on young fathers, let us dance
while the singing kettle heats
then watch me dip this double twix
into that warming mug of tea

strip the chocolate from the biscuit
let the softened toffee melt
until its once solid foundations
collapse inside my mouth

then i will watch you curl
your muscled tongue
inside that purple shell
till all the pips of the passionfruit
are lovingly licked out

things that remind me of the sixty-niner

holding hands on a trampoline
with a best friend who bounces just a bit too
high

cream eclair stuffed into mouth as
the waiter comes to
ask if you'd like another wine

a train ride down the coastline, window
besmattered by a seagull
as the sea comes into sight

chew your favourite garlic sausage
blindfold and hand tied,

lozenge almost rhymes with orange,
but not quite,

distracted by the trapdoor
actor struggles with her lines,

can you scuba dive
and
masturbate
at the same time?

once your legs are in the air,
no matter how you try
the seesaw   always   picks a side

MAKING LASAGNE

One rainy Sunday afternoon I found myself lost among Catholic sex problem pages. Not a normal hobby of mine. I had been googling 'how to receive cunnilingus' and stumbled upon them.

I know how physically to receive cunnilingus. Mentally, I was finding it tricky to let it happen without offering to help somehow or make him a coffee or say thank you continuously because I was ever so grateful, or checking for the fiftieth time if he was definitely OK and not finding it too disgusting. This, despite his constant, caring confirmations otherwise.

Even with the support of the Outhere Brothers, there are only so many times you can see fem fresh wipes shout: *your pussy is a stinky bitch*, or your heterosexual sex education yell: *just get to the 'real' sex* or the two-second film orgasm nudge you into believing: *you're asking too much of him, you're taking ages, when are you gonna cum already?* as if pleasure were a sprint race, your own brain standing on the sideline with a stopwatch.

Our bodies must get really sick of our minds being such killjoys all the time. If only I could have the mind of a cat for just one day, laying itself confidently over a companion's lap and just taking two hours of stroking with not even a hint of any guilt; minus the murdering mice bit.

So I was literally googling how to receive oral sex. I then googled the average length of time for a female reaching orgasm, just to check once more that I definitely *definitely* wasn't abnormal not cumming as soon as I felt a tongue or finger or penis touch my skin.

Ian Kerner's book *She Comes First* has a great section on the ticktock of pleasure:

> Few, if any, of the world's problems can be solved with a mere twenty minutes of attention, and yet here, in the complex socio-political landscape of the bedroom, we have an opportunity to create bilateral satisfaction. When put that way, in the context of sexual peace and equality, is twenty minutes of focused attention, applied appropriately, really too much to ask, especially if it can save your sex life?

Twenty minutes. The idea that this is a long time to ask to be pleasured for is ludicrous. Less time than an episode of *EastEnders*.

Sadly, scouring the internet, there is a whole lot of demand for 'how to receive cunnilingus' articles out there.

There are fewer articles about the guilt of getting your penis licked for long enough, though I do know those worries exist.

Despite the 'imagine a guy worrying about that' comments among girl friends, they do. Some guys have a whole lot of insecurities about this stuff; about giving, as well as receiving oral sex, about people seeing their penises, about the taste, about staying hard, as well as about not wanting to ask for oral sex because they think it might seem demeaning, because well, in our current culture, fellatio is mainly portrayed both in porn and unfortunately kid-reaching pop songs and therefore classroom conversations, as little more than gagging on a dick.

Some experienced adults like this and all good if genuinely consensual but I'd say the vast majority of fellatio givers are not into the head-pushing vomit on a cock. If you don't love gagging, yes, you can still love oral sex.

The main gist of the articles about how to accept cunnilingus were:

- Your vulva does not stink. Clean gently with water.
- If it does actually smell strongly or abnormal, see a doctor.
- You deserve to feel good too.
- The time for women to cum depends on the woman and the day and the mood but most studies suggest an average of ten minutes of focused attention on the right areas after a good build-up for the clitoris to puff up.
- Know your body. Trust it, not TV. If it feels nice, it feels nice.
- Anyone with their face in your pussy loves having their face in your pussy.

This last one was the most difficult to believe.

It would be lovely if it were true and it really should be true that if someone's doing something sexual it's because they want to, but when people tell me 'if he didn't like it, he wouldn't be doing it', it doesn't prove the point to me at all.

All my life women around me have been complaining about giving blow jobs while still giving them; female comedians doing sketches about how much they hate doing it, how all women hate it (untrue) while still implying they are giving them; conversations about how annoying it is when you're on your period and he thinks it's blow-job week, one friend complaining that she had to go cos it was 'blow-job Sunday'.

Looking back, there were so many jokes in my childhood and youth about wives who didn't enjoy sex more generally but were still doing it. The idea of the wife having 'another headache' was so constant and mainstream it was even used in adverts for household cleaner. If women have so much sex they're not wanting to have that it becomes almost a national joke, then men giving cunnilingus could be exactly the same, I thought. So no, that last one unfortunately didn't help.

another headache, is it?

the comedians on the tv
joked of headaches once again
and all the married women
laughed, and the husbands
nudged one another and i sat,
cross-legged on the rug,
not getting the jokes,
wondering why we couldn't
just say no

After an hour or so searching 'I love cunnilingus why can't I just enjoy it', I stumbled upon a letter from Karen (named changed so God doesn't find her). Karen was Catholic, married, and had written quite a desperate letter to a Catholic sex problem page.

It appeared that Karen enjoyed oral sex with her husband but wasn't sure if she was also allowed to 'see the light' through cunnilingus, by which she meant orgasm, I assume. She was concerned that she might go to hell for this, which I imagine, if you believe in hell, is pretty daunting, so she wanted to make sure it was OK. She repeated how much she would really love to 'see the light' as well, explaining that Nigel (invented name for Karen's husband) always 'sees the light' when they have sex.

Of course he does. He has to. Apart from the no sexual activity before marriage rule – yes, that includes anal – the most important rule of Catholic sex is that it must always be 'open to life', which means that any sexual activity must result, to be blunt, in your husband cumming in your contraception-free vagina. Basically, the guy has to cum. Lucky fucking Nigel.

So while Nigel is loving Catholic life, 'seeing the light' inside his wife's warm, wet vagina every single time they make love, Karen is weeping into the problem pages with the fear of hell at her back.

'Of course,' she reiterates to whoever is replying to these letters, she would only 'see the light' as part of the journey to her husband 'seeing the light', she would never just 'see the light' on her own. Is that OK with God?

After this very long and quite desperate letter, the Catholic sex agony uncle replied:

No, it isn't.

A short further explanation ensued.

Nigel *must* 'see the light' for the sex to be 'open to life', but for Karen to 'see the light' would be purely for pleasure and has no role in baby making and is therefore sinful. So, no, Karen, you cannot orgasm because your orgasm has no reproductive purpose. Nigel, go ahead and orgasm all day long, spread your holy male cum. No, not alone. No, not in your sleep. No, not on her tits. Just in the vag, Nigel, get it in the vag and you're all good with God.

Perhaps these folk writing lamenting letters might take some advice from the short-nosed fruit bat or Indian flying fox, both bat species, which according to *National Geographic* regularly engage in fellatio and cunnilingus, mainly, it appears, to prolong the amount of time they can engage in penetrative sex.

With the short-nosed fruit bat, there is an idea that the oral sex is used to ease entry, and transport the sperm better because of the increased secretions from the female – all conducive to fertilisation.

In humans too, though we tend to ignore it on every biology sylla-bus in schools, vulval and vaginal juices help sperm travel faster and more easily up the vaginal canal. Like those water squirts at the top of the flumes at Swindon Oasis (or whatever your local waterpark is). Imagine how much slower it'd be if those flumes were dry. Imagine the flume burn on your arse. So female pleasure does have a role in reproduction, albeit not as essential as Nigel's.

I ended up spending weeks reading these Catholic sex problem pages as if they were a bedtime story. If I thought my relationship with cunnilingus had been made unnecessarily complicated by society, I had nothing on Karen.

Finally, I came across a cunnilingus-friendly Catholic minister. *Karen! Over here, come read! It's OK! Tell Nigel!* I wish I had saved Karen's page and could have contacted her.

This minister responded to another woman, also wondering if her own orgasms were allowed, by saying that the Catholic Church welcomes healthy sexual relationships in marriage and that pleasure between husband and wife is all cool, really good, God loves it, absolutely A-okay we want you to praise each other, so long as (let's sing it together) it *always ends with your husband jizzing inside your pussy.* It wasn't worded like that, but that's what it said. Open to life.

In this minister's view, one which I imagine elated a number of Catholic wives, a wife could be pleasured and orgasm with her husband as many times as the Bible has pages, with God's uttermost blessing, because there's no life spilled from a throbbing, shaking vagina, so long as it is all still in the name of that final intercourse cum fest.

In this respect, cunnilingus is drastically more acceptable than fellatio because, with fellatio, there is a much higher possibility of a husband spilling his life seed accidentally into his wife's mouth or over her stomach rushing en route to the holy vagina, thus throwing his possible future Catholic children to certain 'anti-life' in her stomach acid. Poor Karen, I thought, if only she'd written to this minister she'd be 'seeing the light' all over the shop:

Oh Nigel, I'm cumming.

Good, my love, but are you still thinking about my hard cock inside you?

Yes. of course!

OK, cool, continue then.

I was pretty sure I had mastered the art of holy Catholic sex when a complication came into my mind.

What if you're having what you think is open-to-life cunnilingus and Bryan (new married couple name) is licking you in all the heavenly ways and then you orgasm and he, so excited by the way you shouted his name as you did so, cums right there and then, accidentally, on your right thigh, your vagina now empty of possibility?

Obviously, Bryan has sinned, but does that mean that your cunnilingus orgasm, holy two seconds ago, is now also a sin, your pleasure posthumously descended to the furnace?

And is that going to worry you while he's licking? Are you gonna be thinking the whole time, *you better not cum before you get there, Bryan.*

And what if he does it on purpose just to fuck you up in the afterlife cos he hates the way you've started loading the plates in the dishwasher the wrong way? Is there a Catholic equivalent to stealthing, doing the opposite of secretly removing a condom (yes, this counts as rape despite its catchy label) and instead slipping a condom on during sex without your partner seeing, thus making the sex anti-God because he really wants to shag but really doesn't want a sixth child?

My mind was running.

What if you're getting the cunnilingus and thinking of putting his hard penis inside you, all open to life and lovely, and then your neighbour knocks on the door and you have to stop because she has dementia and you're a good Christian, I mean person. Can you carry that cunnilingus over to the next penetrative ejaculation or has your neighbour, by calling mid-lick because she's lost her keys, just damned your pleasure again?

And what about wet dreams? What if your partner loses their erection because of a cold or a sudden worry about his ill mother but you've already orgasmed on your way to the dick? What about having sex when you know you're not ovulating, because we have all these apps now? What about having sex on your period when the chance of pregnancy is at its lowest? What if one of the partners is infertile? Is sex not OK any more if every sexual activity has to be open to life and you know you can't conceive? And what about after the menopause? Do Catholic couples have to stop sex altogether when menstruation stops? Are they allowed to buy Viagra?

Also, what counts as sexual? Like, if all sexual activity must be open to life, ending in possible procreation, how far do you have to take that?

Is a bit of fingering while watching *Succession* OK, or does everything have to end in intercourse? In which case, how do Catholics define sexual?

Personally, I find making lasagne really sexual, layering the pasta and thinking of the way it's going to wetten softly into the melting cheese as the oven gets hot. Sometimes it's as sexual as fingering. I recently read Audre Lorde's essay on the erotic, passed over to me by a brilliant friend and writer Gemma Cairney. It opened up my eyes to all the aspects of life I find erotic, sensual, sexual that are in no way limited to 'the bedroom'.

I'd be in trouble if I were Catholic, calling my husband to quickly come and penetrate me every time I brushed my hair slowly or wrote a poem about the feel of the sun on my back, or poured the final layer of hot garlicky tomato sauce on the pasta sheet and waited for it to bubble up in the oven.

If every sexual activity has to be open to life, I'd possibly have to try for a baby after every lasagne I ever made.

As I reached the end of the cunnilingus-friendly minister's response, I hit another hurdle. Having thought we'd reached agreement, he caveated: but even if all sexual activity does lead to intercourse, it's *not* OK if that activity satiates the couple so much that intercourse is simply a 'final release'.

Basically, if the other sexual activity is too good, or feels better than the actual intercourse, you're still not all right, because that's turning oral stimulation, which is OK, into oral sex, which is not OK.

Stimulating the genitals, fine, but not too well, because if it got so good that it became sex in itself, oral sex, then no, that's too much, and the penetration-only God will weep at being second place and send you to hell again. So yes, you can have oral sex, but you can never, not even for a moment, prefer the cunnilingus to the penetration. I'm thinking that might be tricky for a hell of a lot of women.

four-page poem about friends which is probably too long if you're anything like me because i often skip the poems in poetry books that are longer than a page but i didn't edit this down because my friends have done so much for me

when i was scared of starting school,when the gates loomed
far too large; you took my hand in yours, my friend,
skipped me to the swings till i was certain we could fly

when sad on the sideline, you passed me every ball
when pushed in the canteen, when tripped in the hall
when the crush was just a bitter joke,
when i did not want to go alone to buy myself a bra

when blood came unexpectedly and we had no bloody clue
there you were, tampons-ready, counsellor of the cubicles
tiptoeing next door's toilet lid, whispers through the wall
encouraging me on like some menstruation football coach

aim towards your backbone   take it out and try again
one leg up on the lid you shouldn't feel it when it's in
without your words of wisdom, what would i have done?
when the outfits *did* look shit on and i want the bloody truth

or, panicked in the changing rooms, the dress a size too small
jammed around my shoulder blades, straightjacket stuck,
tugging fabric just enough to sprint out of the shop
before anybody sees how quick our stitches rip apart

when our bonfire scrapyard hearts need the dark to dance
douse stinging flames with stamping feet, you are lipstick-
pouted-ready friends to strut-red-carpet-pavements friends;
when all we need are ears to vent, silent-lack-of-judgment-friends

when stars are muddled guidance, constellations lost in light
when our hearts are hung to dry when all hope is out of sight
when foundation is not correctly rubbed into our jawlines;
face and neck a different colour; skirt tucked into knickers;

toilet paper stuck to shoe –
when we are smiling unaware of spinach in our teeth
there you always are, my friends
you gorgeous fucking beasts

in each downpour in each downpour
stumbling drunk against the slanting pain,
you band of bloody brothers!
hyenas shrieking chatter to brighten waning moons

when the blue line doesn't come
when a blue line comes too soon
when we miscarry again
when smears are inconclusive

when bruises can't be hidden
and we beg a space of refuge
when stitches still not healed
when divorces still not willing

when thrush when cystitis
when years of ivf
when pregnancy when birth
when recovery when prolapse

when mothering when mourning
when babies do not sleep
when we are desperate for a coffee

praying for some peace

an hour from our chores
without crumpling in guilt
body bloody shipwrecks searching island sands
to moor onto in storms that start at midnight;

when we need someone to call
before starlight drags our flailing minds
back gasping to the shore, there you are, my friends,
kettle clicked, already on,

umbrellas clutched in palm
to shelter one another from those
constant
thrashing   hailstones

and no, we're not offered any gemstones
nor showered in confetti
but who needs a diamond ring
to prove how sweet this love can be

you are everything i ever need
except for cunnilingus
the greatest love of all
is surely that of friendship

so if you ever need a shoulder
mine are very, very sexy
(it was you who told me that)
so lean in any time

we can chat until the moon
skinny dips back to the dawn
problems sunrise-warmed –
i've all the biscuits in the world

and if you ever need a lifeboat
i've a thousand in my pockets
to pass below the cubicles
anytime blood comes with unexpected tales

and if you ever need a hand to hold
to walk through unknown gates
chances are, i do as well

A COMIC BOOK WORKSHOP
CHANGED MY LIFE

I was performing at Cheltenham Literature Festival. This is one of the gigs my whole family often come to; for my mum, because she's really interested in loads of the talks, and also the green room has really good free food and coffee and wine all day. For my dad, it's mainly the green room and the chat and the free cakes. He can give or take the talks. He likes to remind me of this, scones in his pockets, as we leave.

Part of the deal performing at Cheltenham is that I get up to ten free tickets to other events. The morning of my gig, I booked my kid and me into a comic book workshop aimed at eight- to ten-year-olds. It changed my sex life forever, though I don't think that was the aim of the workshop.

It was run by Neill Cameron and was called 'How to Make Awesome Comics', the name of the book he had just written to help kids design their own comics. It's a great book. We all went in, adults looking a bit awkward as we too were dished out pens and paper.

Neill stood at the front, sketching an amazing dinosaur on a pen board. He started explaining his theory of awesomeness. According to his brilliant comic, the best way to make an awesome character is to take one thing that is awesome and add another thing that is awesome and together they will make something that is totally super awesome.

The kids were into it. Me too.

For example: mermaids are awesome and robots are awesome so a robot mermaid will be totally super awesome. *Fuck*, I thought, *Neill is right*. I do believe a mermaid robot *would* be totally super awesome.

We were told to get a few ideas down and we all started scribbling. It's so nice to draw. I never draw. I forgot how fun it is. At first, I was totally on track with the exercise. I think monkeys are awesome. I think butterflies are awesome. And yes, a monkey butterfly would be totally super awesome.

A ninja and a hummingbird. An octopus and a ballerina. Cunnilingus and a head massage. *No, Hollie, concentrate.* A pirate and a whale. A foot massage and eating Quavers. *Stop it!* A dinosaur and a space rocket. Cunnilingus and Quavers and my favourite song by B.Miles playing in my headphones.

I was gone.

Masturbating is awesome, I thought. *Getting my feet massaged is awesome.* A masturbation foot massage. *Super awesome.* Cunnilingus is awesome. Watching the sunset is awesome. The scent of jasmine in spring is awesome. A back rub is awesome. Kissing and roller skating. Shampooing my hair and fellatio. Spooning and strawberries.

For the rest of the workshop, my mind wandered more and more. As I sketched monkeys in scuba diving gear and triceratops on roller skates, which I also did think was awesome, my head buzzed with the myriad of possible sensual and sexual combinations of awesomes plus awesomes plus awesomes that I had never tried in my life. The mathematics of pleasure was multiplying by the minute. There was so much I hadn't tried.

I stared at the roller-skating butterfly on the page in front of me. *This is all meant to be fun*, I thought. Like *all* of it. Actual fun. Your body. Touching. Sex. The tastes and smells and sounds and feelings that you can combine with all of that. All of it. All of sex. It should just be fun and pleasurable and relaxed and totally super awesome. That's the whole point. That's the only fucking point.

Like robot unicorns who eat cupcakes sort of awesome.

Like pterodactyl ducks who scuba dive awesome.

By the end of the session, I had invented a very cool comic story with a character who was a frog who rode on a flying canoe to collect clouds and had made a new life plan of awesomes plus awesomes: full body massages while gazing at the dawn breaking, brushing my hair as I ate a peach as the rain pattered on the window as I warmed my toes by a log fire as I . . .

These weren't my actual ideas, those are for me alone. I share enough, and that's my business. I'd highly recommend you buy Neill's book.

HAPPINESS

Shit in Glitter

This is not a dress rehearsal.

Aunty June, on a pool noodle

wasting time

*for those who don't know, lemmings is a computer game,
the best one*

don't waste your life watching crap tv
i tell my child, pulling out the plug
switching off the screen face the huffs
remind her once again in the adult voice
i'm bored of too, to do something other than
play computer games with friends –
i offer up ideas of going outside
bounce a ball, draw a picture of a boat
because those are less a waste of time
though i'm not sure why that is

sunday mornings as a child were bliss –
my parents still in bed, the whole lounge
to myself, i watched shit tv for hours
omnibuses i'd already watched every
day that week, and after school at julie's
we played lemmings till we couldn't focus
on the screen then stayed up chatting
watching slightly famous people
sleeping, sometimes moving, in real time

sadly, i too, wasted years of my younger life
on many purposeless pursuits –
played cheerleader to needy guys
laughed politely at jokes i did not find
in any way amusing, stressed over how to look
for those who didn't stare, spent nights with boys
who did not care about the clitoris,

smiled once again as my boss explained
in belittling self-righteousness how to make him
proper coffee as my lifetime rattled past
like landscapes from a train

if i could live those years again
i would not waste one second
on such purposeless pursuits
but not one moment would i give back
watching crap tv on sundays
or at julie's after school, building bridges
till the screen rotted our reddened eyes
so that as many lemmings as possible
could safely cross the sky

friendship at its best

i'm too tired to talk today
i've nothing interesting to say
please still come round for tea
i'd love your company
we could read our books together
i might take a nap
i would love to see your face
i just can't be arsed to chat

love, the tobacco industry

the kids stopped smoking
so we invented vapes
in bubblegum flavour
sold them in sweet shops

MONEY CAN'T BUY HAPPINESS

is a phrase generally said by people who have enough money; enough for life's basic needs plus extra spending and savings to support themselves and their dependants, and have fun. I think really we mean 'having money can't save you from unhappiness' rather than 'money can't buy you happiness'.

Having money, whether money you've earned or more likely been born into or a blend of both, does buy you happiness, but only, most studies suggest, up until a certain level – as much as you can prove anything related to happiness.

There are always factors relating to happiness independent of any financial effects – the King still gets diarrhoea – but as a general rule, most findings assert that it's tricky not to be really fucking miserable most of the time when you're really fucking poor all of the time, and that having more money more quickly affects your happiness the poorer you started off.

Being financially poor is stressful, scary, dangerous and difficult. The suggestion of the very poor person who can more easily find happiness in the simpler things in life is, it seems, a patronising load of shit.

Most people I see on television being praised for focusing on happiness through a simpler way of life – sustainable farmed gardens, growing your own food, pottery, crafting, watching rivers run into the sea – most often were bankers in the city for twenty years, made money, gave up the job and moved to a simpler lifestyle in country houses with names and not numbers.

Yes, it is lovely to grow basil on the windowsill, but is it the basil that makes you happy? No, it is not. It is the basil mixed with the fact that, if those basil plants don't survive, you can go grab another one at the local shop, no problem.

benefits

with money, second-hand is vintage
without, it is embarrassment
it is arguing with parents about brands –
even the socks must have nike ticks now

with money, furniture is antique
though the car is always new
bought in full, and therefore cheaper;
who came up with that idea?

with money, clutter is eccentric,
muddy wellies in the hallway
are 'country', whole rooms to hang
your laundry in

with money, spending is forgiven
objects invite compliments
without it, eyes roll at every little luxury
on benefits and he's even got a tele!

Once a certain level of wealth is reached, it seems that more money has less and less effect on your happiness, though the level of wealth at which this comes into effect is disputed. Despite what our obsession with the world of the super-rich may have us believe, it's a joy to have the money to invite friends for dinner but the jokes are no better if the cutlery is gold sort of thing. Some have even suggested that, again after a certain very comfortable financial level, more and more money can also add to unhappiness, which makes keeping it anyway pretty vomit worthy.

When I was at school, I did this annoying as fuck thing where I'd pretend we had a test and my friends would stress for like a minute and then I'd tell them we didn't have a test and they'd be really relieved. I wanted to make them happy and this was one of the ways I thought I could do it for free. What a pain.

I love the book by Julia Donaldson called *A Squash and a Squeeze*. The woman in the story thinks her house is way too small – a squash and a squeeze – and asks a wise man to help her make it bigger. Each time she asks for help he tells her to let another animal into her house until her house is full of different creatures. Then, finally, he tells her to take them all out and she's like 'woah, my house is fucking massive'.

Of course, if your house is really small and full and the rent keeps going up, adding a goat and a pig and then taking them away might not always help, but I think this uses the same mentality as my fake tests. Every year I think my lounge is massive after I take out the Christmas tree.

In terms of advertising, the opposite is done to us constantly. Instead of showing us what's already good about what we have, we are bombarded by photos of bigger houses or glossier hair or a fancier, faster car. This really fucks with the happiness graph, especially for people with less money but also for people very comfortable financially. That's the whole point.

I once cried about cushions. There's a lot in my life I'm ashamed of but this is up there.

My kid was at primary school and I had to make friends with

other kids' parents so my kid would have play dates. Trying desperately to make friends with people who you get on with and whose kids your kid also gets on with is mathematically challenging and should be given more respect as a parental task, especially when you have more than one child. I have a friend who has moved four times for her husband's job and has had to do this each time, constantly make new friends that fit her children's lives and her husband's place of work in between her own work. So tiring, especially if you're shy.

Anyway, I was starting to invite other adults to my house.

Looking at my lovely rented terraced house, which really is lovely, I suddenly noticed all the shit bits. It came furnished and the sofa stains I couldn't get out were covered with a throw but suddenly the throw kept wrinkling in the wrong places and the cushions didn't match and the floorboards had holes in that I'd stuffed with tissue because of a mouse, and I started to cry, sure that I was a failure of a mother and no parent would come round again because the cushions didn't fucking match the throw that covered the sofa I didn't choose with stains on.

making a fuss

house is rented
furniture included
kitchen smells like farts

oven needed scrubbing
drawers of the wash machine
treacle mould thick

the scent of fart still lingers
perhaps a mouse is decomposing
behind a cupboard

just complain to the landlord!
and i know at once
you've never been afraid to make a fuss

A few hours later I realised that I had watched the television show *Grand Designs* the night before, a programme in which people build amazing houses to live in because they have money to do this and they pay designers and builders to help them.

Fine.

What I hate about the show is how much praise these people get for being wealthy enough to get a whole wall of windows built into their kitchen by skilled workmen who don't get as much airtime on the show because they're northern and not as rich. That day I vowed never to watch *Grand Designs* again, no matter how cool the houses looked.

When I was a kid, I was obsessed with TV adverts. I once asked my dad if there was an advert channel so I didn't get all the annoying interruptions of programmes in between. I loved the jingles, and remember many of them and still find it tricky not to believe that a Mars a day really would help me work, rest and play.

In my adult life, advertising was at its fiercest when I was pregnant. I found it so hard to handle the pressure to look like a perfect pregnant mother, with a perfect summer dress over a perfect bump (I recently learnt that most 'pregnancy' models are just normal models with fake neat pregnant bumps tied on under their clothes so no wonder I felt like shit). The guilt of marketing hits doubly hard when the 'you're not good enough' combines forces with 'you don't love your unborn baby enough', as if the appearance of your pregnant body, baby's clothes, nursery, is proof of love and care.

I felt guilty about not being a good mother before I'd even had my daughter. I felt guilty when I didn't look pretty and pregnant.

Advertising, like cults, targets the most vulnerable and susceptible;

kids, teenagers, expectant mothers, and so on. It plays on anxieties, creates them even, and then offers you an apparent solution.

We're too harsh on ourselves for not being happy with what we have, or for letting our kids buy shit we know they'll throw away the next week and so on. Marketing is powerful. If it didn't work, companies wouldn't spend billions on it. They're not stupid. The sweets are at the checkout for a reason and the reason is your breaking point.

decorating the nursery

poem for a pregnant friend stressing over which bookshelf to buy for the baby's nursery after reading an article that said book-shelves where the books face outwards are more fashionable in nurseries these days and better because the children can see the covers of the books and here's some books by illustrators to show off on those shelves but in the nurseries on the '96 Best Nursery Shelving and Book Display Ideas' they were more like standard bookshelves because they can fit more books on and what about the design of the nursery rugs on pinterest and the '234 best nurs-ery images of 2019' and the 'Best Nursery Ideas with Cute and Playful Designs' article and the 'how to paint the perfect nursery wall fun diy project idea for expectant parents' blog

no baby gives a fuck

It's not human to be happy all the time, but it's definitely harder to find happiness at all when there are billions of pounds spent every year to convince you your face is shit or your house is shit or your children are stupid or you're ageing too much or your shit isn't glit-tery enough as it comes squeezed out of your arsehole, which is too hairy for anyone to love; to make you believe you need specialist leggings to go for a jog or a £100 dildo to be able to cum or a treadmill to run on instead of just, you know, running on the spot; to make you cry about cushions as if anyone you'd be vaguely interested in befriending would give a shit about the way your sofa looked.

I mention glittery shit because apparently there is a pill you can buy that makes your shit glitter. I don't know if this marks the peak of human genius or the fall of civilisation.

I was saddened, and still am, about all the adverts my kid will see. I am not the sort of parent who bans TV or phones or city billboards from her sight. I think it's extremely hard to do that now and, anyway, I don't want to protect just my own child. I want society to stop being a fuckshow for children in general and for governments to step the fuck up, starting perhaps with sweet-flavoured fucking vapes.

I daydream about working for the Advertising Standards Authority. I have heard that adverts are not allowed to mislead or lie and I'm constantly fascinated by what is allowed, especially in terms of language. I would like a big stamp that says 'Not Passed'.

For example: the 2022 Coca-Cola slogan: Real Magic.

If you like Coca-Cola, fine. But Real Magic it is not. The word magic would not be allowed by me unless it was OKed by Gandalf. Magic is the preserve of witches and wizards and the Houdini museum in Budapest where I saw my first magic show, which I loved. Not Coca-Cola. Not a drink of which the main ingredients are water and sugar. **Not Passed.**

Happy is another word. It's too big for products to claim ownership over. Happy Meal. Nah: **Not Passed.** Can't prove it long term. The 2009 Coca-Cola slogan: Open Happiness. Nah: **Not Passed.** Come on, guys. Don't get above yourselves, you're a fucking soft drink.

Ditto dream. Is that my dream toilet? Is that my dream kitchen? No matter how much I'd love one of those Japanese toilets that cleans my arse with warm water and also, I discovered, gives many women very easy orgasms with the front spray, or how undeniably amazing it would be to get a spanking brand new kitchen or bathroom fitted that you can lather in and love, you're still not having the word dream: **Not Passed.**

dream bathroom

do not tell me this is my dream bathroom
unless there's a brass band singing nat king cole
with grandad in the sink; unless the cold tap
flows prosecco and the shower transforms
into a giant see-through rocket so i can
exfoliate my arse whilst speeding between planets
unless the bathtub turns me mermaid
the light switch ends all war, and the flush,
when double-flushed, makes *all* shit disappear

I would like to caveat here that ELS Bathrooms in Muirhead, Scotland, can use whatever words they want because their bathrooms and kitchens really are absolutely gorgeous and the staff incredibly helpful and handsome.

There was a Ribena advert a few summers ago I kept seeing in London en route to my lovely friends Jamie and Juliet's house. It was advertising 'Ribena's Latest Masterpiece'. As far as I could tell it was a more watery version of Ribena.

Latest Masterpiece.

What would you call mediocre if that's a masterpiece? If you were advertising the human body, or Lisa Aisato's paintings then maybe, but not water and blackcurrant cordial. **Not Passed.**

oh to have the confidence of ribena's 'masterpiece'

i wish, for all good people struggling with self-belief,
the confidence, for even one day,
of ribena's latest ad campaign, which appears to proclaim
a pre-watered down version of its original recipe
cleverly rebranded as 'blackcurrant water'
rather than 'ribena',
the ingredients of which are basically ribena,
but with less ribena in
and much more water
and a few extra flavourings,
advertised on summer billboards everywhere
across this city's sweating commuter routes
as not simply being
slightly more diluted ribena,
but in fact, being:

'ribena's latest masterpiece'

a slightly crapper, weaker version of itself
but with the unrivalled confidence
of a psychopathic millionaire
tweeting from the white house

Perfume adverts are my favourite, a product which we apparently buy to smell like the celebrity who has ordained the scent, because it is swaddled in the most amazing amount of advertising bullshit. Lifestyle branding. The best.

With most other adverts, there is at least some sort of visual or audible product which can be shown. With perfume they're trying to sell us a scent, and so far nobody has found a way to get smells to emanate through video screens or billboards.

The actual idea of scents and putting scents together is pretty fascinating. But none of this appears in the adverts. There is no smell, only posing and supposed aspiration. No people just sniffing each other, going 'Jesus, Linda, you smell fucking gorgeous.' Except maybe Lynx, but let's not go there.

The women's faces are so smooth and line-free in perfume adverts it's like they're pre-pubescent or painted. The lines on men's faces in the adverts are most often the opposite; actively and purposefully chiselled, I assume accentuating their busy and full lives, the sexiness of having lived and explored and shagged and beaten tigers and crocodiles to death with their bare foreskins.

The fact that lines are erased on the faces of almost all the women implies the opposite. How sexy not to have lived. Not to have grown up. To have no stories or experience to share or compare you with. All to sell something, which is meant to be about how you'll smell.

Big brand advertising is mainly bullshit. I know this. But it is impossible to escape its effects. By the end of every airport perfume section I am mainly convinced that my face is a hideous ancient relic failed since it passed the toddler phase but that my boyfriend's face is a gorgeous lived in adventurer's which will become more beautiful with each new line of intelligence. I hate being jealous of him for this. I also tend to have a headache after squooshing every tester on offer over my body.

There are pressures put on men for sure; the muscles, the money, the North Pole exploration expectations even for those who don't like the cold or walking with crampons (rhymes with tampon, this is why I wrote it); the expensive watches you have to aspire to wear because it's the only jewellery you're allowed.

If you ever find yourself believing that men have none of these issues, watch any hair-transplanting or baldness treatment makeover video; the sobbing of young and older men who've felt like shit sometimes since their late teens or early twenties because of receding hairlines and balding is heart-wrenching.

I appreciate those difficulties I hope, and I really hope men appreciate being allowed to have a face.

I cannot express what a difference it would make to my happiness if woman-skin in adverts was the same as man-skin; because in real life, our skin is literally the same. I cannot imagine how good it would feel for my soul if we accepted that. But that's not the point, is it? The Botox and skincare and foundation industry would suffer horrendously if living was also seen as sexy and exciting for women to do. It's really fucking dire we can't be seen to have lived. And it's annoying because the opposite is death, but that would make our skin even worse.

Is that really her face, guys? Does she really have the skin of a ten-year-old at twenty-five because she's sprayed herself with floral scent? Nope. **Not Passed.**

A child I know, at eleven, eleven, ELEVEN, asked me how to prevent wrinkles after watching a TikTok skincare for girls video.

How do you avoid wrinkles? she asked.

Well, there are two ways to have your face remain the face of a toddler forever. One, you remain a toddler forever, which is either impossible or utterly tragic. Or, to keep wrinkles to the utter minimum, you drink water a plenty, eat very healthily, don't smoke and most importantly spend your entire life sleeping and never moving your face. This would have to include never smiling, laughing, singing, talking, grinning, scowling, eating, among other activities. Cool? Let's try.

We practised walking without moving our faces for a while and it wasn't very easy and it wasn't very fun.

life choice

keep laughing, my love
and those wrinkles will deepen

do you:

a) stop laughing
b) stop listening

I tried to give my child a quick talk on how a lot of advertising works so she could be prepared not to believe, want or feel like less of a human for the rest of her life.

We were in a park café and there were cartons of sugar-free (aka sweetener-filled) blackcurrant drinks, one covered with Tinkerbell images for the thirsty girls and one with some other cartoon, probably sharks or guns or something else that we associate with killing, for the thirsty little boys. I was telling her to remember that bright packaging like that doesn't mean she'll love what's inside, and that generally the brighter the packaging and the more advertising around the product, the more shite and unnecessary what's inside. I used the word shite because lessons work better if you swear.

She said *yeah, if someone wrapped a poo in a glittery smell-proof Tinkerbell box I'd probably want it.*

Good. Understood. I bought the drink though. I really like Tinkerbell.

poem scribbled whilst worrying about something

outside my window, there is blue
inside my bedroom, there is bed

at the far end of the kitchen
a kettle steams in hope

at the back door sparrows chat
over the fence my neighbour waves
pegging up her pants

in the park, plum tree buds slowly turn to plums
soon, i will bite into one

then stars above will show
once the dark allows them space and time;

everything is fine
today, everything is fine

uncomfortable everyday pants
for michael, who did make an effort

you are not sold uncomfortable everyday pants
as if the purpose of pants is a portrait of your arse crack
even with no audience present for the viewing

arses like yours – i assume – have never heard friends
say things like *oh god! i hope i am not knocked over*
by a bus today or a car today or a truck today
my bones smashed to confetti on the pavement
the concrete covered in satin red rivers
of my mangled body's blood, forever to be dead
because today i am wearing the WORST underwear,
how embarrassing that would be
to be smashed onto the pavement in smithereens
in front of strangers wearing these

worst, most often meaning comfortable,
perhaps large or baggy, the likes of which women,
for some reason, call granny pants, to be worn only
when elderly, or, but with an implied negativity,
our 'comfy' pants as in, *oh i think maybe i'll just wear*
my comfy pants today which men seem to simply call pants,

neither are you sold pants designed to give the illusion
that you are in fact not wearing any pants at all
the line of your pants being seen slightly through clothes
or blatantly above the waistband has not been given
the shameful slang of a vpl, oh the embarrassment
that someone strolling behind you may know
that you are wearing underwear underneath your clothes

no, i've spied just two everyday types of underwear for you
depending – i'm guessing – on preference of air flow
or the comfort of tighter elastic cradling your balls
and yes, you must occasionally adjust, choose a side
for your penis to loll at, as i pull lace out of my arse crack,
cotton from my perineum, satin from my inner lips,
itching from the gusset, wondering if any women
having dressed in the correct sort of uncomfortable
underwear, matching and satin,
ever walk out their front door thinking:
right, if there's a truck coming, pray let it be today

smart

written after a disappointing night out

in between checking your phones
we talk, sometimes we laugh
waiters come and go, the sun rises then sets

birds leave nests, find berries
and return
in between checking your phones

earthworms that remain
are thankful for another night
we order starter, then dessert, eat,

go dancing, stroll through cities
phones laid beside the spoons like a last request
awaiting silent moments;

a sudden message mutes the conversation
extinction of the daydream
in between checking your phones

you wait to check your phones again
you wait to check your phones again
what is the first thing you touch

in the morning, what is the first thing
you think of touching?
is it desperate if i scream?

yank the tablecloth until all the glasses shatter
is anybody out there?
don't be a nag, this is how it is now

waiting for the school bus
the children do not talk
no one is ever bored, everyone is bored

we all walk into lampposts much more often
i am jealous of no one but your phone
every friend you've ever known

every message every story every joke
the weather
no need to open up the windows

to check if it is raining, it is raining
and tiring, the humiliation of competing
with the entire robot world

in between checking your phone
you wait to check your phone again
in between checking your phone,

sometimes you notice,
if you look up – mostly you don't –
i am gone

owning outer space

currently, there are men (i assume)
sitting in locked rooms (i assume)
dressed in expensive suits (i assume)
discussing how to slice the moon
the way they sliced up earth
sliced up seas sliced up soils
sliced land up into countries
sliced labour from its wages
sliced species from their seeds
into pieces, like a birthday cake

fidget spinner

once all my flesh is rotted from the bone
i think – tucking in your sheets –
and my bones ground down to dust

once nothing whole is left of me
but minerals to falling leaves
that piece of useless plastic
you begged me for for weeks
(because *the advert at tia's house*
because *kamila is allowed one*
because *everybody has one*
because *please mum* because *pleaaase mum*
because red-faced at the till again
because everybody's watching
because perfect product placement
because *don't you even love me?*)

once i am gone, i think,
as i watch you fall asleep,
that grinning fidget spinner
now abandoned in the same drawer
as every yearly plastic fad:
the loom bands, the shopkins,
the popping stress relief thing
shaped like ice lollies or ice cream

even your fidget spinner,
even your squishy emoji poo

will outlive me, my love
and outlive you

WATCHING CHILDREN PLAY

i am a mature adult now
i am trying to embrace this
but i still cannot accept
there's a planet called uranus

My mum always says she learnt more from her kids than she taught them. As her daughter I don't agree; as a mum, I do.

Watching my daughter enter the mighty age of toddlerdom was the greatest reminder to me of what happiness could look like in human form. I don't mean the parenting part of that; looking after a toddler is beautiful and challenging. I mean literally watching a toddler play. It made me question almost everything I had come to feel, or been told or made to feel, about what makes me happy as an adult.

As I write this, the little boy on the picnic table opposite me (I'm working in an outdoor park café while my now teenager is in town for two hours) has just shouted, 'I need more blackberries, Dad', his mouth already lipsticked with purple autumn sweetness, and then run off to the bush screaming in delight as if he's just won the pools. This is the shit I'm talking about.

I didn't love every single second with my beautiful toddler while I was in the thick of early parenting, much more tired and uncertain than I am now.

But I did absolutely love it and, looking back, I learnt so much from stirring mud into hot chocolate in leaves for twenty hours a week. No matter how gorgeous it is seeing your child enjoying themselves, their love of repetition: the same favourite book each bedtime; peekaboo for five hours straight; role playing being a dog for three years; turning a teaspoon into a best friend simply by putting on a voice and making it hop across the table; believing your teddies are sipping secret tea from plastic cups; one puddle and a stick to occupy an entire day; can be hard to keep up with, enthusiastically, when you are most likely struggling from sleep deprivation while juggling life and time and love like a manic circus act.

But I did love a lot of it, and I was often totally in awe of my daughter. Being with her made me wonder over and over again what I actually enjoyed in life; like really, truly enjoyed. One thing I learnt for certain – I fucking loved doing puppet shows and I made an exceptionally good horse.

problem is, i'm still really fucking great at being a horse

it took me nine months to get used to being pregnant and then my body changed again and it took me another year to get used to carrying a baby on my body then the baby learnt to walk and run and wanted to play games and it took me two years to become comfortable at peekaboo in public, pouring pretend tea to teddies, pretending to be a horse, oh how i galloped for hours and hours and hours and hours around the living room

and then the games changed again and it took me a year to become expert at ball pits and puddle jumps then daisy chains and loom bands then climbing frames and diving into swimming pools then talking dolls and stringing beads and just as i got good at those the games changed again again to building avatars then castles on computers out of blocks and

just as i finished my pixelated house your avatar moved on, and i cannot
keep up, my body and these games, how quickly it all changes, and now its music and sleepovers and can you run us into to town please and i love to see you happy and i'll run you in of course, it's just sometimes i get a little sad how no one gives a shit that i'm still really fucking great at being a horse

Of all the people on the planet I have spent time with, I am certain that toddlers are the overlooked gurus on how to be happy.

More importantly, because, no matter how many fad toys companies invent each year to end up in landfill soon after, what toddlers actually get the most pleasure from is largely free; you can't package it or sell it, though we sure as hell try to.

Toddlers could easily be the downfall of our economic capitalist model, content as they are most days to throw stones at icy puddles, chase pigeons, break sticks if allowed the free run of a woodland or park and rest in the evening playing with a wooden spoon and being tickled.

What makes humans truly happy? Is it really the stuff we've been told is fundamental to happiness: handbags, six packs and so on?

From the years I spent looking after babies and toddlers, happiness seems to begin mainly with sucking on nipples while fondling warm breasts (let's be honest, many would still enjoy that) or sucking on rubber teats shaped like warm nipples; sleeping; being hugged; making noises; banging stuff; farting when you've got a sore stomach; ditto any toilet relief; sticks; puddles; making dens; mud; dancing; more hugs; eating (fruit is an absolute joy to most kids until they taste the sugar-sweet stuff adults have invented); fiddling with their genitals (yes, kids do this for pleasure, we really need to get over this fact); looking around; learning new skills like talking and walking and running and skipping; being tickled;

being held and swung through the sky with your legs in the air; playing with friends; having raspberries blown on your neck and belly; pretending to be a dog; pretending to have a dog; climbing trees; playing catch; falling in snow; screaming and running round in circles shouting *ahhhhhhh* with a stick in your hand. The sort of shit a lot of adults pay to do in therapy sessions or exclusive kink clubs later on in life.

The problem is that toddlers are also often selfish, uncontrollable bastards who also have no mind jumping on real dogs' backs and trying to ride them like horses around the living room; pushing other kids off slides when they are bored of waiting for their brief descent of joy; screaming that they hate you because you won't buy them a comic with a plastic mermaid on the front; sticking wet fingers into plug sockets if ever left alone for five seconds so you can change your tampon in peace.

Toddlers are also very bad at cooking and their desire for party bags contributes, in my estimations, to 30 per cent of global carbon emissions and landfill, though it wasn't toddlers who invented those plastic bags full of plastic shit; it was us adults. They were overjoyed with a slice of cake on a napkin to take home until we showed them what other shit was on offer. We all were.

Watching my kid in her pre-give-a-shit-about-social-mores-days made me so aware of all the things I used to just feel happy doing and then stopped doing. I don't mean like pissing in a nappy, or trampling on the neighbour's beloved tulips to fetch a ball, I mean things I would definitely still enjoy and that could have been hygienically, harmlessly and consensually carried out as I grew up.

For me, the end of carefree, non-self-conscious fun was the biggest blow of my childhood. The unashamed, there's-a-good-tree-to-climb-I-think-I'll-climb-it or I-fancy-plaiting-someone's-hair-so-I'll-ask-my-friend-to-practise-on-her sort of fun that dwindled within the awkward claws of puberty.

Ideas of 'cool' shifted so suddenly and hit so hard between

primary school and a one-thousand-person comp secondary school. I had a lot of fun as a teenager, but it was more rigid, more ruled over. Everything was judged, and not fitting in could be dangerous, both in terms of being outcast from social groups and also in terms of being physically bullied for doing things or wearing things or thinking things deemed uncool, even if you loved them. Wear an anklet on the wrong ankle and you're a slag. Wear your backpack on both shoulders and you're a loser. God, I hate the term loser. I wore a heavy backpack on one shoulder for years and walked around with a constant ache.

At some point of teenage life, it was no longer 'cool' to admit to enjoying anything. Even smiling proved tricky at times. I feel sorry when I see kids at the school bus stop now, stood in cold rain without jackets on. This is not through poverty (I know their parents), that would obviously be way worse. These examples are because it isn't cool to wear a jacket. But, it *is* cool to be absolutely fucking freezing and damp all day.

My god, the difference between dancing freely as an eight-year-old in whatever clothes you fancy wearing at the time – tutu, snorkel, glitter eyeshadow and a pirate eyepatch – versus dancing awkwardly as fuck as an older kid or adult wondering who's watching and if you've any sweat marks appearing.

Things kids have told me are 'sad' (aka you're a fucking weirdo loser dickhead, not like emotionally upsetting) for adults to be into: computer games, roller skating, trampolining, dancing, going to parties, going to nightclubs, birthday cake, laser quest, having sleepovers. When I had my friend Kasia to sleep over at my house recently, I was told it was a 'bit weird' by one of the kids who was having a sleepover with my daughter.

I am trying, I am really trying to just do things I enjoy, especially things that are free, and I'm finding it odd how hard it is. It is mind-boggling how indoctrinated and concerned I am about what other people will think of me.

A few hurdles I've attempted so far:

1. Handstands
When my daughter was six, on tour with me, we had to wait two hours for a train. We went out onto a grassy patch outside the station. It was a lovely, sunny day.

My kid filled the time by doing handstands. I watched her for a while. I desperately wanted to do handstands too. I really like doing handstands. I used to spend hours walking round on my hands as a kid (village life) and I loved it and I can still do handstands and often do, onto my couch, at home, in secret. It feels good and it stretches my back and I just enjoy it and always have.

I commented to my daughter, without thinking, that I wished I could still do handstands. She was genuinely confused. She'd seen me a lot doing them with her in the house.

You can, she replied, looking at me like I had lost my memory.

I smiled, forgetting she was six years old and didn't know the adult rules of acceptability.

No, I mean, I wish I could do them now, I replied.

She looked even more baffled.

You can, Mum!

She shrugged and leapt to her hands again.

I laughed. I watched her, happy she was enjoying herself, imagining joining her like I did in our own small garden.

Come on, Mum! She smiled, flipping once again onto her hands and then feet, ever straighter each time.

I stood, staring, as if this, of all moments in my life, was the decisive one; life crossroads, in between time portals, *what will your future hold, Hollie?* Handstands or no handstands, fun or standing watching children having fun? *Why can't I do fucking handstands here?* I thought. *Why can't I do some handstands while waiting for this train rather than standing, once again, doing nothing because I am an adult and not a six-year-old who can get away with having certain types of fun?*

339

Because of other people's opinions.

Because people will think I'm weird.

Because it's not the *done thing*.

Because I'm an adult and that's for children.

Because it will look like showing off because other adults can't do this.

Because I might fuck up and fall on my face and get laughed at.

Because if I fuck up, people will say *arsehole* or *show off* and be pleased that I fell on my face cos why the fuck am I doing handstands anyway because I'm an adult?

Or maybe they won't. Or maybe it doesn't matter anyway.

I stood for an hour watching my kid lovingly as she twisted and flipped and stretched and exercised, free and happy and not spending any money while I, proud parent, stuck stiff like a statue at the beginning of a sprint, questioned the entire trajectory of my life. Seriously, is this going to be it forever, doing the 'done thing'? *Come on, Hollie, hands on the grass, put your hands on the grass and get your handstand-loving arse up in the air.*

I did one handstand. It wasn't my best, but it was a start.

2. Roller skating

I love roller skating. I roller skated loads as a kid, up and down the pavement outside my house if none of my mates was free. I love being on wheels. I don't really like walking, possibly because my legs are shorter than most of my family or friends so walking just means I'm constantly trying to catch up. I also hate running, and it annoys me that running's seen as OK to do but not skating. Who makes these rules up? Also, once I started skating and cycling, walking just seemed so slow. I'm also more scared walking on my own than being on wheels because I've been followed too many times not to be nervous constantly.

I taught my kid to roller skate when she was about four. Once she was good enough that I didn't need to basically drag her along the pavement, I sometimes roller skated alongside her. Once she got really good, we began roller skating to school. Or rather, I ran or cycled (acceptable) and she roller skated. It was about a fifteen-minute skate along a really smooth cycle path.

The reason I didn't skate was because of the return journey. It was one thing skating your kid to school but what would I do on the way back? Skate by *myself*? In front of *other adults*? I had a word with myself and thought, *fuck it*, skated beside her and it was all fine, a few comments from parents, a few embarrassing stumbles but all good. On the way back, though, I chickened out, took my trainers from my bag and walked back sulking because I don't like walking and could have been skating.

The second time, I didn't take my trainers.

When I got home, happier now I'd had a morning skate, I got a text from a friend saying I was being talked about, or she thought it was likely me, on the village Facebook chat. I'm not on this village chat but she sent me a screenshot of the discussion.

It read:

I have just seen the most dangerous thing ever! What looks like two girls crossing the very busy [road name] on ROLLER SKATES! I assume they are going to the junior school. If you know these girls please have a word with their parents. This road has already had its share of deaths!

Underneath a long thread unrolled discussing how terrible it was that parents allowed young kids to roller skate alone across this road.

I'm glad there are people watching out for our kids. I would have felt the same if I'd seen two ten-year-olds crossing the road. It is a busy road, but it is also a road that many pedestrians cross each day, on bikes, scooters, foot, unicycle once. There is a pedestrian crossing island thing in the middle. I had held hands with my kid to cross the road.

I'm a little worried about the woman's eyesight if she thought I was a ten-year-old. Or maybe it's just that our adult brains assume that someone on roller skates must be a child. One friend said what a compliment it was that she thought I was a ten-year-old. I get that we're in a society obsessive about looking younger, but I'm really not wanting to appear pre-pubescent.

Either way, that was the end of skating to school: having spent two years building up the confidence to do the school run both ways on my skates, I stopped after two days.

3. Swimming

I love swimming. Or rather, I love being in water. Mainly, I love jumping in, diving in, swimming underwater. I love going under and playing catch and then floating like a starfish on the surface staring at the light waves on the ceiling. If flumes are on offer then I'm at my most ecstatically happy. I fucking love swimming pools and no, I don't care about the piss because chlorine kills it. I don't love doing lengths. I hate the manky changing-room floors but, hey ho.

I was so excited to take my kid swimming and took her the first week you are medically allowed to take a new baby into water in the hope it would make her love pools as much as me. I signed up to one term of baby swimming lessons, so I knew what was and wasn't OK and after that just asked my friend, who was still paying for one-to-one lessons, what they did each week and copied it. My kid learnt to swim slower than kids still in lessons but she still learnt.

By the time she was two it paid off and the crying stopped and it was glorious. We would jump in. Make faces underwater. Pretend to be pirates. Splash each other. Go head first down the toddler slides until I was told that we weren't actually allowed to do that by an embarrassed lifeguard who had seen me coaxing my kid into it.

The flumes were only for over fives and I can't remember anything I was more excited about than our first visit after she turned five. I felt like both of us had been waiting five years for this moment. After that, we spent most swimming sessions going on the flumes and jumping into the pool and very little actual swimming.

Six years on, I was a little unprepared for the realisation that now my daughter would rather go on the flumes with her friends, which in itself is perfectly understandable, but it meant that if I still went on them, I would now simply be the 'weird lone adult on the flumes'. I sulked my way back to the adult pool to do lengths. There are no slides into the adult pool.

I did try once to go on the flumes when swimming alone on a lunch break. I was on my own and noticed the flumes were open. They're not normally until after school hours, although I wish they were. Nobody was on them, which meant I wouldn't be stared down by a bunch of kids who view adults queuing for activities like this as basically taking up their flume time.

After doing some boring lengths, I got out and walked up the spiral stairs, trying to look as confident as an adult going alone on the flumes can possibly look. When I got to the top, the lifeguard looked at me and smiled and I honestly felt like a total arsehole. *Fuck it. FUCK IT!* Come on. I am an adult. One of the privileges of this surely is the freedom to do the things I love.

I held the metal bar and swung myself into the water shoot, my arse sliding side to side gleefully, grazing over the adjoining lines and I whizzed through the daylit green portal into the final splash of water pool at the bottom. I got up and went on again but facing the lifeguard for a third time was too much to handle. Still, an achievement.

exactly as i like

my daily life is beautiful, but not much for conversation
i've taken out the washing and hung it in the sun
ran my child to football, watched small feet pass or miss
after bedtime, stayed up to read a book

i haven't been to any exhibitions i could talk about
there wasn't any time left once i'd cut my nails, replaced
the light bulb in the toilet, or maybe there was time
but instead i tried some earrings on i probably won't wear

the bread i burnt this morning smelt exactly as i like
i rode my bike to buy a melon then cut it into slices
placed it in the fridge, then got excited three hours later
when i fancied something quick and there they were

When I told my mum I was pregnant one of the things she said was how excited she was to eat a fish-finger sandwich again. She'd made them for us as kids, until I, much to my family's annoyance but very sweet acceptance, turned veggie at five years old, and stopped eating them.

Had my mum gone without a fish-finger sandwich for almost twenty years because there was no child to make one for?

I sometimes wonder how many people on this planet are stopping themselves doing things, things which they could easily do and love to do and which hurt no one, just because they feel they shouldn't any more?

How many adults are currently doing lengths in the adult lanes of a pool gazing over at the flumes? How many adults are waiting for their kids to have kids so they can have a fish-finger sandwich for dinner? How many people aren't going to see bands they love for fear they'll seem too old to simply enjoy music and dance?

my friend doesn't want to be in your bookclub

says it's a waste of her time
she's not enjoyed one of the books

you don't even have wine

my friend is too frightened to tell you
she's always been shy;
so if she stops turning up to your bookclub,
that's why

As we grow older, we don't lose all the other versions of ourselves. We're not caterpillars dissolving our young bodies into new butterflies.

The kid that liked puddle jumping hasn't fled my bones, she's there, just bigger, expanded, with tax to pay and more worried about death as it approaches, but also freer, not told to tidy her room any more, more skilled at doing Excel spreadsheets and drawing elephants and travelling on trains, more at ease with her mind and body, smarter, wiser, worse at handstands and imaginative games with toy cars, better at masturbation and making lasagnes and actual driving.

'Act your age.'
I fucking am.

lit

for anyone who uses childish as an insult

you lob childish at me, mocking
as if no child should linger here

as if our skin is not pegged up in dens
more elaborate each year

as if each wick lit on each birthday cake
as if wildfires don't expand

as if each year, just one new single flame
the others molten wax –

toss childish at me, scornful
as if my child can just walk out

pull these grown up bones apart
like, *thanks, i'm off, don't wait around*

a snake scuttles out of skin
each time the earth skips round the sun

as if every larger russian doll
gobbles up the littler ones;

but this shoebox of a body
is stuffed fuller every day –

ticket stubs and photographs
sea glass, shells, mistakes

first steps, first words, first love notes
written, scrumpled, salvaged, kept;

newborn me is wrapped up there
cheek still squashed to mum's warm chest

toddler me is in there too
scared to take a second step

the four-year-old is reading
a pile of dusty picture books

the nine-year-old has found a stick
woodland scent now lost

teenage-me is sleeping
new-mother-me is not

a thousandth kiss is ling'ring
beside a fading pressed forget-me-not

toss childish at me, once again
i'll place it in the box

next to the birthday badge and bottle cork
and a thousand mismatched socks

and when – world-willing – i am old
ninety candles on a cake

there will still be eighty candles
and there will still be sixty-eight

and there will still be fifty-seven
and there will still be seventeen

and there will still be five
and still be two and still be

that one single
newborn flame upon its wick

glowing just as bright
as the first year i was lit

I'm not pretending to be younger when I do things I love, an accusation I hear so often thrown at adults. I just still enjoy roller skating. I'll be fucked if all those years of falling on my arse skating up and down the pavement outside my house on my own as a kid, desperately trying to learn this skill, is now to be banned from my life because of some cultural idea we've devised of what adulthood ought to look like. And even if you didn't roller skate as a kid, you're still allowed to try new things after the age of ten.

I love rope swings stumbled over in forests. I love jumping into swimming pools and going on flumes, preferably with friends. I like hanging washing in the sun. I get excited by maths puzzles and cherish Excel spreadsheets to do secret sums, which only appear with a double-click. I love playing board games with my kid. I love watching videos of other people giving maths hacks. I love applying mascara slowly and straightening my hair and finding words that only exist in certain cultures and I love learning idioms in other languages. My whole day was made recently when I found out that the English phrase 'it costs an arm and a leg' has a French equivalent but without the leg bit.

And I love doing handstands. I really, really love doing hand-stands and I always have and I do them most nights before I go to bed and hope my arms will be able to hold me up above my head until the day I die, preferably peacefully at about 102 years old, preferably after having shared a really good jacket potato at a garden centre café with my daughter, because by then we'll both get half-price lunches.

I tried to find out who the oldest person to ever do a handstand was, but I couldn't. I just kept getting referred to the longest hand-stand, which is debated to be between a few hours and a day, though the longest one actually recorded and proven is by Gordon Lindsay in 2015 for twelve minutes and five seconds.

I did discover that the oldest person to ever do a backflip is Walter Liesner, who did one into a swimming pool in Wetzlar, Germany, at the age of ninety-four years and 268 days. He was a gymnastics teacher and was famous at seventeen for doing a handstand on the handrail at the top of a church tower, so yeah, he's always been pretty good at it. Still, seems he wasn't embarrassed to continue. I am from now on invoking Walter's spirit.

life is too short to iron

unless you like ironing a lot

or need collars uncreased
to make the impression you want

or perhaps slipping into ironed bedsheets
undoes your whole day of its blues

so maybe life is too short to lecture others
on what life is too short not to do

not puddles though, not jumping

i do not know the exact day i last rushed into a puddle
but there must have been a shift, when

i saw one, a good one, and jumped gladly,
not knowing this would be the final time, not knowing

that one week later, maybe even just the next day
after a night of heavy rain, the morning sun beckoning

my mother and me for a walk in the park,
path dotted with puddles, good ones, lots of them

and me, in the same rainbow wellies as the week before,
or just day before, for the first time, would walk past them,

like a party hat no longer dashed from the cracker to my head
a teddy bear suddenly refusing conversation

i do not know what happened between those moments
perhaps, a tree climb more alluring

perhaps it is a natural progression
to stop finding joy in water spilled over thumping wellies

perhaps another child had called me *silly*, whispered *baby*,
the heavy threat of not acting my age finally begun

to follow me for years, this never-ending erasure of love
as *baby-ish* then *child-ish* then *immature* then

acting like a teenager then
it's like she still thinks she's twenty

then '*what to wear at forty*' columns
then *at his age!* declarations as he dances to a band

perhaps, today is the twenty-fifth anniversary
of the final time i ever saw a puddle, a great one

and jumped in it – and what other unnoticed
anniversaries of endings have i missed –

the final bedtime story i begged for
final plate of purple jelly

the final time i sat topless in the sunshine
making castles out of stolen sea and seaweed

the final snog in a cinema; the final moony
from the back of the last bus;

the final picture i painted just for fun
not worried it wasn't good enough or pointless

one day i will stop bleeding, the menopause
is only one day long, i didn't know that until recently

one single moment, the exact day
one year after your very last period

i don't know how i'll feel then
perhaps bereft, perhaps elated

one day, i will never bleed again
not even if i start to eat black pudding

not even if i hold a newborn baby
and make cooing noises

some things are like that; irreversible
not puddles though; not jumping

testing my kid's socialising skills on adult friends

instead of asking *how's your husband getting on*
with his job? i ask *if you had to snog, suck or marry*
one of the dads on the school run, which dad would it be
and why?

instead of saying *what tea would you like?*
ask *do you want to go to the shop*
buy a bumper packet of monster munch
and share it on the swings?

instead of sitting, dance

instead of offering a biscuit
thus stoking a conversation about how you shouldn't
oh you really shouldn't and the body parts you both hate,
take turns attempting bum drops on a trampoline
or just lay together, holding hands on the undulating surface

instead of speaking, take a pillow
hit her in the tits

instead of asking *how's the kids' gymnastics*
or *did you get that email about the new school dinners menu*
or *have you filled out the form about GCSE options yet*

scatter one hundred beaded letters
and form them into bracelets
spelling out phrases like: friends forever
or *fuck life*, or maybe just your names

friendships in adulthood

i would ask you to come over
plait my hair for an hour or so
plait the way friends plaited
before adult rules took hold
plait without purpose
take it out plait again
but i can't, so i ask you
for a cup of tea instead

the problem with ageing
is that by twenty-one years old
everything's allowed: every film,
every spirit, every sexual position –
and all you have to wait for
is a free ride on the bus,
and half-price half-size lunches

if i were minister of culture
i would alter legislation:

beer and wine with food at sixteen;
vodka jelly, nineteen; gin at twenty-one;
twister lollies, twenty-three;
hot-air balloon rides, thirty
candyfloss at thirty-eight
cocktails only when you're forty-one
baileys, sixty-seven

imagine the parties; frantic groups
of adults, skin still too unlived
to buy martinis at the bar, calling up their elders
for tips on how to contour wrinkles
guys pleading with bouncers
they are *definitely forty, even forty-three*
grey hair dye flying from the shelves
grandmas begged outside the offy

friends telling friends they're so lucky
to look fifty when they're only
early-forties so they can finally get into
the penguin enclosure at the zoo

and at the fun fair,
queues of sixty-year-old lovers
old enough at last
to ride the ferris wheel at night

outside the cinema,
just-retired friends scrunching faces
fake walking sticks and wigs,
to sneak into the new erotic movie;
certificate eighty-seven

and at ninety-five,
for those lucky few who make it
hobbling to the sweet shop
legal age at last
to buy watermelon bubble gum
and blow it in the street

how to be a happy woman

they said *have you met the one yet?*
they said *aw, don't give up*
they said *spinster* and *confetti*
they did not say live alone eating toasties in your knickers
knitting cardigans for nephews and nieces who visit monthly
they said *relationships take work* – they only meant marriage
they did not say friendships are as significant a love
or that even married people can die with an unheld hand;
that living with a lover can be lonelier than living with a cat,
they said *swans make heart shapes with their necks*
they said *swans stay together for life*, they said *penguins*
they said *penguins* they did not say *ostrich* or *duck*
they did not describe the way fruit bats love cunnilingus
or how female bonobos masturbate
to distract the males from fighting
they said *body clock time is ticking*
they did not say miscarriage or prolapse
or post-natal depression
they said *your body is a temple*
they did not say your body is your temple,
they said *wrinkles* and *menopause*
they did not say the majority of women
are at their happiest after forty,
they did not say don't worry, they did not say
there are many ways of living,
choose your own, life is fleeting;
they didn't say anything about sleep

CATCH 22: THE CHILDLESS
SPINSTER HAG

what is the male word for slut?
what is the male word for slag?
what is the male word for skank?
what is the male word for whore?
what is the female for player?
what is the male word for prick-tease?
what is the female for rugged?
what is the female for bachelor?
what is the male word for spinster?
what is the female for ladies' man?
what is the male for old biddy?
what is the male word for nag?
what is the male word for bitch?
what is the human for tired of this shit?

For many years of my life, the sadness of the spinster future was engrained in my psyche; the weird, elderly woman living alone, unloved and childless, clitoris retreated into its lonely, untouched hood, weeping into her amateur tapestries, dying a sad and passionless death with no one to hold her wrinkled hand as she drowns in a heap of her own lonely ugly man-hating tears.

When my daughter started primary school – the local school was a C. of E. school – she was taught about marriage before she was taught division. She was taught that people in love get married. She questioned the unmarried couples in our family before she'd learnt what half of seven was.

The first recorded use of the word spinster was in the mid-1300s – initially to simply mean a woman who spins for a living (as in thread and yarn, not her own body or a bicycle stuck to the floor of a gym). Around five hundred years later this word slowly morphed, supposedly for economic reasons, into use in legal documents to refer to unmarried women: *married tradeswomen had greater access to raw materials and the market (through their husbands) than unmarried women did, and therefore unmarried women ended up with lower-status, lower-income jobs like combing, carding, and spinning wool.*[*]

By Victorian times, the word spinster was considered one of the most vicious insults that could be hurled at a woman.

In 1889, a British weekly magazine – *Tit-Bits* – ran an article, discovered over a century later by historian Dr Bob Nicholson, asking women the question: Why Am I A Spinster? It was in response to a previous Why Am I A Bachelor? call out from this same publication, which had asked men why they were not married.

The editor received many more answers to the spinster question than imagined, and much more passionate and amusing responses than expected so that instead of printing the best response as was initially advertised, the prize money was split between twenty-one winning responses.

Some of my favourites include:

Because I have other professions open to me in which the hours are shorter, the work more agreeable, and the pay possibly higher – Miss Florence Watts.

Because (like a piece of rare china) I am breakable, and mendable, but difficult to match – Miss S.A. Roberts.

---

[*] Merriam-Webster dictionary.

Because matrimony is like an electric battery, when you once join hands and can't let go, however much it hurts; and, as when embarked on a toboggan slide, you must go to the bitter end, however much it bumps – Miss Laura Bax.

Or, arguably the most poetic:

Like the wild mustang of the prairie that roams unfettered, tossing his head in utter disdain at the approach of the lasso which, if once round his neck, proclaims him captive, so I find it more delightful to tread on the verge of freedom and captivity, than to allow the snarer to cast around me the matrimonial lasso – Miss Sarah Kennerly.

Modern studies would tend to agree with these responses, the fact that the effect of marriage on women is still such a hot topic proving somewhat tiringly that the stereotype of the spinster has still not been defeated.

In contrast to the 'having it all' idealisation of the mother, wife, working woman, the therefore fulfilled and happy woman, the evidence shown by a study from behavioural scientist Paul Dolan suggests unmarried, child-free women are the happiest sub-group of the population, and that they are even likely to live longer than their married and child-rearing peers, all else considered.

I'm not sure if this includes the likelihood of being murdered, which for women is unfortunately higher if you're in an intimate relationship with a man, pregnant, post-partum, trying to leave a man or recently having left a man.

clutching keys

for years, you warned us of strangers
men in shadowed corners hiding threats inside our drinks
if we ever wore our minds above the knee

we listened. clutched our keys accordingly
to quickly open doors. it is true;
there are men who wait in shadows

for years, you warmed us towards marriage
men at hallowed altars giving meaning
to our lives; happy ever after never leave

we listened. clutched our keys accordingly
to quickly open homes in which
statistically, we are most likely to bleed

Motherhood is also particularly gruesome, despite being pushed alongside marriage as the pinnacle of female happiness. Physical and mental complications and illness resulting from pregnancy and birth aside, according to Best Beginnings, over one-third of intimate partner violence starts or gets worse when a woman is pregnant.

Another report suggests 'women are at greater risk of experiencing violence from an intimate partner during pregnancy and post partum'.[*] A study in 2021 found that homicide is the leading cause of death for pregnant women in the US.[†] The American College of Obstetricians and Gynecologists says that one in six abused women is first abused during pregnancy.

Sorry to go on, but I really feel it's important to happiness to stop covering all this up in Instagram photos of big weddings and baby nurseries. Marrying and/or having a family of your own can be utterly gorgeous, fulfilling, thrilling but is not the clear path to

[*]   https://aifs.gov.au/cfca/publications/
domestic-and-family-violence-pregnancy-and-early-parenthood.
[†]   https://www.insider.com/pregnant-women-in-the-us-homicide-leading-cause-of-death-report-says-2021-12.

happiness we have been sold for, erm, a very long time, and certainly not if you're female.

Many parents around me don't let their kids listen to sexual song lyrics. Fair enough. There are a lot of songs I think are extremely dangerous for young people to hear, mainly songs about strangulation during sex, which seems to be becoming more and more 'popular' for mainstream adult record bosses to release to children with absolutely no intimate sexual experience.

But so, in my opinion, are the other 'love' songs that we mainly deem totally fine.

Romantic even. Romantically dramatic. Possessively suicidally 'romantic'. The 'I'm nothing if you leave me, without you I'm a pointless piece of shit so don't ever leave me' sort of theme. Don't get me wrong, it's a feeling many have, but the extent to which we romanticise it irks.

dipped in fire

i'll not say you're my everything
– you're not

if we broke up, i would stand in hail
howling, once my daughter slept
missing you like midnight snow
stripped of moonlight's sun

while i carried on loving
other things i also love;

like hailstorms; like doughnuts;
like a touch in early evening
like hugging friends i haven't seen for years

like hearing children laughing
like dreaming i can fly
like marshmallows dipped in fire

Personally, I'd rather my kid hear Ashnikko singing about giving cunnilingus on somebody's couch (would prefer it not be someone else's 'girlfriend') than the very catchy and positively upbeat Diplo song 'Suicidal', which I sang all through my youth, that told me that a beautiful girl would make the singer suicidal if she ever left him.

At the end of the day, cunnilingus on a sofa doesn't kill anybody. Jealousy and possessiveness in romantic relationships sure as hell do.

After writing this flippant cunnilingus comment, I spent some time researching if cunnilingus has actually killed anyone. Thankfully, despite comedians making increasing references to face-sitting, I couldn't find it suggested anywhere.

For men, in contrast, marriage appears overall beneficial, with married men suggested to live longer than their unmarried counterparts. Every married woman I told this too simply said, 'Duh, of course.' Also, for men, starting a relationship or family with a woman does not increase your chances of being abused or murdered.

In his talk on the subject at the Hay Festival in 2019, Paul Dolan summarised his findings thus: 'We do have some good longitudinal data following the same people over time, but I am going to do a massive disservice to that science and just say: if you're a man, you should probably get married; if you're a woman, don't bother."

---

*   *Guardian*, 25 May 2019, https://www.theguardian.com/lifeandstyle/2019/may/25/women-happier-without-children-or-a-spouse-happiness-expert

for anonymous

your husband has not had to change
one single thing about his life
to work around your children

you have given up nearly everything:
your passions pastimes pelvic floor
your freedom prolapse pay rise pension

you say you've *lost your sex drive*
you say *it's probably lack of time*
i think, it's more the fact you hate him

The study, as does everything that is seen as a threat to picture-perfect family values, received backlash from both people who hold some sort of political or religious stake in forwarding married life, as well as those who *are* happily married with children – of which of course there are many – as if the finding somehow negated their happiness, which it doesn't.

The solution seems to be to only get married and have kids if you really, really want to. This perhaps seems simple. But even if you are able to make a conscious choice to not put a ring on it, or a bun in the oven, which many people can't due to familial, legal, religious or cultural pressures, according to Paul's study, even those who can make these choices and *are* happy in those choices still have their happiness diluted or even reversed due to the social hierarchies around love.

As in, it's not necessarily *not* being married or *not* having your own kids that prevent you being happy, it's not being married and not having kids in a society that deems getting married and having kids as the standard of success, the pinnacle proof of love, without which you have somehow failed.

I have conversations all the time with friends who, despite being happy, constantly apologise for being happy despite not being married, or despite being single, or despite not having children. Always despite, as if they shouldn't be happy, but somehow, and guiltily, they are.

My own recurrent 'I'm sorry but I'm happy' is about having only one child. Obviously, I don't get as much shit as child-free women get about having kids, but the amount of times that I've been told, especially when my kid was younger, to 'give her a little brother or sister to play with' as if birthing a second child were akin to buying her a fucking colouring book from Asda is incredible; as if there is no such thing as friends or cousins to share time with and be close to in life, only siblings; as if all siblings get on.

Am I happy with one child? Yes. (World whispers: *Really though, Hollie?*) Yes! (World whispers: *Selfish mother, poor child, lonely child, only children aren't in the holiday brochures you just flicked through.*)

For years, I have swallowed back every response I have to people who tell me I should have another child, so as not to make those with more than one, who are always the people who tell me I must have another one, and whose choices I have never dared criticise because it's none of my fucking business, feel bad.

For all anyone knows, I might have desperately wanted another and had several miscarriages. I might have had such a traumatic birth I couldn't consider doing it again despite wanting to. You just don't know. I didn't go through those things, I just don't want another kid. In fact, I really love having one child. I'm sorry, I apologise again, I really do. I love having one child and I never ever talk about why, but people so often praise the joys of bigger families. I'm sure there are positives for all sizes of families so if you're currently pregnant with your second or third, that is also fine, and great.

because i only have one child,

my hands are rarely too full
desperately attempting to grasp
more than they can carry,
the laundry basket's often empty,
my one face never turning its attention
to another set of screams
no ping-pong game of childcare
as the walls behind my back
are not painted with crayoned scribbles
of why do you love her more?
and it's my turn in the front! and
he was darth vader last time!
and middle-child syndrome
and sibling rivalry, and therapy at forty
as the oldest or the youngest
or one of three or two of seven
or never enough attention;
mealtimes at mine are mostly peaceful,
always have been
holidays both easier and cheaper,
the school run so much quicker
playtimes are patient, never arguing
which games each child
does and doesn't want to play
my savings do not hyperventilate
about the future; i can get the underground
in london without fainting with exhaustion,
friends pop over for dinner all the time,
i can offer piggy backs to everyone
if everyone is tired
and each time we cross the road

i have an entire extra safety hand
simply dangling at my side
in case of sudden scares; but hollie,
but hollie, you once again declare
as if i asked for your opinion,
as if i've ever given mine about the
toddler yanking at your trouser leg,
your baby in my arms again,
our three-year-olds yelling for us
to watch them on the swings –
don't you worry that your only child
your poor and lonely, only child
will grow up to be a spoilt and selfish prick?
it's a risk, i smile once more, *it's a risk*

As well as feeling like your happiness is not good enough if it doesn't adhere to the wife-mother-family fantasy, the opposite guilt is also true. If you *are* living the picture-perfect family life, have a kitchen island, your children play the flute, you have a husband and two or three children, but you don't feel overjoyed constantly, you're more likely to feel more guilty and confused because on paper you *have it all*. The pressure affects everyone.

In Paul Dolan's words: 'You see a single woman of forty, who has never had children – "Bless, that's a shame, isn't it? Maybe one day you'll meet the right guy and that'll change." No, maybe she'll meet the wrong guy and that'll change. Maybe she'll meet a guy who makes her less happy and healthy, and die sooner.'[*]

In terms of happiness, it seems there is one sort of relationship that makes a huge difference to all people. An exhibition in 2021 at the

---

*   *Guardian*, 25 May 2019, https://www.theguardian.com/lifeandstyle/2019/may/25/women-happier-without-children-or-a-spouse-happiness-expert

Wellcome Trust on joy and happiness forwarded this notion, with a quote from Robin Dunbar, Professor of Evolutionary Psychology, University of Oxford, stating: 'One of the surprises of the last decade or so has been the number of studies showing that how many friends we have and especially the quality of those friendships has more effect than anything else on our mental and even physical health, our sense of wellbeing and happiness, how much we trust those among whom we live, even how long we live.'

loneliness

if everybody had a gemma –
arms open as a cove
whatever weather beckons
toes would tiptoe to the water
dip timid skin in cheering tides
laughter of receding storm
tango to the moonbeat

if everybody had a gemma
loneliness would be antique;
an out of fashion trinket; *out of usage;*
obsolete, and future teachers,
on seeing pupils' puzzled faces
as they stumble on this ancient word,
would explain:
imagine, no gemma in the world

Perhaps, instead of dressing us up in wedding gowns at pre-school (as we were made to do) or teaching us in primary school that when two people love each other they marry and have a baby, we should have been teaching children how to make better connected friendships; that when two people love each other, they go for a walk in the park and share a bag of Skips and ask each other how they're doing and then have a game of whatever game you wanna play and don't punch each other and call them stupid if they cry or make them promise to be their best friend and no one else's forever.

This is perhaps especially important for little boys.

A 2019 YouGov survey found that one in five men have no close friends, and 2021 research by the mental health charity Movember suggested that almost one-third of men felt as though they do not have any close friends – or any friends at all. If friendship is so crucial to life's ills then marriage is being used to fill in the gaps, and maybe this is why we're all still encouraged to get hitched, to rescue men from this often devastating loneliness, female knights carrying away our male damsels from their isolated towers to nurture and hold this mental burden of men who find making meaningful friendships difficult.

One of the weirdest things for me that our society often romanticises is the death of two old people at the same time.

I get the idea – the couple loved each other so much that they couldn't live without each other, and so when one died the other died in broken-hearted solidarity, and that is supposedly a lovely thing, to rely on one person so much that you drop dead if they die before you. Pure. Love.

But, personally, I'd rather people didn't drop dead in sync with their partners, even if they're really old. I'd rather no one dropped dead because they couldn't live without someone else. I don't think that makes me an unromantic bitch. I just prefer it when people stay alive when they are able to.

As much as I loved both of my grandads, I'm really glad my grandmas didn't drop dead in lovesick heartache when my grandads died.

I don't think this implies that my grandmas didn't love their husbands with the strength that those who died in sync did, or didn't miss their husbands terribly. It's not unromantic to keep living, no matter what the powerful love ballads might say (Adele excluded), or films where men hang from big wheels threatening their own death for a date.

Instead, they both had what seemed to be many more years of happiness with family love and love of friends and birds and tulips and travel to new countries or garden centre cafés and, in my gran's case, her first try of a mango smoothie, which I was so thrilled to be a part of, as well as a bit of romance, mainly in the form of perving on the sixty-year-old decorating guy who seemed to repaint the hallway more often than paint could ever chip.

seashells

some days are hard
some days friends feel far away
some days they are

some days lovers leave
lungs lose the art of easy breathing
sleep a skill forgot

tomorrow might be better
it might not

either way i am here
if you want to talk we can

but i hug just as willingly
through awkward
sobbing silence

if you'd rather weep in peace
i'll read a book downstairs
slip biscuits through the letterbox

distract you
if that's better
with facts i learnt last week

about the way
a seashell opens

i know things about the husbands

the one who weighs his wife each night but not himself
the one who bought the boob job as a surprise birthday gift
because she didn't look the same four kids later;
the one whose dinner must be at eight,
must be different every day, must be fresh, must be tasty,
is it your children who tire you, really?
you say you'd be happy with beans on toast most days,
so would they –
i'll just check with him, i'll just check with him, i'll just –
there's the one who marks the kitchen calendar with
when you last had sex to remind you with a smiley face,
although you do not cum that way
there's the one who has his own chair
and needs his chair back and we all have to leave
and my mum sat on the floor; there's the one
you have to ask to hold his own newborn baby
every time you want to eat and the one who still earns
more than you because you turned down the promotion,
the one who waits, watching tele, for his wife to return
from work to ask her what's for dinner,
and there's the one who does half the childcare
and brings in half the wage
and we all say *what a saint what a saint what a saint*
you are so lucky you are so lucky you are so lucky
there's the one who reciprocates oral sex and we all say
what a saint you are so lucky where did you find him?
last week, your mother marched you to the chapel
where you married him, the one who asks you why
you bother painting, who always waits five minutes
before he comes to the table just to make a point,
eats the dinners tepid before joking to your kids

that their mother never learnt to cook, and he's right
you didn't, because you're a teacher, not a chef
they say it's different now. perhaps it is, but do you know
how many times i've been told that my cousin tim
is actually the one who cooks the dinner in their house,
like actually *all the time*.

for the sake of the children

for my most despised piece of advice
given to couples wanting and able to separate

won't you just stay together
until your kids are in college?

sit round a table pretending to smile
save the truth till they go out with friends
when silence repeats its marital beggings
like stage understudies;

doing the dishes
like wringing out blood

wouldn't you just stay together
pretend *this is love*,

until your kids are in college
until your kids are all gone
until your kids are having kids of their own

until your grandkids are grown
until your house has no bones
until the fig tree is rotten

until storm clouds burst open
the stars spat their last; sun fire imploded
planet sucked into a vacuumless hole

and your lips, pretending so long to pucker
for someone who scoffs at your skin

have forgotten the point of their softness

coffin nailed shut
body ash cold
and the funeral guests,

unaware of the tears
in your cinder grey eyes
can comfortably make their way home

punch

on the beach front, we giggled
crowds of cross-legged kids,

as punch, pleased as punch
beat the shit out of his wife

and we yelled: *that's the way
to do it!* and the dog stole

all the sausages, and we
begged for a screwball

because there's
bubble gum beneath

**poem written after hearing the comment
'*if it was that bad, why didn't they just leave*'
during a discussion on domestic violence**

if it was that bad, why didn't they just leave?
you accuse, chewing on a chicken thigh
flesh stuck between your teeth

genius that you are, if only they
had thought of that, if only they
had had your intellect

knew how handles work
how to open doors, how to run
in the opposite direction

i imagine you researched this
fully
before offering your opinion

that you know the most likely time
a person will be beaten
is on trying to flee the fists

and if they do escape unscathed
which statistically they won't
will you be there to help them –

offer up your home?
a bolted bedroom door?
bouncer for protection

from the demons, i mean human,
who does not just disappear
once doors are closed?

have you ever tried to leave someone
who promises to find you
wherever you may go?

fire stoked
each time
you tell them no

like breath blown onto flames
sometimes, if it is *that bad*
it is safer just to stay

pray help
not judgement
comes your way

dishwasher

you tell me it's the little things –
the way she picks crisps from her teeth
watches tele half involved
how she bites her thumbnails, breathes
the way she stacks the dishwasher

the way she stacks the dishwasher
it's always back to that

knife blades upside down; plates stacked backwards;
backwards! no matter how often you tell her!

i hear you,
still, i'm suspicious of your reasonings

does anybody really hate the way
a person stacks plates?

does anybody *really hate* the way
a person stacks plates?

I LOVE YOU, MY FRIENDS

One of my favourite songs is Louis Armstrong's 'What a Wonderful World', possibly because it diverges from the standard love-song lyrics and actually talks about other subjects like the sea and sky and roses and friendship.

My favourite line of the song was the line about friendship, the one in which it is claimed that friends 'shaking hands, saying how do you do' is really their way of saying 'I love you'.*

I've never shaken hands with friends, it feels like such a formal gesture. I guess we didn't have to revert to handshakes because no one, if the girls hugged, would call us names. For many boys and men, a handshake or a falsely soft but still violent backslap was perhaps the closest they could get to hugging in our culture as they got older without being ridiculed in some homophobic way. I imagine this was even more evident in the era in which Louis Armstrong sang about the wonderful world.

This song was also the first time I had heard it suggested that friends did in fact love each other and that gestures that friends make to each other can be seen as gestures of love. Like, 'I love you'. That line is so stark. It's not I love you, mate, or I love you, you know. It's total. I love you.

I said I love you to just about everything I harboured passion or excitement for when I was little, except my friends, despite the fact

_____
* From 'What a Wonderful World', written by Bob Thiele and George Weiss, 1967.

that through childhood and into adulthood, I have loved friends more than most other people or things on this planet.

I think in reality, I *was* often telling my friends I loved them when I told them I loved the new skorts they were wearing or new posters of Take That they were putting up in their bedrooms. Did I really love Julie's wooden model whose arms and legs moved, or did I love Julie? Did I love the photos we were looking through in Laura's exceptionally well-organised photo album, or did I love Laura and all the friends I was looking at in the photos? Oh, I love your side ponytail! Oh, I love the soda stream flavours you have ... your hair that colour ... that CD you lent me! Even 50p scrunchies from New Look. Perhaps especially 50p scrunchies from New Look.

As an adult, it seems sometimes that friendship, or putting friendship first, is seen, like roller skating, as embarrassing or childish. I can't think of anyone who's done it. We put partners first, have children, get married. We move away for work and romantic relationships, for the work of those we are in romantic relationships with but rarely for friends.

I was trying to think at what point these love hierarchies started to shift as I watched my toddler hold my hand less, grabbing on to other children's hands at the park instead. Once my daughter noticed I wasn't the only one who could chase her round a park, make daisy chains and play peekaboo, spending time with friends who played with her began to take precedence over family ties.

Realising that my daughter would increasingly prefer to be with her friends than with me, whether in playparks or, as now, talking on the phone or texting or snapping or gramming or DMing or – the list is endless these days – has been a hard heartache sometimes. Sometimes, of course, it is freedom. I can spend more time with my own friends. I can be alone more. I can actually do work in the day and not wait till she's asleep. But it is hard on the heart. I've never had someone need me so intensely as she did. If any romantic partner needed me that intensely, I'd run.

I love my daughter with every inch of my bone marrow and I hope beyond much else in life to have a long and loving relationship with her. I hope she will always feel she can come to me for anything. I do not want her to want to be with me more than with her friends, even if I secretly also might. She no longer grabs my leg and cries when I leave her, just as I no longer grab my mum's leg and cry when she goes home after visiting us.

But when those arms, once inside your body, then clinging every moment to your body, start to ease off, it is a heartache like little I have known or want to know again.

nostalgia for the toddler

no one will ever love me as much as you did
before you realised i wasn't perfect
before you realised other people
could string daisies into jewels

When parents, myself included, bemoan the amount of messaging kids do with their friends, I try to remember my early teenage days. I was exactly the same.

How many times was I caught on the phone to my friends, clogging up the line and wasting the family money? *What if someone's been trying to call, Hollie? You've just been at school with Kathryn all day, do you really need to phone her?*

Yes, yes I do. Because Kathryn walked home with Jo and Julie and sometimes stuff happens on that hour walk that I miss and need to be updated on before the morning.

And sometimes, I needed to know straight away if they, also watching *O-Town: Making the Band* on Saturday morning, also knew 'Liquid Dreams' was about sleep-wanks.

I was reminded recently by my boyfriend of the trope of a father holding the phone bill in front of his kids with numbers that he didn't know highlighted. *Which of your friends are these numbers?* I hardly remember my own mobile phone number these days, but I still remember each one of my school friends' home telephone numbers as if they were a secret code to happiness, because they were.

If I wasn't physically with my friends or allowed to call them, I was very often sitting in my room writing letters to them to give them the next day; letters of important information such as the top-ten pencil cases that we could check out at the weekend, new music I liked or my new celebrity crushes.

And I know friendships can be utterly brutal. Falling out with friends and losing friends and being shunned by friends. Friends can be clingy and unforgiving, obsessive, cruel. I still panic when I think of the note I got from a girl in school asking to be my best friend with a yes or no tick box. Her sister was one of the hardest girls in the year above. I didn't want to sign a best-friend treaty with anyone. I didn't want to put promises to paper.

Yes, for some, friendships, or 'friendship dramas' as we called them at school, have been the bane of their lives and the idea of being in a more isolated couple or family, blissful. For others, friends are quite literally the family we choose, and sometimes a crucial lifeline out of toxic familial or romantic relationships.

I have always loved my friends. I just don't think I knew I loved them until Louis Armstrong whispered it deeply into my eardrums. Or, that the love I had for my friends was just as real and just as significant as the love I had for Leonardo DiCaprio as he sat on a beach smoking in the Baz Luhrmann remake of Shakespeare's classic tragedy. I'd be too old for him now, of course.

and

you took a bite out of my birthday cake
before mum put the candles on
and i forgive you, my friend
because i love you

you gave my garfield annual back
fifteen years after i lent you it
and i forgive you, my friend
because i love you

you got boobs before i did
which i assumed you'd done on purpose;
but i forgive you, my friend
i hope you forgive me too

and i'm sorry i never thought
how hard that was for you
and i'm sorry that i let you
take the blame for the malibu
and i'm sorry i never gave
your two-tone jacket back
or the troll with the pink hair
or your point horror book

and i forgive you for your face
when i told you i was pregnant

and i am sorry i did not
make it to your wedding

and i forgive you for never
remembering her birthday

and i'm so sorry i forgot
your third kid's name again

and i forgive you
and i'm sorry

and i'm sorry
and i forgive you

and i love you
and i hope this never ends

If the life of children is often built around friendships, adult life is presumed to be built around work, family and lovers, not friends. Friendship takes a firm back seat. But love is not a competition and it's odd we seem to have made it such. Giving friendship equal status to romantic or family love does not negate the others. We have space to let everyone in, if we want. We really do, even if we don't always have the *time* we want to be able to give to friendships.

Relationships take work is a phrase I've heard a lot, but never about friendships, as if that work doesn't matter. Staying in touch with friends takes work. Being a good friend takes work. Remembering friends' kids' birthdays.

Parenting also takes work. A lot of it. Being a kind neighbour or grandparent or aunty or cousin. But it's never about that. It's always about working hard when it comes to romantic relationships, sticking through it, mainly about marriages, which is perhaps why we make such a fuss over these anniversaries as if reaching ten or twenty or fifty years is some sign of higher achievement, harder work; the phrase 'happily married' still a necessary appendage.

Imagine saying you're in a 'happy friendship' – it would sound ludicrous.

So yes, of course, happy anniversary if it is, marriages can be gorgeous, glorious, a life bonded in mind and body with one chosen soul. Beautiful. Work for it and reap the benefits and beauty of that time you've put in.

But is it still a joyful achievement, is it still an achievement at all, if the people married are miserable or worse or, you know, just born at a time when divorce was so shameful or financially and socially impossible that they 'stuck it through', as previous generations, especially the women, are so often heralded for having loyally and lovingly done, getting a ruby for your troubles.

divorce rates go up

the headlines tell it
like a tragedy
forget the word finally
forget the word can

Around the world, many news outlets are currently pissing their panicked pants about the rise of single women, both young and, gulp, older, refuting claims that they are 'happy living alone' or 'happy to be single' as if they are perhaps mentally unstable or protesting too much.

South Korea now has a declining population rate, with thousands of headlines pointing fingers at South Korean women's 'refusal' or 'rejection' of marriage and children, with articles delving into the curious conundrum: why don't South Korean women want to get married and have kids? Hmm, tricky. Your guess is as good as mine.

Relationships take work. But what if you'd rather put that hard relationship work into being an excellent aunty? Into looking after stray dogs? Into caring for kids in a classroom? Into petitioning for lower air pollution? Into sitting alone, happily, learning to knit jumpers? Into friendships? The work put into friendships, which are often the most long-lasting and healthy relationships of people's lives, is rarely celebrated in gemstone timelines.

Saying all of this, during primary school and into the first few years of secondary, I bought best-friend necklaces from Argos quite often, with forever friends bears or hearts on them. You keep one half, your friend keeps the other half and you are forever bound in £5.99 eternal harmony.

It mirrors the exchange of rings or hand binding, I guess, but with fewer rules about going ice skating with other people and no government or church interference should you decide you no longer get on as well as you did; no official documents to sign and no name to change on every social media platform if best friends come and go, as often is the case. Imagine having to ask the government every time you wanted to swap the Argos half-hearts.

I am grateful that our social codes haven't managed to have quite as much a hold over friendship love as they do sexual and romantic relationships. I imagine standing in a government courtroom trying to break up a best-friend contract for two friends grown apart:

'And what are your grounds for this separation?'

'Well, basically, yeah she said that she was on the Oasis side of the Blur/Oasis divide, but actually I found out from another friend that she'd actually gone to the Blur concert and she didn't even tell me that she liked them so I'm just so upset that she lied to me because she swore that she thought that "Morning Glory" was the best song ever made and I made her a T-shirt and everything. Also, she thinks Peter André is fitter than John Leguizamo, which is ridiculous.'

I still have one of those necklaces. Half a coin. In all honesty, I can't remember which one of my friends I gave the other half to because I dished out quite a few. Still, it felt very special at the time.

As well as Argos jewels, we also made bracelets plaited from wool or thick colourful thread or bought from tacky tourist shops on holidays. Friendship bracelets.

As we grew up, we didn't give them out any more; the world of jewellery taken over by the romantic ideal of wedding rings and rubies, or a diamond necklace being draped gently round your neck before you walk down some stairs into a casino and everyone's head turns to gaze at your beauty.

I used to find this a bit sad, the gradual slowing of friendship-bracelet making, but I'm now thinking that love which doesn't need gemstones is maybe the most glorious of all.

titanic

though i have never snogged you sober
or with serious intent
you are still the greatest romance of my life

if i were romeo, my friends, and you, juliet
that curtain
would never have fallen when it did

i would have known without a twitch
that the poison were a trick
and if you were anakin, my friends,

and i, pregnant padmé,
we would have talked our feelings through
you would not have joined the dark side

you would not have spent half your life
slaughtering young jedis
heavy wheezing through that dreadful mask

and if you were jack and i were rose,
once you'd sketched my lovely tits
or maybe just my lovely face, i would have

made space on that raft,
because there *was* a bit of space
and when, eighty-four years later

some patronising fuck in a diving team
asks us if, by any chance,
we can remember anything at all

anything at all about a giant diamond necklace?
we'd shake our heads in unison
fingers forever crossed behind our backs

how octopuses shag

there are friends you go out dancing with and friends you chat
with sipping tea and friends good for both; friends you love
to see in groups but would never meet alone; friends you've
known since childhood and friends you met last week; friends
you might not see for years but feel utterly at ease every time
you do; there are friends who lend you shoulders; friends who
lend you shoes; friends you only ever text; friends who phone
you as they pee; friends who leave twenty-minute messages
each week; friends you call when passion dies; when cakes
don't rise; mealtimes burn; when tulips wilt; war begins; when
shadows grip your ankles; when your boss has been a bastard
and you're late to get your kid from school; friends you can
pop into and friends you have to book; friends who know your
favourite tune, your bravest move; your secrets; friends who
give you flowers; friends who write you cards; friends who send
you articles about how octopuses shag; there are friends you
call for gossip; friends you call to sob; friends who broke your
heart; friends you wish you hadn't lost; friends you're glad you
left; friends you miss every day;

friends you haven't met yet.

pluviophile love song

pluviophile: a lover of rain; who finds joy and peace of mind during rainy days

i love you like frogs love rain
but if you changed your mind about me
i'd be ok, after a while

there's a lot i'd do without you
– not die, though
your life is no more precious than mine

i think of you each sunrise
and sunset and often in between
and when i touch my skin in gloaming haze

or eat or walk or breathe
but if you wanted someone else
i hope you'd leave

you're not everything i need
that would be weird
and slightly creepy

i wasn't nothing before you
i'd not be nothing if you left me
but i'd much rather you stayed

some say i'm unromantic; i am not
your conversation turns my nipples
rosehip ripened after frost

and when you sit by me on trains
or whisper-eat my neck
gasps satiate my ribs as if

each zoo cage in the world
broken open by a storm;
set every wild beast free

you are the man of so many of my dreams –
like the one where we fly topless
on the silk-scaled purple dragon

or the one where you are my optician
and you say i must be patient
as you change the filter on those clicky glasses

and come so close to my face and put your hand
over my left eye and ask what i can read,
and i slowly tell you PEZOLCFTD

or just the dream where you are you
and i am me and we sleep bundled
as if our bodies cannot dream alone

but not the one where i eat cherries
with frida kahlo
in a rowing boat, or the one

where all my friends come to visit me
in cuba, where i live because i'm cuban,
and george michael's still alive

and if you found somebody else
i'd be so jealous of that next love
but i wouldn't key your car

cos you don't have one
and i wouldn't key her car
even if she did

i love you like frogs love rain
like you love frogs so let's have fun
until we don't, let's kiss till we don't want to,

let's talk until i bore you
or you bore me, or we both just
change our minds,

or the world becomes uninhabitable
to humans, which, right now
i am certain will come first

gemstones

chiselled

from
their rock
they do not care
if you and tim are still
together, as if your life times
were a test, swap the ruby ring
for cash, they're not bothered,
they do not sit in courtrooms
scowling at your divorce
they are gemstones
nothing more,
content
within
their caves
before, chisel sharp
we smash them
into shape

Never Wear Navy with Black

At thirty-two years old, while getting dressed one very normal weekend morning to go for a walk into town, already in my comfiest black trousers, I noticed my favourite navy sweater on the bed, its softness the kind that only very worn clothes give and I shuddered, realising it was not a scientific truth that these colours – navy and black – could not be worn together as I had somehow believed since an article I read in a magazine when I was eighteen years old told me to never combine navy and black in an outfit. Next to this article were photographs of celebrities wearing these colours together in public, giant red crosses slashed across their grotesque choice of outfit to highlight the disgusting faux pas.

Never, it said, *never wear navy with black.* The message was written with such confidence, as if this rule was akin to: *never put your fingers in a plug socket, look both ways when crossing the road, don't masturbate after chopping chillies, never give oral sex to someone with gonorrhoea.*

For the first time in my life, I put a navy sweater on with the black trousers and the sky remained sun-filled, vultures did not swoop to peck my heart out, God did not make thunder of clouds to punish me for the sin of awkward colour coordination, no wolf cubs howled as I passed, no children, petrified by my choice of hues, sobbed behind their mothers' legs; daisy petals remained open to the sun; raindrops still fell, hugging into puddles, my boyfriend did not refuse me cunnilingus, vomiting into my vulva, disgusted at the colour combination of the outfit he had just unbuttoned, and I wondered, what other opinions, spoken as if ancient proverbs, had I been following for the last three decades of my life?

Do not wear horizontal stripes if you are apple shaped?
Avoid cropped hairstyles on a square face?

Opt for a wide-leg if wearing lace?

Put your tongue to the top of your mouth to avoid a double chin in photographs?

Always love him less than he loves you.

Sorry, Grandma, I have never managed that one.

All the advice I had swallowed all these years. All the 'rules' I had learnt from over-confident so-called 'beauty' magazine articles and their advertising sponsors and other people who had read the same lines as I had.

So many things I had not enjoyed as much, especially in my late teens and early twenties, as I should have for worrying about whether my outfit matched while I was out dancing, or my body was the right fruit shape while having sex, or my hair was silky enough for anyone to really love me. Such a terrible, terrible waste of time.

A week after the navy and black rebellion, I gazed through a shop window at a summer dress patterned in peaches and peaches are my favourite and I treat myself to one new dress each summer. My boyfriend offered to buy it for my birthday and I turned to him, as if a perfect programmed robot, and said *thank you, but my legs are too short for long dresses.* Then I burst into tears.

The realisation you have listened to such pointless crap for so long was overwhelming. I have put my tongue to the top of my mouth in every family photograph ever taken. I tried on the dress. It didn't fit.

BEGINNINGS

Birthing Dragons

I gather intelligence by sniffing his bum.

CLARE POLLARD, 'Soft Play'

the day i gave birth

was not the best day of my life; far from it –
today, for example, i ordered two half orange juice
half lemonades for us and we walked along
the river path chatting about which comedy
we'd watch tonight with dinner and what to buy
your friend for her eleventh birthday gift;
my stitches no longer bloody, insides no longer raw
you, no longer vomiting milk excess upon my shoulder
me, no longer wiping sick from skin in supermarket toilets
you no longer wailing wordless in the street
me no longer petrified to close my aching eyes
in case you perish in my dreams

if you think it's hard now

before your lungs had sung in air
still scuba-ing inside me
as i scratched my life-stretched belly
and vomited once more

they laughed *if you think it's hard*
being pregnant, hollie,
wait until the baby's here!

and then you were here, and it *was* hard
i bled, the stitches slowly healed
you smiled as blossom fell on grass
your toes a prayer. i did not sleep
some days, no more than leaking tap
the constant drip of milk and tears
your giggles mending each tired night
you screamed again. i did not sleep.

and they laughed: *if you think it's hard*
having a baby, hollie,
wait till she can walk and speak

and then you spoke and walked, and it *was* hard
i held your hand, you held mine back
your fingers gripped my own like life
summer rain turned winter frost
you screamed as a first snowflake fell
and melted on your hoping palm,
and you giggled and you wailed
and a ladybird strolled past your feet
and you screamed in shops and slumped

404

on streets and your fingertips popped bubbles
and that, that was enough for you;
the world a mad magician
through which i saw each hour anew
and remembered how to talk to toys
make people out of forks and spoons
how to stop at every single daisy
how to sob when you said mum

and they laughed: *if you think a toddler's trouble, hollie,*
wait till she can run and jump

and you ran, and we ran arm in arm
and you jumped and we jumped crashing seas
and you skipped and we skipped to the moon
and you sprinted, sometimes far from me

and they laughed
if you think this is tricky, hollie,
wait till she's a teen

and now you *are* a teen and your eyes *do* roll
and hugs don't come so frequently
and your toys get bored and you go out more
and you like your friends much more than me
and you close the door to sleep at night
and you sigh as i blow kisses through
and we sleep in late at weekends now
but snow still falls as beautifully
and i can borrow all your jumpers
and your chat is much more interesting
and your laugh still mends each tired night
like the most enthralling magic trick

and yes, sometimes it's difficult
because sometimes it always is

and they laughed, *if you think it's hard now, hollie,*
but i'd finally stopped listening

for Catrin

you knew before a single breath
this world was not for you

no wonder, i imagine it was
wonderful within her

songs swimming through the waters
like whispers under sea

you left love letters inside her
forever there to read

so beautiful you were. are.
will always be

THE BEST DAYS OF YOUR LIFE

The day I gave birth was not the best day of my life. I said this to a friend in front of my daughter and my friend looked at me like I had just slapped both my child and motherhood across its beloved face.

You can't say that! she exclaimed later.

I didn't really understand. It seems evident to me that the day you birth a human through either your vagina or a cut open womb and can't walk or wee properly for days or weeks and are possibly suffering from a multitude of serious physical and mental traumas, wouldn't be up there.

I didn't mean it as an insult to my daughter, whose presence in my life is undoubtedly one of the best things that ever has and will ever happen to me.

My daughter was eleven at the time. At that point, we'd had about four thousand days together. That's a lot of great days.

The idea that the day I gave birth, or those subsequent early days or weeks, during which my vagina was bleeding, I couldn't wipe myself with loo paper, I couldn't stand for long periods of time without possibly instigating a prolapse in later life, worried my stitches were not holding together a battered and terrified body, added to the now almost unimaginable lack of sleep ... no, they weren't the best.

Saying this does not mean that I didn't find my daughter astounding in babyhood or didn't feel magically blessed by her and her healthy delivery onto this Earth. But no, they weren't the best days of my life with her. Not even close. I also find it fairly insulting to her; the idea that I should have had better days with her as a baby. She is so much more brilliant to hang around with now than when she couldn't even talk.

I feel like this expectation of bliss is one of the issues I had with new motherhood.

Whereas often in life we 'prepare for the worst' so that whatever we are readying ourselves for goes, hopefully, better than expected, with new motherhood, we seem more often to force mums in particular to do the opposite. We make new motherhood seem heavenly. And all the bad bits, we're told not to talk about, for fear it will put people off having kids, or scare women or upset us all or just, you know, be a bit much.

I saw so many idealised images of mothering – on products, brochures, book front covers, social media – photos of women, mainly white women, mainly white women wearing white clothes, mainly white women wearing white clothes with white husbands, mainly white women wearing white clothes with white husbands with very white teeth in very white kitchens looking nothing but ecstatically happy holding or feeding or rocking or staring lovingly at mainly white babies in mainly white sheets and white blankets in a white bedroom with white angels and a white God with a white beard.

Of course there are people who don't want to know certain things. I'm not talking about giving a pregnant woman a two-hour graphic detailed talk about your possible perineum stitches, but the idea that not talking about any of the possible traumas somehow protects new mothers is bollocks. It was for me anyway. It also ruined some of the great moments of pregnancy and new motherhood, of which there were so, so many, because they still didn't live up to the holiday brochure I'd been sold.

You are pregnant. And morning sickness isn't only in the morning, and maternity leave doesn't cover vomiting in the office every day and you are possibly really scared as well as really excited but everybody tells you it's your hormones, and you are a crazy and forgetful mess, and maybe it is some of the hormones but blaming them for every feeling also kind of belittles the huge task you are undertaking and all the other reasons you may be more vividly emotional than when you are not growing a fucking life inside you and preparing physically and mentally to give birth to it.

But you have the advertised bliss of new motherhood to look forward to. It must be spectacular. It must be the highlight of your life. The best ever days.

Then you have the baby and your teeth still aren't white enough to smile like that mother on the breast-pump packaging and you don't orgasm with joy every time you hold your baby and sometimes you stand with baby shit on your arm and cry.

tap

my tits are leaking milk
my nose is leaking snot
my pants are leaking blood
please someone turn me off

And it's not that it's all terrible, it is also incredible in so many ways, but giving the impression that it is *supposed* to be blissful and joyous and mess-free can also add so much guilt and pressure even when everything is going well. And by well, I mean, everyone is healthy and has the help they need.

Best days of your life. It's a bogus concept anyway. Most days are a mixture.

Some of my best life memories have definitely been forged from the fires of early motherhood – my baby's first laugh, woah; the feel of her sleep-hot cheek settled against my chest in a cradle, snoring soft as freshly rising dough as I wandered around the shops feeling like something utterly magical was happening to me. But even those days, the days in which some of the best moments lingered, were also interrupted by screaming I didn't know how to deal with, fears of choking, boredom, isolation and so on.

Sometimes the exact same activities had opposite effects on me depending on the mood I was in, mainly based on how much sleep I'd had.

Like . . . 5 a.m. wakes. I wake up to my baby daughter standing up in her cot, smiling, eager to play at 5 a.m.

Some days the sight of this made my heart melt with love and gratitude.

On these days, I would stumble to her room and look at her smiling eager face and think *oh you are so in love with the world look at your gorgeous excited face, I am so in love with you of course I will get up now, the sun is shining and I am your mother and I love everything about you and you are teaching me to love the mornings more than I ever have before.* Other days, I thought: *5 a.m., are you fucking kidding me? I can't do this any more. I can't fucking do this, I cannot fucking cope* and then sob the entire morning.

When people label any period of life 'the best days of your life', often telling you to 'cherish them' because, so the implication seems, the rest will be much, much shitter, it makes me want to vomit.

I was told this about my 'youth' for years by a variety of people. Oh those days! Schooldays! The best days of your lives.

I was also told it about my wedding, that my wedding day would be the best day of my life, which is doubly weird because I've never been married, or even engaged.

Similarly, as a new mother, I was told constantly that having a baby, as in literally the early new motherhood baby years, would be the best days of my life, so cherish them, cherish them, cherish every single minute of them because otherwise you are a terrible selfish mother who does not appreciate what you have and what others desperately want and cannot have so you better never fucking moan.

eden

for mine and any other unfurling ferns

i put a bird feeder on my window
filled with bird feed i had bought
now birds sing at my window
– they never did before

put bulbs into the soil
filled with hibernating blooms
the bulbs grew brightly coloured
bees came flying down

sliced an avocado flesh
cleaned the stone already cracked
put it in a glass of water
watched a tiny tree expand

i pushed a baby from my body
fed her milk and sleep and hugs
watched her skin uncurl beneath me
as ferns unfurl in sun

When pregnant I had constant nightmares; vivid, fiery, fierce recurring nightmares the likes of which I had fortunately never had before. These nightmares continued for months after I gave birth; I dreamt I was still pregnant and had to do it all again. Seeing that my baby was indeed already born when I woke up was a relief like no other.

I later learnt that pregnant women are said to have some of the most frequent nightmare-filled sleeps. When I heard this, I felt a weird sense of elation. Like it wasn't just me being more negative than others. I also thought, *of course we do*. I just spent nine months with a baby growing inside my body, getting gradually much larger than the supposed exit pathway, nine months worrying about every single detail. Of course I was petrified.

But I did it. We did it. She arrived and was healthy and we came through all the blood and tears and stitches and late nights and early mornings and we were living.

It's not the done thing to act as if giving birth teaches you anything, but I'm tired of that attitude. No, growing and birthing a baby does not make you a better or more accomplished person. No, it is not OK that every female politician or public figure is seen as uncaring if she does not have or want children of her own. No, being a mother does not mean you are more loving or that you do more good for children in general. But: giving birth does give you a view of life that cannot be replicated or understood by those who haven't done it. I'll be fucked if I'm going to keep denying this any longer. Pregnancy and birth are a big deal. My body has gone through something massive and both the trauma and the awe of it have changed my outlook on life forever.

It's all very tricky because it is possibly too insensitive to people who desperately want the experience or who had much more traumatic birth experiences. I don't know the balance.

It annoys me to say nothing, because it was a massive deal and because I really, really want to talk about it and because, while glamourised in many ways, the realities of pregnancy and birth and raising children are still given so little actual status in our society. The famous quote *there is nothing more burdensome to art than the pram in the hallway* has been cited to me so often, as if nothing amazing or inspiring resides in any of these experiences.

correction

the pram in the hallway is tiring
i do not have much time to write
scribble down poems in play parks
and the still of nights

every piece could be edited better
but the baby needs fed
i'm sure there are many more beautiful words
i could find if i'd slept

the pram in the hallway is stirring
put down your pen
do not bother yourself with the endings
you're about to forget

the pram in the hallway is waking
what a beautiful fight
a million more wonders to write about
in a tenth of the time

Pregnancy and birth were so frightening and so painful and so extraordinary and such hard work and I did them and I know that a huge part of that was luck, luck that my body was OK and luck that I have the NHS, and luck that the baby was OK and that I am a white woman in the UK. But I still want to brag about it a bit.

Also, my friends brag about so much shit that is nothing compared to this.

Marathons, for example.

I know lots of people who have run marathons. They talked about it all the fucking time – the training, the bleeding scabby feet, the need to piss sometimes when still running, the after effects of it, the five-day body cramps and aching and blisters.

I listened to all the gory details and I was proud of them, despite not understanding what the point of ever doing a marathon is when instead you could not do a marathon.

But then I guess people might say that about choosing to have children and self-inflicted bleeding vaginas or Caesarean scars or worse.

Another example: some of my friends do dry January every year and fuck me, if they don't go on about it.

When pregnant, I did a whole year of dry Januaries (I'm not shaming those who don't stop drinking when pregnant, but I did). I didn't pose about that at all.

Not only did I do thirteen dry Januaries, but while being sober in nightclubs I also carried a life inside my body and I cycled to work vomiting and I carried on working (this was out of necessity, it was totally shit to work when vomiting and sore) and my back ached and I took on all the strain of this child's development inside me and the worry of my body stretching out of control and then I gave birth, I gave birth, and it took twelve hours and my body fucking heaved and I pushed and pushed and I pushed and my feet didn't bleed like in a marathon but other parts bloody well did and the baby was born and I tried to recover with uncomfortable stitches and bleeding and breasts leaking and I got on buses while my breasts leaked and I fed my baby in places where people looked at me like I was murdering kittens in front of them and I know I am lucky that it all went OK and I know I chose to have a child but you chose to do a marathon and my body is also a goddamn champion and I want to scream it every time someone uses the word pussy as a weakness because I have felt my pussy burn and push life through its eternally stretching gateway to our galaxy and I want to tell people what I did and what I'm still doing, but I can't.

I can't say any of it.

So I sit on my healed vagina and watch another documentary

about the strength of a woman called Tamsin who has climbed a mountain in Kathmandu followed by a fifty-person film crew, or a man called Nigel who is holding up his shirt to show us all the scar where a shark bit him because he is an amazing adventurous wealthy explorer who swims with sharks and I look down at my body and I think I fucking swam with sharks and I have scars. If my vagina had been scarred by a shark bite not a baby's skull, I'd be interviewed on every fucking programme on television.

Some of my mates even brag about cushions they bought on discount in Dunelm.

I thought this feeling would ebb as the memory of birth and breastfeeding and those most intense of newborn months all but faded, but it hasn't.

Eleven years on and I still want to shout it from the rooftops for my former twenty-seven-year-old shattered self.

I want to shout at the doctor who said I might as well go home when I was crying in the hospital after birth and didn't know what to do.

I want to punch the other doctor who compared childbirth to stubbing his toe.

I want to pull the passengers off the tube by their hair who would not give up their seat on the train when I was eight months pregnant and could hardly stand without pissing myself.

I want to storm into National Rail and ask why the fuck we design trains that left me as a newborn mum, not meant to even be standing up because I had a gaping wound between my legs and a womb which may more likely fall through it eventually if I don't rest, the choice between sitting on the floor in the vestibule like a bag of shit or waking up my sleeping baby to scream and wail at passengers for the next hour as I folded down the pram.

I want to tell myself, and every parent and carer in every café and on every bus who are frantically shooshing their babies or scolding their toddlers for simply chattering, that these public spaces are their public spaces too, and that they do not need to continuously apologise for having had a child.

I want to scream and scream and scream for all the new parents waking up to the fact that we make raising a child so very much more difficult than it could be. Have you seen the trains in Finland!?

Even this motherly love I have discovered within my bones since having a child gives me constant nightmares. Loving another human being as much as I love my daughter is fucking terrifying and terrifyingly selfish. I don't like it. It's too much.

It was terrifying from the moment I got pregnant and it is still terrifying now and my mum tells me it never stops being terrifying.

paranoia

tonight, i'll try again
to watch the silver crescent
through my kiss of open curtain
turn my light off, go to sleep

tonight, i will not sneak back
to your room, stalker at your bedside
search the moonlight for the rise and fall
and rise and fall of lungs

and i will not,
no i will not
because for god's sake,
you are almost ten

i will not, with open palm
cast a net above your breath
till the warm current of living

assures me once again

and, as i fall, i will not
fling off once again my sheets
shine a final searching torch
lighthouse for a heartbeat

until, back below the covers
i watch shadows pace my walls
wonder, should i check on you
once more

So yes, I had nightmares when I was pregnant. And after birth. And when I went back to work. Lots of them. Of course I did.

And over a decade later I still have nightmares, especially the night before I take my kid on a trip anywhere, or go on a plane, or when I don't do a final check or when I go away without her which I do a lot and love it a lot, apart from the nightmares about losing her, which I am guaranteed to have after three days of being away.

It makes sense that the body still shivers a little in my sleep when we're apart. Both socially and, previous to that, biologically, we had been in extremely close proximity for a good while. Closer than anyone has ever been to me before.

I heard Myleene Klass talking in a brilliant radio interview with the excellent Mother Pukka about a process called foetal-maternal microchimerism. I had heard the word chimera in reference to a creature in Greek mythology – a fire-breathing she-monster with a serpent's tail, goat's body and lion's head, and, less excitingly, as an illusion of the mind.

Apparently, however, there is a third meaning, defined in the Merriam-Webster dictionary as: *an individual, organ, or part consisting of tissues of diverse genetic constitution.*

Turning to the *Harvard Science Review* for an introduction to this chimerical phenomenon Myleene Klass was referring to:[*]

> fetal microchimerism describes the presence of living cells from a different individual in the body of placental mammals. The placenta generally serves as a bridge between the fetus and the mother for exchange of nutrients and wastes. But that is not all that crosses this bridge – fetal and maternal cells can cross between the two organisms intact. While maternal cells do end up in the fetus, significantly more fetal cells are transferred to the mother. The result is that the mother carries a small number of foreign cells belonging to her fetus within her body – hence the name 'microchimerism.' While these non-maternal cells are few in number in comparison to total number of maternal cells, evidence suggests that these transplanted cells can actually remain for long after the end of gestation. In fact, derivative fetal cells have been found in the mother's body up to 27 years after pregnancy . . .

In other words, cells from the foetus can and do transfer into the mother. Scientists are still not sure of the effect of these foetal cells on the mother's body. Studies have shown conflicting results, with the cells both improving – in some cases serving as stem cells and helping to heal the mother's body in a variety of ways – and also worsening health outcomes for different diseases in different situations.

What is clear is that these cells can be released early on in pregnancy and remain a long time in the mother's body, then also passing through into other children that mother may birth.

A study by the Fred Hutchinson Cancer Center found that more

---

[*]   https://harvardsciencereview.org/2015/12/04/fetal-microchimerism-2, 4 December 2015.

than 60 per cent of autopsied brains contained copies of DNA from another individual.

We also know that these invading foetal cells are not only found in the mother's bloodstream but can also travel, and have been detected in the mother's liver, bone marrow, thyroid and heart years after pregnancy.

The fact that these cells migrate from early on in pregnancy was what Myleene Klass was discussing, primarily in relation to the loss of miscarriage – that even brief pregnancies leave a cellular mark on the mother for years into the future, somewhat poetically with the potential to heal her, as well as cause havoc, or at least settle in her, even as part of her heart.

miscarriage

at the school gates, we congratulate
comment on her bloom
her child has told the whole class
he will have a little sister soon!

at the school gates, one month on
children play, her bump is gone
adult silence strikes again
she carries on

A friend recently told me very early on that she was pregnant. I was told not to do this, because of the higher possibilities of miscarriage. I had taken this as a sort of rule. Do not tell people you are pregnant before a certain number of weeks have passed. My friend said she was telling us for exactly that reason. Because she was sick of hiding miscarriages. She was sick of going through them alone. She wanted us to know she was pregnant because why on earth should she hide it just so she had less support, as she saw it, if a miscarriage occurred.

I'd never thought of it that way. Of course, many may want this to be a private matter, but this very rigid rule of not telling even close friends before miscarriages were less likely was something I'd never really questioned.

When I was pregnant, I knew very little about my body in general, and even less about all of the fascinating feats of pregnancy, birth and breastfeeding. I feel like if I had known more, I would have been less disgusted by, and more in awe of what my skin, blood and bones were going through. The idea that cells from my daughter will stay in my body for years, my entire life even, blew me away.

Or that, if able or wanting to breastfeed, my body would produce a milk that changed depending on messages from my kid's saliva as she sucked my nipple, and that the milk then produced would contain differing levels of nutrition and antibodies in direct communication with these saliva-produced messages. Seriously, what the actual fucking magic is that?

Or that those nightmares I had did not make me a bad or ungrateful mother; that both the wonder and the fear of motherhood were totally understandable and much more common than the brochures suggested.

What a beautiful, mind-boggling, hellish love this is. It is incredible and it is petrifying and I wish it, rather than flowery maternity dresses and designer prams, were celebrated and supported much more.

> **often,** when getting on with my day
> pavement cold beneath my feet
> leaves in trees, bags of shopping in my hands
> i remember that time i grew a baby
> in this body, then pushed it from this body
> and i'm amazed, then carry on

421

I posted a poem about one of my most prevalent nightmares in pregnancy and had a host of other dreams and nightmares sent to me. Here are some of my favourites:

Emily Buchan
Before I discovered I was pregnant I had a very vivid dream in which I was a dragon protecting my nest full of eggs . . .

Chris Baxter
Postpartum, delirious with lack of sleep, I half dreamed that I was breastfeeding a rat (I am very scared of rats), had to quickly switch the light on to reassure myself it was my tiny daughter! That memory still freaks me out 7 years on!

Jo Hartley
About a week before I gave birth to my first I dreamt I gave birth to a kitten. Everyone was saying how lucky I was to have had such an easy labour, and how it was the cutest kitten they'd ever seen (it was remarkably gorgeous), but I was so disappointed.

Beastie La Stick
One of my daughter's teachers had a dream she gave birth to Mick Hucknall from Simply Red when she was pregnant. Whenever she talks to me about her son I see her child as a mini Mick Hucknall.

Jen Hall Smith
My reoccurring one was that I'd had the baby and it had somehow shrunk and kept shrinking and shrinking and I kept losing it in the bed or in the house and I could hear it crying but couldn't find it anywhere because it was so tiny.

Reply from Rosie Hogan
I had exactly the same dream! Again and again. I kept finding my baby though, in the shed under all the garden tools. It was super strange.

Ellie Crane
I had this one too!

Jackie John
With my first child, I kept dreaming she was born with pointy teeth, sitting up and talking, but the worst were when I dreamt she was a bubble. She kept floating away from me and I knew if I touched her, she'd pop.

pregnancy nightmare number 1:
the night you were born a goat

the pushing part was easier than expected;
but when they wrapped you in that blanket –
placed you in my arms: your face full of goat fur

purrs full of bleat
teeth full of goat teeth
feet full of hooves

eleven zombie midwives cooing at my bedside
as if you weren't a goat at all
heads nodding in slow motion with calm,
concurred denial, silent to my pleas that:

this is not my baby girl!
this is not my baby girl!

gloved hands stretched towards me
to soothe my sweating hair
assuring me in unison:

not all mothers love at first, hollie
sometimes it takes time –
now be good and take your child
now be
    good   and   take   your   child

pregnancy nightmare number 27: the exam hall

the exam hall is the same hall from school.
there is only one desk.
the midwife invigilator hands me a test sheet and pencil.
the pencil lead breaks.
i watch the hands of the clock spin minutes from seconds.
the lead is still broken. i put up my hand.
the midwife invigilator sighs and walks over.
she laughs at my paper.
tells me every unanswered answer is wrong.
i tell her the pencil was broken.
she tells me i've failed as a mum.

pregnancy nightmare number 289:
breastfeeding the dragon

it was clear something was wrong
when the fire did not stop
i had assumed it metaphorical
the feel of flames inside
must be the ripping of my flesh
ten dilated screams until i heard you
snarling from between my legs,
head twice the size of humans'
scales instead of skin,
wing-limbed and grinning;
one midwife on each ankle
pulling my legs as wide
as bones can break, creaking
with the weight of you till
dragon, you are born,
snort, slither up my skin,
bring your lips to my breasts
lapping milk till you are
strong enough for flames;
your first cry sets the labour ward alight
then every patient, every midwife
till us alone, in bed amidst the cinders
you cuddle to my chest
whisper *mummy*
suckle on my nipple

post-birth nightmare: no you haven't, hollie

for months, i dreamt you back inside me
arms cuffed behind my back
dragged back to the labour ward
screaming in the corridor

i've already given birth!

as the doctor, holding giant forceps
slowly moves towards me
and my belly, still unborn-baby-full

recurrent nightmare after returning to work: boiling

*(these dreams began after my boss told me, soon after I returned
to work, in front of the entire management team meeting that I
was serving the coffee to, that I'd obviously forgotten how to
make coffee since having a baby. He then followed me to the
kitchen and talked me step by step through how to make coffee
 using the cafetière 'properly', watching me as I did it)*

for months, after that first week back at work, when,
returning from my 'leave', during which i grew
a second heartbeat in clockwork with my own,
heaved it screaming through my shapeshift bones
as death crawled close as shadow and i, bloody, loved
and broken, pushed a thousand cries by day
a shawl of stinging stars each night,
sang daytime bedtime lullabies, as milk
spilled from my insides through honeyed heaving breasts,
my entire being burst with a terrifying love
like nothing i had ever known before,
and you said:

*christ hollie, you've obviously forgotten how to make coffee
since you've been away,*

for months, after that, i dreamt your death
in countless brutal ways: most often, boiling coffee
sometimes, you, tiny in my womb, your little bossy fists
punching inside out, pleading for a breath,
me, cross-legged at my desk refusing your release
once, i dreamt a forest, each bark bearing your face
each trunk your overbearing flesh
a lumberjack those nights, i took an axe happily

428

to your kneecaps till every tree of you was felled
two times, poison in the staff room biscuits
i'm not proud of this; never been a fan of violence

the last time i remember woke me sweating from my sleep
bedsheets drenched
hands still clenched around your phantom neck
screaming as i stirred,

have you ever given birth you prick? have you ever felt a skull
rip your grinning dick apart? do not patronise a mother
make your own fucking coffee you useless piece of shit

Fresh

If you don't like poo stories, move on

I have never seen a sky of stars as clearly as the sky of stars I saw as I stood outside holding a Tupperware box filled with my own shite.

The first time I left my flat after having a baby it was three o'clock in the morning. It had been three days since we'd come home from hospital, my body working out how to reconfigure the spaces inside where a baby had been playing for months before being suddenly and much less slowly released.

I'd convinced her dad to take a gig and my mum had come to stay the night.

The moment I stepped outside, the vastness of the world around me struck: the stars spilled glitter across the blackness of the sky; the sudden sense of cold air on my skin; my lungs gasped without asking; air rushed in.

I didn't realise I had become so accustomed to the stagnant inside air; that I'd forgotten the difference between closed and opened windows; that I'd lost the taste of frost in my throat as I breathed in. I felt as close to a re-released prisoner as I hopefully ever will.

I stood just outside the flat doors, staring, awestruck, at the above. I spotted Mars in the centre of the sky. Mars, or the red tip of a plane wing. One of the two. It didn't matter. I was outside, without a roof above my head; remembering an entire universe that surrounded me, a universe that I had almost forgotten after three days inside, staring nervously down at a newborn, attempting to catch glimpses of sleep in between feeds and being too scared to venture beyond my front door.

I momentarily forgot the Tupperware box smelling of rotten animal carcass, clutched in both of my hands.

I hadn't gone to the toilet for three days since giving birth. I woke up suddenly, just before 3 a.m., desperate to empty myself.

My baby was asleep next to me. Her dad was out working until sunrise. My mum was sleeping on the couch. I was so worried that this fresh little human being on the bed next to me might suddenly learn how to roll just as I made it to the bathroom, that she might have rolled off the covers and over the cliff top of the mattress onto the carpeted ocean below. I had already imagined her death numerous times. I'd never felt so desperate to go to the toilet. I called out for my mum as if I were five again, desperate for the toilet, scared of the imaginary monsters in the corridor.

My mum came running in as she had done all those years ago. I apologised for waking her as many times as I could before she stopped me. She fell into my bed, asleep again next to her new grandchild within seconds.

With my mum on guard, I ran down the corridor and sat on the cold seat and breathed out.

The first poo after birth is one of the scariest things I've ever encountered. My life has not been full of trauma, but I still think this moment counts. I still felt a sense that my body had done all the pushing that it ever could do and that one more push would split it open.

When I was done, I looked down and began to shake. I think half my body weight had now emptied from between my legs. I wondered if I would die. I had no idea what was and was not normal after you'd pushed a large amount of new life from your insides because nobody spoke about this. There was no way on earth this would all flush. The bathroom floor would have overflowed, flooded, curled up, heaved and died.

I wiped painfully, rinsed myself in the shower, washed my hands and ran to the kitchen desperately searching for any container before another member of the household needed to use our single bathroom. I found a trusty Tupperware.

I scooped, gagged a few times, tiptoed out the front door and down the communal staircase as if I were doing some horren-dous new mother's version of the school egg and spoon race.

Once out the front doors, the night air momentarily stunned me, before I realised the task at hand and looked around, praying that none of the other neighbours were also out emp-tying three days' worth of post-birth trauma into the shared bins behind the garages.

I made my way on tiptoes between my second-floor flat bathroom and the communal bins seven times that night, emptying the small Tupperware box straight into the bin – I'm so sorry, I was panicking and horrified – and refilling it from my toilet remains.

Once I had thrown the last lot of waste away, plus lunch box, into the bins, I turned, my heart slowing with the lessened possibility of now being caught. I could finally feel the air fresh and take my time to look up at the stars again, a vision now blurred not by shit stink, but by the tears now streaming down my cheeks in total self-disgust.

I went upstairs, scrubbed my hands with soap and a cleaning brush until they almost bled and fell back into bed beside my new baby and my mother, wondering whether my mum had also forgotten the existence of stars for a few days after my birth; wondering if any other mothers' insides had also fallen through the earth like mine.

Today is ten years since that day and though I realise the story is perhaps an unnecessary one to share, I am tired of ignoring the horrors of motherhood. I am tired of denying the hardships of birth on the body. I am tired of chasing ideals of parenting. I am tired of pretending I have never stood shaking, holding my own blood and shit in a Tupperware box beneath the stars.

newborn

it's worry i often feel
spying newborn mums;
loneliness creeping up
nights awake in silent stares
zombie-pushing pram on street
strolling with no place to be
a feeling after gifts are done
that few folk really give a fuck
a body she's now told is mess
standing, when she needs to rest
mixed with pressure for these days
to be the best days of her life
and so i check, as she stares
bearcub hugged to hips,
if that smile is from her eyes
as well as lips

**if the loudest two guys of the stag party i met
on the train to newcastle had just given birth**

you call that a fucking stretch mark?!
mate – these are fucking lines!
you give birth to a mouse or sth?
eleven pounder, mine

five-hour labour, did you?
i pushed three solid nights
at best, you've got some tom-cats there
these here are tiger stripes

vaginal, yeah? nice one, dude
nah, not me, a perfect cut
check the scar out, still pretty raw
spotlessly stitched up

pumping are you? yeah, me too.
how much you getting out?
i've got so much fucking milk
my kid's been getting gout

tits like fucking tankers, mate!
you need some – let me know
you trampolining yet?
nah, me either. soon tho'

missing time/watching children grow

Time moves slowly, but passes quickly
– ALICE WALKER, *The Color Purple*

for Faith

you're here, and i love you
still, i miss the you before
from three years back, from yesterday
from the first springtime yawn

in your face, i see them all
each age you've left behind
silhouette so quickly shifting
callous prank of passing time

and you're laughing, and i love you
still i miss the times you laughed before
more easily, or louder
or at jokes i hadn't made before

how glorious to see you now
swimming far ahead
but then i miss the you of jumping waves
clinging to my steady legs

and i love you growing up
but still, i mourn the fleeing time
and i can't wait to know you older
but i still rock in shopping lines

body cradling a memory
unable to keep pace
so tomorrow, and in twenty years
i'll miss the you today

PEEKABOO

One of the most tricky parts of new parenting for me, aside from the physical effects, was that it got quite repetitive; a bit boring sometimes.

I have never met anybody that likes repetition as much as a child does and the extent to which they love it is both fascinating and also, at times, when you are the sole play companion, mind-numbing: the same story asked for every night, the same joke made over and over again, the same games to be played. Sometimes it was so enamouring and I couldn't think of anything more joyous than dancing in the same puddle all day. Sometimes, I felt like my brain was going to lose the ability to string an adult sentence together.

One of the games which I, and most other carers on the planet, will recognise is peekaboo. A phenomenon the world over. Don't get me wrong, there is little better I find than making a baby or a child smile or laugh, but spending years playing games aimed at the intellectual level of a baby then toddler then young child has its effects, however much my child's happiness spills into my own.

I had a play date with one of the pre-school kids' dads once. As in, with our kids, for our kids to play together. We were doing crafts with them and when they left the room after about an hour, he said to me, guiltily, that he just didn't really enjoy doing the crafts. Our children were about three.

I laughed a little, thinking he was joking.

He continued to tell me how he just didn't find it very interesting.

When I replied that I also didn't find repeatedly cutting triangles out of paper or colouring in colouring pages aimed at three-year-olds intensely motivating, he looked genuinely surprised. Relieved, but surprised. He told me that he thought 'mums loved that stuff'.

I've been told the same by a few other dads, my own included, that they also thought mums loved most or all of the care they do for their children, games and crafts and wiping shit included.

Don't get me wrong, I really mean it when I say I absolutely loved hanging out with my daughter when she was little and I still love it now she's older, but the idea that mums in particular, mums and not dads in particular, women not men in particular, would be completely fulfilled spending their days repeating tasks aimed at a child's brain is almost insulting. Dads, they'd understandably not be completely and intellectually fulfilled by twelve hours of peekaboo, but mums, sure, their brains don't need anything more than that.

Being a bit bored of peekaboo does not mean you are not enraptured with your child or negate the fact that on many, many occasions watching them draw scribbles on paper will fill your heart with a love of Everestal heights. It did that too. But it is also sometimes mind-numbingly tiring, because even if you're just sitting watching them get on with their own thing, you cannot look away for a second. Like driving down the A1.

I made a pact with myself when my daughter was very little to explore or perhaps make peace with this difference in our ages and hobbies.

One day each week, I would scrap all plans of my own and do absolutely everything at her pace. I would stop feeling guilty for getting 'nothing done' as I repeatedly referred to these days of keeping a baby and then toddler alive, occupied, loved and learning. 'Nothing'. Seriously. I want to run back to my new mother body and shout, *it's not nothing Hollie, it's everything and it's important!*

I realised that most of the time, it was me who stopped games.

It was me who moved us onto the next thing when my daughter was perfectly happy still staring at the daisy or opening and closing the gate to the park over and over and over again, rather than playing on the designated playing equipment.

After a few months, I found that I loved these child-paced days.

A walk that took me five minutes (to the shop and back) when alone, on one occasion took four hours with my daughter.

Every single flower was stopped and stared at.

A bush was used for hide and seek for over an hour, the exact same level of surprise and laughter issuing from her lips each time I acted surprised at her jumping out from behind it.

Once I relaxed a bit more into it, once I designated this one day to just throw everything aside and go slow (I realise this is easier with an only child) and perhaps most importantly once I realised that this time is for her not me and that there was no need to feel guilty or unmotherly if you didn't always feel utterly fulfilled by these games, parenting became much more fascinating; or rather my child's development became fascinating.

One thing I wish I could tell all parents and carers who sit similarly worried or guilty because they are a bit bored of playing snap on a loop all day, is, firstly, that that's normal for an adult but, secondly, that those repetitive games – the opening and closing of gates or peekaboo over and over again – is essential work. You are not doing nothing. You are doing so, so much and you must remember that.

Sometimes, I felt ridiculous playing peekaboo, especially when in public.

I remember once sitting in a café with my daughter playing peekaboo over and over again while other adults chatted adult chat and people on laptops typed up important essays or reports or stories or whatever they were tapping with their adult fingers.

I had not played this game before, at least not since I can remember, and was not well-practised in exclaiming *boo!* within earshot of adults I didn't know.

I felt embarrassed speaking to a baby who didn't answer back. At times, I felt almost stupid, like I was no longer using my brain and as if everyone in the café would think I was useless.

My baby, of course, was loving it, laughing every time my face reappeared into view and, of course, I loved hearing her laugh each time, but I still felt sort of silly. A bit redundant. It seemed like the other people were doing important things and I was not.

If anyone had asked me what I had done that day, I would likely have replied 'nothing'.

I would definitely never have replied, 'Oh, I played three solid hours of peekaboo in order to develop my child's neurological knowledge of object permanence.'

For me, this was one of the problems: what I was doing all day was considered at worst nothing and at best nothing intelligent.

I recently researched more about peekaboo.

According to a survey carried out by the BBC,[*] peekaboo is the most popular way to make babies laugh the world over, and laughter is one of the essential first forms of communication and conversational skills.

The game gives children the giggles for about the first five years, for differing, essential reasons.

In the first six months, babies are genuinely surprised by your return; then they learn to anticipate it and are pleased that their predictions come true. By the time they're toddlers, they're often playing to humour you. Throughout this period the basic elements of the game remain the same. It is all about

---

[*] https://www.bbc.co.uk/tiny-happy-people/speech-lab-peekaboo/zqntxbk.

441

eye contact – which is pure social interaction, stripped down to its barest elements.

Crying is another form of communication, more obviously a sign for something they want stopped. Laughter, they say, is the opposite: babies laugh when they want you to continue to interact with them. That way, they learn more.

One of the loveliest things in this study was the effect of other people on the level of laughter.

The scientists filmed toddlers as they watched a funny cartoon in groups, pairs or on their own, and found that toddlers laughed around five times as much if even just one other child was present. The resulting theory: *even in infancy, it seems, a joke is best shared*.

In his book *In an Unspoken Voice*, scientist Peter Levine goes further, suggesting that 'one of the earliest ways we build our emotional resilience as humans when we come into the world is through playing Peekaboo'.

More specifically, he explains how as the sequence of this game, the disappearing and then reappearing face, is repeated and repeated and repeated and, ah, repeated, a playful pattern emerges, where a baby's trust in being 'saved' deepens and deepens with every disappearance and reassuring reappearance of your face from behind your hands. As in, your baby is like, *ah, I thought you'd gone, phew you came back*.

Scientifically speaking, the 'momentary startle and threat response of the nervous system' through playing peekaboo is experienced over and over again in a way that is safe and not as scary or traumatising as it would have been if the adult had just left abruptly and not reappeared again.

In his words, the baby's brain, from playing peekaboo a lot, starts to understand that: 'Sometimes good things disappear for a while and sure enough, they then reappear again and I'm OK. Life is fun like that and I can trust in the disappearing and eventual reappearing of people that care about me.'

I think most of us could do with that sort of reassurance now and then.

peekaboo

is a phenomenon
and you
an exceptional professor

please remember this
as you collapse into coffee
your days full of peekaboo

wondering if you'll ever
use your adult brain again –
do not feel stupid

as you play peekaboo
and peekaboo, your palms
performing wonders

hear the baby's laughter
ecstatic each time hope returns,
this is stunning work

neuroscience at its best –
eye to eye contact
momentary relapse

re-establishment of hope:
absence is not death
things will be ok again

broken hearts will mend
sometimes we all
need reassured of this;

that every storm will one day calm
this is not nothing
right now, this is everything –

covering your face to uncover it again
covering your face to uncover it again
covering your face

no stones in her stomach

everything she crawls past
she grabs   everything she grabs
she wants to swallow   so

when you ask what i was doing
all day long   why i've not got any
work done   no fresh cookies

in the oven   not wiped my arse
nor brushed my teeth
i will tell you that this week

i have saved this baby's life
at least one hundred times –
look at her! i'll cry   look inside

her stomach! no stones! no feathers!
not one single jigsaw piece!
no ladybirds! no foxglove!

just one small piece of sick
she sucked up from the carpet
in the twelve-second interval
i ran to take a piss

terrible mother

you never even taught me how to bake bread
a terrible mother, you apologise again
and i wonder if it really bothers you
as much as it doesn't bother me

i love bakeries now
and cafés that sell sandwiches
and people who specialise in single skills
like baking bread really well, and you

walking through town, holding your hand
was like strutting red carpets
every second person a patient
with something new to thank you for

drink water; for the love of god, don't smoke
if fear seems overwhelming, wait
smile at people passing; you've no idea
what they are going through

each week,
you brought home presents patients brought you;
dvds, ferrero rochers, apples from allotments
i scoffed them, wondering, watching

each bedtime, as you'd try desperately
to finish stories open-eyed; three minutes per appointment
but everyone wants more of you
then complains you're running late by ten a.m.

those glorious evenings, waiting for you after school,
singing solo in the nurses' room, doing homework,
gobbling biscuits, beg you check my blood pressure
once all the patients left

imagine if we all knew how to bake bread
thank god you never taught me –
all those bakers with no jobs! all those cafés
that might never have opened

for me to sit in, eating toasties
writing poems like a wanker
about what an excellent mother i have got

our house did not smell of bread

no, our house did not smell of bread, freshly baked in the morning or the afternoon, or evening. no, i have never sat around a table, wooden or otherwise, learning from my mother or my grandmothers to shell peas or boil celery into soup or twist the green from strawberries before stirring it to jam, our fingers sticky as we giggled, passing down ancient recipes i would one day whisper deep into my daughter's ears as she sits with me, rolling dough across a floured table's surface, soaking up the stories of her foremothers before her, before us, serving the dishes upon plates as if paper trails sauced with inky blood. no, like me, she will likely never recall in later years that smell of bread freshly baked in the morning, or the afternoon, or evening by her mother – do not worry, there are other ways to make memories outside of baking bread; after swimming, we always shared a bag of chips, do you remember? salted and ketchupped; every time i jump into a crowded pool i am back tiptoeing the counter of the café, pound coin in my small delighted hand, your hand in my other, anticipating the heat of fried potatoes in my palms; do you remember when we tried pesto for the first time and then bought it once a month as a treat? do you remember when you tried to teach me to make mashed potato and apple sauce but i didn't listen and went out with my friends or when, once a year, you let me buy a small bag of the expensive jelly belly beans from the local garden centre; and at grandma's, once hugs were done, the way she nodded us the all clear and we sprinted to rummage in the bottom of the freezer where, cradled between the frozen peas and the frozen supermarket bread that none of us had baked like tiny treasures in thin paper packets, the choc ices awaited us again

PUT A TIT IN IT

Despite learning French all my life with the dream of living by the sea in southern France, I've never actually moved out of England and, because of Brexit, am now much less likely to be able to. I often think that this means I've wasted years of studying, but the things I've learnt from learning other languages, even the very few European ones I stumble over, have still helped in ways I never expected.

In Spanish, one of the common translations of 'to give birth' is *dar a luz*. This literally means 'to give light', not to be confused with Karen's 'seeing the light' Catholic orgasm metaphor.

In English, I gave birth. In Spanish, I gave light. How fucking cool.

Something I learnt too late was that one of the German translations of 'to breastfeed' is *stillen*. This literally means 'to calm'.

When I learnt this, it opened up a completely new way of looking at this act.

I often felt quite weird breastfeeding, or rather was made to feel weird by how not normalised it was for me; never seen in real life, never seen on screen except in the *Rugrats* cartoon, not even, when I was doing it, seen in an emoji. Sometimes, don't get me wrong, it was utterly incredible to feel your body produce this milk. And then other times I felt so strange and I hated that I felt that way, but I did.

I felt weirder still when my baby wanted to suck on my nipple for other reasons; to go to sleep mainly; to fart sometimes; to calm down. Nobody had told me that a baby might just want the comfort of a breast, even if they didn't necessarily want any milk.

The idea of putting my baby on my breast just because she was agitated or upset made me feel like such a, I don't know, pervert I guess, because language had taught me that when a baby went on your breast it was for 'breastfeeding'; feeding from the breast. Feeding, as if that, because the word says so, is the only reason for the breast. This isn't true.

When a baby's on your boob, to them, it's like the motherfucker of all comfort blankets, with all the smells and warmth and softness and heartbeat that a baby can recognise. It's what a dummy does, which is why dummies are shaped like nipples and are so helpful at shutting kids up.

Finding out about this German translation made me wonder if I'd have been less awkward if I'd become a new mother in German and not English. I wondered what it's like for German speakers who have the ability to answer '*Ich stille*' instead of 'I am breastfeeding' when confronted with questions about why the kid still has their lips wrapped half-arsed round your nipple despite being fast asleep.

Even the other more literal translation of breastfeeding in German – *die Brust geben* – meaning literally 'to give the breast' – still doesn't highlight this definitive idea of feeding being the reason for the breast. I wondered if this makes a difference to mothers who might not be producing milk the way they want but could still comfort their baby, if they want, by putting it to the breast, without feeling so weird about the minimal feeding going on. I've never heard that discussed. I think England is just too confused about women's breasts to even attempt the conversation.

There is a perfect summation by Iris Marion Young of this weird attitude we have towards women's breasts. She stated that 'Breasts are a scandal because they shatter the border between motherhood and sexuality.' I think this is perfect, and something that we really need to get over. Babies suck tits. Lovers suck tits. Both are fine. I would like this slogan on a billboard please.

The German word for placenta is *Mutterkuchen* (literally 'mother cake') and a word for cervix is *Muttermund* (mother mouth). Also the German word for 'slug' is *Nacktschnecke*, which literally means naked snail. Snail is just *Schnecke*. In German, slugs and snails are the same but one is less embarrassed of their body.

When my daughter was about ten, we got the train to Newcastle and were sat opposite a very confident-looking couple I'd say were in their mid-thirties, but who the fuck knows. They had a newborn baby with them.

When the baby started crying, the woman put the baby to her breast and the baby drank and then fell asleep with the woman's nipple basically still hanging out the baby's open mouth.

I expected the mum to then put her breast, as I was always petrified not to do when in public, and even sometimes when in private, 'back', so to speak.

Often, my baby woke up and started crying when I did this, thus fucking up the rest of the possible nap-time journey, but I still did it whenever I was out for pure fear of what people would think if I had a baby on my boob who wasn't sucking.

This woman didn't do that. She sat for about an hour and a half with this newborn baby hanging off her tit, mouth loosely around the nipple, the baby looking as relaxed as I do after an hour-long full-body massage.

When I'd sat down at first, in all honesty, I'd thought, *fuck, a baby opposite us for five fucking hours*. But the baby was the most content I'd ever seen. I guess the way a baby, if fed by bottle, is when it goes from bottle to dummy. But in this case it was nipple to, well, nipple.

I was in awe of this woman. I would never have done that and the only reason I wouldn't have done it would have been social stigma. That annoys me a lot now. I woke my baby up loads by putting my boob away.

The other thing was, she didn't look the way some other mums, and me, inside, looked when with a small child we were feeding with our own bodies.

She didn't look like the weight of having a baby permanently attached koala-like to her flesh was weighing her down, sucking the freedom out of her, making her uncomfortable on outings, making her feel like sometimes she needed to run to the forests and hide in dens she'd made when she was a kid, just to have one fucking moment when her body was her own again, not the grabbing, sucking, feeding, loving station of another being.

Perhaps she did feel like that, but she didn't look it. She was chatty and reading and drinking coffee and wide-eyed, laughing at the world that swept past the train windows, baby mouth still wrapped round her nipple.

I wondered if – all being well – this would be how it might feel as a mother feeding a small child if a baby hanging off your tit was as socially accepted and unencumbering as a handbag at your side.

I dream that one day we will start getting more offended by big companies selling our own water sources back to us in plastic bottles which take more water to make than is actually inside them, and less offended by kids sucking milk out of zero-carbon environmentally friendly mothers' tits.

And maybe, in a society where a kid simply tit-chilling on the breast, as I will now translate *stillen*, wasn't quite so difficult to do, choosing to breastfeed would not be quite as isolating as it often seemed to me. Maybe it's not the baby on the tit that brought me the feeling of claustrophobia, maybe it was the wide world watching and judging that and therefore me rushing to hide or worrying every time I needed to simply feed or calm or settle my kid.

Whenever I see a baby peacefully chilling on some mother's breast now, whether drinking or sleeping or just putting its feet up for a wee bit of time out, I think back to that time when I was so embarrassed to do this, especially when I was alone without the support of family or friends, and I think about all the fuss that people have made about women doing this in public, and I am constantly enraged and so damn sorry for that twenty-seven-year-old new mum that I was worrying every day about where it might be OK or not to nurse or nurture my child.

I look at the calm-as-fuck babies and think how no one in the world is being hurt by this and how normal it should be and I think very loudly in my head: *what is the fucking problem with this world!*

There's a word in Italian, *abbiocco*. It translates roughly to 'the drowsiness that follows eating a big meal'. This word, when I learnt it, reminded me so perfectly of the look on babies' faces after their bellies have been filled with warm milk and they pass out, heads back on your arms or the cot, tiny smiling drunkards. It also made me wish that I could nap after every meal, food-full adults in restaurants allowed to sit finally face down on a table pillow, no talking for ten minutes.

milk-glazed

main course finished, we force conversation
though blood is all draining from brains
to our stomachs; if only we could pause for a moment;
take leave of convention; untie the bows
from the corners of cushions; floors turned to bedrooms
for our bones to spread out on;
unbutton buttons now strained by consumption,
let zips open locks from the torment of fullness;
silent prayer for the god of digestion
a ten-minute nap before pudding;

but we can't; etiquette says so
so we sit there, bellies still flat-packed into boxes,
talking politely, dreaming of dreaming,
hallucinating tablecloth duvets
watching the baby with jealous respect

who, milk-glazed and drunk, lays its head
on the softs of a chest, self-consciousness
not yet passed down by its elders,
and shamelessly tilts back its neck,
eyes sunk, mouth open in song

Italian seems to have a lot of cool words and expressions related to resting and napping and dozing that English doesn't. Another one of my favourites is the verb *meriggiare*, which means 'to escape the heat of the midday sun by resting in the shade'. A combination of *abbiocco* and *meriggiare* sounds like a perfect afternoon. When a language has specific words for things related to resting or simply being, it weirdly makes me feel less guilty about resting. Like no, I'm not doing fuck all, I am resting in the shade of a tree with a full stomach and heavy eyes, duh.

abbiocco

nothing better than a food-nap
bellies plump with cheese and bread
picnic crumbs like sun-formed freckles
splayed across your sun-kissed chests

head rested on a lover's lap
lover laid in shade of grass
eyelids sunk in feast-fatigue
clouds kindly tiptoe past

If, in theory, I did have another child, I would try to rest in Italian, feed in German and have a midwife in French, because in French a midwife is called a 'sage-femme', which literally translates as 'wise-woman', and I think is more reassuring and accurate. Be nice if there was a male version. Perhaps there is.

After watching the baby hanging off the nipple on the train that day I also scribbled down a poem about letting Boris Johnson suck on my nipples.

I wasn't sure whether to ever share this poem because it is a bit, well, gross and I don't want people to think that I actually want Boris Johnson anywhere near my tits or would shove my nipples randomly in anyone's mouth.

But seeing that baby and thinking of the German *stillen* reminded me how calm and silent my own baby would suddenly go when I put my nipple in her mouth when relaxing at home; what power my tits once had to put my kid to sleep or calm her down or stop her from bawling or to ease her ears popping on an aeroplane.

While thinking about this, I was reading an article on the train about some of Boris Johnson's thoughts on single mothers, women, religion, race and young people, among other opinions. You can find all the quotes online. I'm not wanting to repeat his words.

The memory of this tit-effect on my child, mixed with the urgent desire I felt for Boris Johnson, among many others, to shut the fuck up, merged into the thought that the phrase 'put a sock in it' really ought to be 'put a tit in it'.

I started imagining the effect my breasts might have had if placed into other people's mouths to calm them down or put them to sleep (not as in kill them, just make them sleepy and quiet) or just shut them up for a while; the woman shouting about pushchairs taking up too much space on the bus – put a tit in it; the man standing outside the primary school yelling at any little kid who walked near the corner of his front garden – put a tit in it. Any billionaire giving budgeting advice – put a tit in it.

I would like to make it clear, I don't want Boris Johnson sucking on my tits. Saying that, if it stopped him talking any more crap, or just at all, I might sacrifice the wonders of my milk-producing motherbody for the greater good.

breastfeeding boris johnson

when watching boris johnson speak
i reminisce new motherhood
the speed she calmed and fell asleep
each time i put a tit in it

her peachy cheek upon my breast
my heartbeat to her panicked lips
subsided tides of fear or need
each time i put a tit in it

and watching him, i wonder
if this magic trick were one size fits
would he, if i could just get close,
unfasten that old feeding clip

peel off the leaking cotton pads
nipple in his open mouth
like *come to mummy, boris*
shh, i think it's nap time now

THE END

I am writing this final page because I realise I have just ended a book about learning to love things I want to love, and trying to stop hating or being disgusted by things that cause no harm or hurt to anyone, with a slightly creepy poem about breastfeeding Boris Johnson. I would like to confirm again that I would never force anybody onto the tit nor condone it as a means of political conflict resolution.

This ending is especially hypocritical because the poem has the word mummy in it and although I guess it is not harming anyone and maybe it is something I need to learn to live with, I really cannot handle adults who still call their parents mummy and daddy.

I am trying to accept it, but it's hard.

I guess we all have fickle and harmless hates we find it harder to dismiss than others.

So I will thank you for reading this book, because I really am so thankful and I will hope that maybe you can join me in giving less of a shit about things that make pointless money for billionaires or cause no harm to anyone or make you miserable.

Here's a final poem. I wrote this one after eating a really good strawberry.

fuck, i love you, and strawberries are perfect

and sheets smell so good when they dry in the sun
masturbation is free and kittens are so fucking cute
and watermelons have too many seeds but they're easy
just to spit out; imagine, all your life as a caterpillar
and then – pooff! – one final butterfly rush

ACKNOWLEDGEMENTS

First, thanks so much to you for reading this book; or thinking of reading it. Thanks to everyone who has read or shared my work or been to a gig or bought or borrowed or gifted a book. I am eternally grateful. I really love writing and it's because of you that this is now something I can keep doing more of. Thanks to all the booksellers and bookshops who've stocked and sold and supported me and especially to Toppings, Ely, for letting me use the desk in your shop when I'm in between errands. Thanks to all the amazing independent venues and staff who've replied to my tour emails and offered such great clubs and theatres for poetry readings – Oran Mor (thanks to Creon), Hoxton Hall (Toffy), Queen's Hall (Emma, who isn't my mum), Summerhall (Jamie), Trades Club (Mal), Hope Chapel (Gerald), Wylam Brewery (Dave) and on and on. Thank you to the Cambridge City and Cambridge University Libraries, for your free space and silence and tea, and to all the other libraries in all the cities where I've found a few hours of writing time while on tour. (PS: I get paid if you take my book out the library so never feel bad about this.) Thank you also to the following favourite cafés and pubs, where I have sat for hours writing and reading and eating and editing when I needed chatter and life around me while working, without which I'd have gotten so bored of my own company sat alone at my desk: Box Café, Cambridge; the Elm Tree, Cambridge; Indigo Coffee House, Cambridge; Café 121, Cambridge; Unwrapped, Ely; the Rocket, London; the Wellcome Trust, London; and Kamila's house, the best shared 'office' I could wish for. Thanks to Becky and Rhiannon for having so much faith in what and how I write from way back, to Clara and Lilly for all your brilliant work getting the books out there, to Jack and Nico for the super cover, to Nithya and all the amazing proofreaders for finding the hundreds of mistakes I have made somehow with your extra-terrestrial eye-scanning abilities, and thanks to Amy, Helen, Howard and Rhiannon again for your most dexterous and loving editing of this book, and others, for years, which always makes me seem way sharper and more precise than I am; and to Helen Mort and Marjorie Lotfi for your much-appreciated help with the poems, and to Lauren Bahroun for being the most amazing producer of the audiobook. Books are never written by just one person; don't believe anyone who pretends they are. Thanks now to my gorgeous family and brilliant friends I'm so, so lucky to have and have written about in here. Oh joy to Michael for all your glorious company and care and much-loved and much-cherished love and for your ridiculous belief and encouragement in me. Thanks to my gorgeous daughter for putting up with having a mum with a pretty embarrassing job, and for being great in general, and very funny, and very calm and understanding about being dragged around various venues and keeping me company. Thanks to my mum for the love and very practical guidance and childcare and for listening to the poems as I write them, as you have always done; to my dad for the love and laughter, and my excellent aunties and cousins for all the love and support and tea and holidays. To Elisabete for being the best neighbour, and to her and Fred for distracting me on the final edit woes. And finally, thanks to the NHS staff who helped me deal with a few mild, scabby issues, which would have distracted me much more from the writing if our healthcare wasn't so free and brilliant. Thanks to all the trees. Sorry.

CREDITS

P 9:   Lines from *Walking Words* by Eduardo Galeano, W.W.
         Norton & Co: New York, 1997.

P 81:   Lines from 'Letters from a Kashmiri Boy' by Geet
         Chaturvedi, translated by Anita Gopalan, in *Modern
         Poetry in Translation*, 2022, https://modernpoetryintrans-
         lation.com/poem/letters-from-a-kashmiri-boy/

P 147:   From Harriet Lerner, 2005, https://lilith.org/articles/
         speaking-the-unspeakable/

P 209:   Lines from 'The Next War' by Wilfred Owen in *The
         Complete Poems and Fragments of Wilfred Owen*, ed. Jon
         Stallworthy, Chatto & Windus: London, 1983.

P 231:   Lines from *Charlotte's Web* by E.B. White, Harper &
         Brothers: New York, 1952.

P 259:   Lines from *She Comes First: The Thinking Man's Guide
         to Pleasuring a Woman* by Ian Kerner, Souvenir Press:
         London, 2005.

P 403:   Lines from 'Soft Play' by Clare Pollard in *Incarnation*,
         Bloodaxe Books: Hexham, 2017.

RECOMMENDATIONS LIST

Here is a list of the main books and poems and people I referenced or read or thought about while writing this.

Books

Stephanie Yeboah, *Fattily Ever After: A Fat Black Girl's Guide to Living Life Unapologetically*

Emma Dabiri, *Don't Touch My Hair*

Sonya Renee Taylor, *The Body is Not an Apology: The Power of Radical Self-Love*

Musa Okwonga, *One of Them*

Fern Brady, *Strong Female Character*

Michael Pedersen, *Boy Friends*

Darren McGarvey, *The Social Distance Between Us*

Neil Astley (ed.), *Staying Alive* (Bloodaxe Books poetry anthology)

Kim Moore, *All the Men I Never Married*

Individual poems

Salena Godden, 'Can't be Bovvered'

Pauline Stainer, 'The Honeycomb' (in *Staying Alive*)

Wendy Cope, 'The Orange'

Seamus Heaney, 'Oysters' (in *Staying Alive*)

Laurie Bolger, 'Parkland Walk'

Michael Pedersen, 'Birds and Blowies'
Geet Chaturvedi, 'Letters from a Kashmiri Boy' (trans. Anita Gopalan)
Jane Duran, 'Miscarriage' (in *Staying Alive*)
Anthony Anaxagorou, 'Futurist Primer'
Sharon Olds, 'First Birth' (in *Staying Alive*)
Andrew Greig, 'Orkney / This Life' (in *Staying Alive*)
Vanessa Kisuule, 'Hollow'

Other things that I watched or listened to a lot as I wrote

Shabazsays – Instagram account
Jen Brister – comedian
Kae Kurd – comedian
Sindhu Vee – comedian
Pink Ladoo Project – Instagram account
Quinn – audio erotica podcasts
Kelis's farmlife – Instagram account
Goodlawproject – Instagram account
The news
Reruns of *The Fresh Prince of Bel-Air*

INDEX OF POEMS